Blowin' Free

Thirty Years of wishbone ash

Blowin' Free

Thirty Years of wishbone ash

Gary Carter & Mark Chatterton

Firefly Publishing

FIREFLY
PUBLISHING

First published in 2001 by Firefly Publishing
Firefly is an imprint of SAF Publishing Ltd. in association with
Helter Skelter Publishing Ltd.

SAF Publishing Ltd.
Unit 7, Shaftesbury Centre,
85 Barlby Road,
London.
W10 6BN
ENGLAND

www.safpublishing.com
email: info@safpublishing.com

ISBN 0 946719 33 0

Text copyright © 2000 Gary Carter and Mark Chatterton

The right of Gary Carter and Mark Chatterton to be identified as the authors of this work has been asserted by them in accordance with the Copyright, Designs and Patents Act, 1988.

All rights reserved. No part of this publication may be transmitted in any form, or by any means, electronic, photocopying, recording or otherwise, without the prior permission of the publisher.

In some cases it has not proved possible to ascertain or trace original illustration copyright holders, and the publishers would be grateful to hear from the photographers concerned.

A CIP catalogue record for this book is available from the British Library.

The publishers would like to thank Paul Widger for copy editing assistance.

Printed in England by Cromwell Press, Trowbridge, Wiltshire.

This book is dedicated to the memory of

John Sherry
(1946 – 1994)

former agent and manager of
Wishbone Ash

and to the legions of Wishbone Ash fans throughout the world who have followed the band over the years through thick and thin.

Acknowledgements

Firstly we would like to thank all the Wishbone Ash fans out there who have helped with photographs, memorabilia, press cuttings and general information: Ian Anderson, Ray Annis, Billy and Steve Auld, Rory Banham, Chris Brennan, Derek Byram, Mike and Margaret Darken, Jill Douglas, Carol Farnworth, Russell Fish, Peter Hingley, Roger Hoodless, Pauline and Mike Holt, Martyn Jones, Neil Jones, Jan Krynski, Steve Lord, Nicky Masters, Phil Matthews, Colin Milburn, Steve Moore, Andy Nathan, John Nixon, Mike Perring, Peter Popert, Alan Pye, Bob Rand, Guy and Sue Roberts, Martin Rodgers, Sandy Russell, Ian Sadler, Ken Stephen, Mike Tarling, Trevor Vanderplank, Alan Workman, Andy Yates and everyone who has contributed to the various Wishbone Ash archives over the years.

In America we would like to thank Dr John at the US ASH fan club for all his help and support and also John Hahn and Fred Renz. Detleff Assenmacher of the German fan club and Bodo Kirf of Trimedia, and in France Christian Guyonnet.

Thanks also to Pete Feenstra at Real Music, Mark Paytress and John Reed formerly of *Record Collector*, Fran Leslie at Blueprint, Martin Hudson and Jenny Allen at the Classic Rock Society, Alan Hartley at Uriah Heep Appreciation Society and Barry Winton, Simon Robinson at the Deep Purple Appreciation Society, Barry Riddington & Malcolm Holmes at HTD, Andy Gray and Mike Gott at Beat Goes On Records, Rob Ayling at Voiceprint, Chris Griffin and Alan Hodgson formerly of MCA/Universal, Dave Ling at *Classic Rock*, Kevin Rowland at Feedback.

Plus the following associates of the band – past and present – who kindly gave interviews and support: Chris Auld, Mike Bennett, Doreen Boyd, Mark Emery (Hobbit), Ben Granfelt, Kevin Harrington, Ian Harris, Max Kay, Derek Lawrence, Andy Nye, Pauline Powell, Nina Sherry, Tacye, Leon Tsilis, Glenn Turner, Susie Turner and Patricia Wisefield.

A big special thank you to the various members of Wishbone Ash throughout the years, especially Martin Turner, Laurie Wisefield and Andy Powell who all gave several extensive interviews during the writing of this book and Steve Upton who, despite declining to be interviewed for this project, kindly granted permission for us to quote from his personal diary. Thanks also to Mark Birch, Trevor Bolder, Jamie Crompton, Roger Filgate, Robbie France, Claire Hamill, Tony Kishman, Andy Pyle, Bob Skeat, Mervyn "Spam" Spence, Mike Sturgis, Ray Weston and John Wetton who all kindly gave interviews for this book.

Thanks also to Bob Harris, the BBC DJ and former presenter of *The Old Grey Whistle Test* who kindly wrote the foreword to this book.

Finally a big thank you to Sean Body at Helter Skelter for all his help and support during the writing of this book.

Contents

	Acknowledgements	6
	Contents	7
	Foreword	8
	Introduction	9
Chapter 1	I'm Leaving To Search For Something New	11
Chapter 2	New Rising Stars	29
Chapter 3	Goodbye Baby, Hello Friend	48
Chapter 4	Locked In... In New England	62
Chapter 5	Everybody's Talking Front Page News	78
Chapter 6	Leaving Is A Sin They Say	91
Chapter 7	The Streets Of Shame	107
Chapter 8	There's No Longer Magic In Your Eyes	121
Chapter 9	Phoenix Fly... Raise Your Head To The Sky	130
Chapter 10	Had Enough Of This Strange Affair	143
Chapter 11	They Sure Do Hit Hard Times	157
Chapter 12	I'll Return Again To Fight Another Day	165
Chapter 13	Wings Of Desire Will Keep Us Flying	180
Appendices	Sources and Addresses	195
	Wishbone Ash Concert Listing	196
	Discography	208
	Wishbone Ash Family Tree	222

Foreword

I'm so pleased to have been asked to write the foreword for this book, because Wishbone Ash helped launch my broadcasting career more than thirty years ago. We go back.

I first saw them play at the Marquee in the early summer of 1970. I was there with my producer Jeff Griffin, checking them out for a possible session on the BBC's nationwide Radio 1 station.

We thought they were absolutely stunning; Ted on one side of the stage, Andy on the other, the two guitarists trading licks with dynamic confidence. That twin guitar thing was new then and it was exciting. Jeff Beck and Jimmy Page had previously test-run the idea in the Yardbirds, but I couldn't remember actually seeing anything like it live before. But there was more to the band than that.

Wishbone Ash music contained a lot of influences that made them hard to pin down. I hate categories anyway, so it was great to see a group that were blurring the edges between progressive rock, blues, folk and just plain heavy. The songs were strong, the stuff of legends. We predicted big things.

We went backstage, introduced ourselves and booked them on the night. Jeff produced the session at the famous BBC Maida Vale studio. The band recorded "Errors Of My Way" and "Phoenix". It was their first ever radio session and was broadcast on my first ever programme, on *Sounds Of The 70's* on 19th August 1970.

We've stayed in touch on and off ever since. In fact Andy was on the phone (from somewhere in Denmark I think it was, backstage at one of the big European festivals) when I celebrated my 30th anniversary on my Saturday night show on Radio 2.

It feels very good to have been in there from the beginning. I'm massively impressed by the way the band and their loyal fans have remained true to each other and the music.

I truly hope you enjoy this book. And that Wishbone Ash will be there again when I celebrate my 40th anniversary in 2010!

Bob Harris

Introduction

It may come as a surprise to some to read that the classic British rock group Wishbone Ash has been in existence for thirty years. "The biggest unknown band in the world" as some wisecrack music journalist once remarked. Contrary to reports in some music encyclopaedias, the group never broke up in the eighties, but has always been around, albeit with ever changing line-ups. Wishbone Ash are a train that has never stopped rolling and throughout the group's thirty-year history band members have come and gone, getting on at one station and alighting at another. All the time there has been one constant factor – Andy Powell – who can rightly be called the engine driver. In fact, he is the only original member in the current line-up.

Formed at the tail end of the 1960s, Wishbone Ash came to prominence in the seventies with a string of best-selling albums; a reputation for being one of the best live bands around; and as the pioneers of the twin lead guitar sound. The band continued through the eighties, being among the first groups to tour the then uncharted territories of Russia and India. After a reunion of the original line-up in 1987 the band continued to evolve throughout the nineties despite an ever-changing music scene and lack of interest from both the music press and the music industry. In spite of this, the group has stubbornly maintained a presence on the music scene – due largely to the dedicated fans who have never given up on "the Ash" (or "the Bones" if you prefer) often travelling hundreds of miles to see their beloved heroes and publicising the band through various fanzines and via the Internet.

Now, thirty years after the formation of this truly great British rock institution, comes the complete story and history of the band whose music still sends shivers down the spines of its loyal fans the world over.

Mark Chatterton

Chapter One

I'm Leaving To Search For Something New

The 1960s was a decade of radical change in Britain – including politics, fashion, people's attitudes and above all popular music. In musical terms the sixties are probably best remembered as being the decade of the Beatles; the group from Liverpool that conquered the world and in doing so changed the face of popular music forever. The fifties had seen the rise of rock 'n' roll with the likes of Elvis Presley, Bill Haley, Little Richard and Chuck Berry. But by the start of the sixties, Elvis was about to leave the army and start on a decade of watered down film scores and the heady days of rock 'n' roll rebellion had been replaced by a plethora of sugary ballads which filled the charts. With the arrival of the Beatles, all that changed. Beat groups dominated the charts from 1963 onwards, to be followed by r'n'b groups like the Rolling Stones and the Yardbirds and the Mod groups such as the Who and the Small Faces all staking their claim in the ever changing pop charts. Outside of the singles charts the blues boom of the mid-sixties brought guitarists like Eric Clapton and Peter Green to the forefront, then as Psychedelic music came through with artists such as Jimi Hendrix and Cream, popular music became ever more radical and diverse. It was therefore hardly surprising that the sixties saw a rush of groups forming and playing in garages and church halls, eager to emulate the latest pop star or god-like guitarist. One such group was the Empty Vessels who hailed from the West Country of England. The Empty Vessels would eventually evolve into Wishbone Ash, a quintessentially English group, who along with contemporaries like Jethro Tull, Led Zeppelin, Deep Purple and Black Sabbath came into being at the tail end of this revolutionary decade.

The roots of Wishbone Ash lie in the English seaside resort of Torquay, a West Country town in Devon more famous for Basil Fawlty's escapades than its contribution to the rock music industry. Local musician Martin Turner (born Torquay 1 October 1947) started playing guitar at the age of fourteen on a "beat up old Spanish instrument" before moving to bass, although he had shown a musical talent from a much earlier age.

"I was trained to read music when I was a very young boy and I sang in a church choir," recalls Martin. "I reached the stage when I was about nine years old where I could read sheet music straight off a page and actually sing it, but I kind of rebelled against that later and I found the written language of music restrictive in a creative sense."[2]

Martin and his guitar playing brother Glenn formed their first band, the Torinoes, back in November 1963 soon after the Beatles had come to national prominence in the UK. The Torinoes soon built up a respectable following in the West Country area playing the music of the Shadows, Johnny Kidd, Chuck Berry, the Everley Brothers, Little Richard, Ray Charles and Wayne Fontana.

"We played youth clubs, town halls, church halls, village halls, and wore a uniform of dark red cord jackets, various trousers, Cuban heeled boots, and sometimes ritzy-glitzy sparkly ties, à la Las Vegas," recalls Glenn Turner. "Our dad used to drive us to most of the gigs in his Ford Cortina – sometimes we'd travel 100 miles with a bass drum on our knees."

Martin Turner finished his schooling at Torquay Grammar at the age of seventeen and balanced his musical activities with a succession of day jobs.

"My first job was at a builders' merchants doing sales analysis," remembers Martin. "After a few months I told them that from my observations the business was antiquated. They thought I was a pretentious brat, so I was fired. I soon fell into the role of 'beach boy'. During the winter I would take a variety of jobs, working in factories, driving vans etc and then take the summer off to sit on the beach, play the guitar and chat up the tourists."[3]

By 1966, the Torinoes had evolved into the Empty Vessels – a three-piece outfit featuring Martin and Glenn plus drummer Adrian Smith. Adrian's stay, however, was to be short-lived. During a visit to a local cafe called "Dirty Dot's" on 16 July 1966 the Turner brothers met Steve Upton, a well-known figure on the West Country music scene who already had a wealth of touring experience under his belt.

Steve Upton (born Wrexham, Wales 24 May 1946) started his drumming career purely by chance at technical college in Torquay. A couple of Steve's classmates were forming a band and one of them asked him if he knew of anyone who could play.

"It was all a big accident," recalls Upton. "I used to sit next to a guy at college who played in a band and, almost jokingly, I offered to play drums for them. When they actually turned up and asked me to start I had to admit that I couldn't play. As it happened neither could they, so we took it from there".[1]

The next stage was the loan of a drum kit belonging to a friend which, as chance would have it, was set up for a left handed player. "I'm not actually sure if he was a left-hander," continues Steve, "but he set his kit up that way and that was the first kit I ever played, so I got used to playing a left-handed kit in a right-handed style. Being naturally right-handed there are disadvantages, I'll admit. I can play the kit the other way round but I now feel comfortable with it set like that. What is rather strange is that I'm right-handed but left-footed." [1]

The band members eventually clubbed together and bought Steve his own kit, each contributing four shillings and two pence a week to pay off the hire purchase repayments. The Scimitars (as Steve's first band named themselves) became fairly popular around the Torquay area, playing covers of the Shadows hits of the day. When the band eventually split up, Steve, together with the band's guitarist and bassist, formed a five-piece blues band called The Devarks. Steve gave up his day job on a building site and the band headed for Germany, where they spent three months touring the clubs until finally going their separate ways. Steve returned to Exeter where his mother lived, renting a small terraced cottage and taking up a regular job but continuing to play with bands at night in addition to pursuing his love of painting.

At that historic meeting in July 1966 at Dirty Dot's, Martin and Glenn Turner invited Steve to join their band, an offer the sticksman eagerly accepted. A week later the trio played their first gig, just before England won the World Cup at Wembley. By 1967, Steve Upton had persuaded Martin and Glenn to relocate from Torquay to Exeter.

"Martin lived in Torquay and I had lived in Torquay, but when we met I was living in Exeter," remembers Upton. "I said to Mart, 'It's time you left home – come up here and live with me.' So he and Glenn came up and that was the beginning of leaving the nest for them." [4]

By 1969, with the Empty Vessels musical style now bearing similarities to the Who/Fleetwood Mac/Led Zeppelin sound of the day, it was decided that the name (derived from the phrase, "empty vessels make the most noise") no longer seemed appropriate, so it was changed – to Tanglewood.

As Glenn Turner remembers: "We took two weeks out in the sticks in a cottage to write a new set and I guess we wanted a name that was more '1969' and marked a departure from the old to the new."

"Empty Vessels was a name that we felt was indicative of where we'd come from – the sticks," adds Upton. "We weren't, as the phrase continues, making the most noise. We felt that our music had a bit more quality than just a noisy band." [2]

It wasn't long before Tanglewood moved to London and turned fully professional, having already built up a reputation on the pub/dance hall circuit in the Torquay/Exeter area (notable venues included the Shiphay Youth Hall, Foxhole Village Hall and the Landsdowne Ballroom) and having opened for a number of major acts.

"We supported the Who at Torquay Town Hall, playing to 2,000 people," remembers Glenn Turner. "We also supported Led Zeppelin and Fleetwood Mac at Exeter Civic Hall. I also remember doing a village hall with the Spectres, who shortly after changed their name to Status Quo."

For Martin Turner, the decision to "turn pro" had been made in the wake of a road accident in Exeter on New Year's Day 1969. As Martin recalls: "I had a nasty accident as a result of staying up all night. We'd played a gig in Cornwall on New

Year's Eve and Steve gave me some stick because I didn't want to go into work the next day, but he made me. In the afternoon I had a big smash in the car I was driving and that really freaked me out. I nearly killed a woman and her baby. That was the point at which I decided you can't work all night and all day – you have to do one thing or the other. So it was time for me to become a professional musician".[4]

"It was a break we had to make," continues Upton. "We were one of the most popular bands in Exeter. We could stay that way or go to London and see the world. As Mart said, the catalyst of the whole thing was working all night and then trying to do it during the day."[4]

Steve, being the conservative member of the group, persuaded Martin and Glenn to hold fire for a few months so that he could get some money saved up before making the big leap. So on 13 May 1969 the three of them relocated to London to try and "make it big". As Steve remembers: "We were leaving the small pond for the big one."[4]

On arrival in London, Martin, Steve and Glenn found themselves in the wrong part of the city.

"Being lost was just part of the adventure," admits Upton. "That day we sat in a van outside a studio which a friend of ours from Torquay worked in. It was in New Bond Street. In the evening he took us back to his flat. By coincidence, a one roomed flat was vacant in the same block, so we took it."[5]

Tanglewood spent the next couple of months playing club gigs around London and trying to secure professional representation, including advertising for a manager. As Martin remembers: "We went to loads of people in London and people would say, 'No, sorry, come back in a couple of years when you've learned to write songs properly'. We went to Apple, the Beatles company, and they just showed us the door. But I was totally one-track minded – 'I'm going to get somewhere in this business. If you can help me, fine. If you cannot and you don't like what we're doing then get out of the way and let me through to where I wanna go!' I think you have to be that single-minded. We had a very positive attitude to everything, in a nice kind of way – not in a nasty way."[4]

Shortly after settling in London, Glenn Turner decided to leave the band and return to the West Country. "It was after much pressure from a girl I was in love with in the summer of 1969," recalls Glenn. "I knew straight away it was a mistake, and tried to re-instate myself with the band after a week, but was told I'd made my decision, so 'Bye'. I felt near suicidal at this point. I split from the band and lost my girlfriend within weeks."

Tanglewood's final gig was at the Country Club, Hampstead in July 1969 as support act to Keith Relf, the former Yardbirds' vocalist. It was here that Martin and Steve first met Miles Copeland III, an expatriate American who had been bought up in Beirut by a Scottish mother and a southern American CIA agent father. Miles explains how he first came to be involved with the band:

"I was living in England in 1969. I went to a club and I saw a couple of the guys, Steve and Martin, in a band. I thought they were great and after the show I went up to them. It turned out that it was their last show with that line-up. We got to be friends and I agreed to help rebuild a new band."[2]

Left: The Empty Vessels,
Martin Turner, Steve Upton, Glen Turner. *Photo: M. Dadley*
Right: Ted Turner playing guitar on the right, 1969.
Photo: Wishbone Ash Fan Club Archives

"After the show I went to the bar and there I met a guy sporting short back and sides, horn rimmed glasses and of collegiate dress," recalls Steve Upton of his first introduction to Copeland. "I thought I was in the presence of a Joseph Smith fan and was preparing myself to argue the virtues of rock 'n' roll, but he was not – he was an American. I told him our story and that this was the last gig and he offered to help. Martin and I went over to his house in St. John's Wood – a well proportioned house at 21 Marlborough Place with its own rehearsal studio in the basement which had been built for Miles' kid brother Stewart, a budding drummer. After several days of discussions, Martin and I agreed Miles should manage us despite the fact that he had no prior experience of managing a group."[5]

Steve and Martin spent the months of July and August searching the country for guitar players. Miles offered to pay for an ad for musicians in *Melody Maker*. The ad read: "Wanted – Lead Guitarist: Must be positive thinking, creative and adaptable, for strongly backed group with great future."

"All these people started to ring us up," remembers Martin. "We'd go into the cellar under Miles' house and have a blow for a while. Sometimes it lasted ten minutes, other times three hours."[6]

One of the replies to the ad came from an eighteen year old Birmingham born guitarist, David 'Ted' Turner (born 2 August 1950 and no relation to Martin). Ted lived with his parents in the Yardley area of Birmingham and had finished his schooling at the Cockshut Hill Boys School. Ted started playing guitar at the age of sixteen but had little experience of playing in bands except for a Birmingham blues band called King Biscuit.

"When I left school I had a variety of jobs – printing, car washing – but gradually the music took over," remembers Ted. "I used to listen to Buddy Holly and rock 'n' roll, but at sixteen I really got into the blues thing. I got into it so much that the only way I could express myself was to start playing myself. I used to listen to albums and play along, and I joined a semi-pro blues band. They weren't very successful – just local gigs. I couldn't have done more than thirty gigs with them over a space of about three months. We split up because we had no finances."[7]

Prior to responding to Steve and Martin's ad, Ted had auditioned (unsuccessfully) for Jon Hiseman's Colosseum. "They were looking for a guitarist in the early days and I went along to the audition," recalls Ted. "They were incredible guys, which was good because at the stage I was at, if they'd said something horrible it would have hurt like hell, but they encouraged me."[8]

Despite his lack of experience, Steve and Martin were amazed when they first heard Ted play.

"Ted lived for and with his guitar," says Steve Upton.[1] "He played it constantly and took it everywhere he went. His greatest goal in life was to get a Gibson Les Paul Sunburst guitar. At the time he wasn't really conversant with a lot of chords, but he had the right feel."[10]

Martin and Steve didn't think that Ted was quite good enough after that first audition and wrote telling him he had been rejected – but a few weeks later they had a change of heart.

"I remember his mum answering the phone and giving me a right ear bashing about how good a guitarist her son was," recalls Martin. "I told her that we were inviting him back down to London for a second audition and then she changed her tune!"

Another reply to the ad came in the shape of the more experienced Andy Powell (born 19 February 1950). Born in Stepney in the East End of London, Andy had been living with his family in Hemel Hempstead, a post-war "new town" about twenty miles north-west of London, where he had played with a number of bands, having taken up guitar at the age of eleven. Andy's first band was a Shadows-based group.

"My original hero was Bruce Welch," reveals Powell. "I always used to play rhythm in the early days, so I could relate to Bruce, because he was a rhythm player too. I do like Hank, but Bruce was the man."[7]

Andy subsequently played with a number of seven and nine-piece semi-professional soul groups such as the Sunsets, the Decoys and the Sugarband.

"We were all Mods," recalls Andy. "I used to wear a mohair suit and a short haircut. When I played in the Sugarband I used to just stand in the background and just chunk away on rhythm during songs like 'In the Midnight Hour'. We were the warm-up for groups like the Small Faces and the Who."[7]

After the break-up of the Sugarband, Andy's direction became bluesier, playing with smaller bands like the Ashley Ward Delegation. He remembers the summer of 1967 as being a key year in his musical development:

"I spent the whole summer going around all the festivals, so I got exposed to what big rock bands could do. I saw Cream's first gig. I saw Fleetwood Mac's first gig. I saw Jimi Hendrix play quite early on as well. I also saw Fairport Convention which got me into the folky thing. I once had to be helped off the stage by a bouncer at a Fleetwood Mac gig for trying to pull Peter Green back on stage for an encore."

After leaving Apsley Grammar School at eighteen, Andy took a job with John Lewis as a trainee fashion buyer, which he stuck for one and a half years. After a

thirty years of Wishbone Ash

Above and below: Andy Powell, Martin Turner, Steve Upton and Ted Turner. An early festival appearance, circa summer 1970 (note home made guitars).
Photos: Courtesy of Martin Turner

short stint as a Tonibell ice-cream man, he decided that he wouldn't be happy unless he was playing with a professional band. He continued working with various bands part-time right up until the beginning of 1969. After his audition for Wishbone Ash, Andy took off for a holiday to Morocco with the idea of "getting out of his head and figuring out what he wanted to do". It was on returning from that holiday that he was invited to come back and play with Ted and to join the fledgling Wishbone Ash.

"There were so many people coming up, it was incredible," says Martin, "but we knew we wanted Andy straight away. He was original; he had a style of his own."[9]

Martin Turner, in an early *Melody Maker* interview, revealed that Ted and Andy weren't actually accepted straight away:

"After a month we didn't feel we'd found the right person to fit into the concept, so we threw the whole thing open again and re-thought the whole idea. We decided that there would have to be changes. We remembered Ted and Andy and asked them to call on us again. They didn't know each other at all but after one afternoon of them playing and talking together, something clicked."

Although not originally intending to recruit two guitarists – they had planned to enlist a keyboard player to augment the line-up – Martin and Steve, unable to decide between Andy and Ted, invited both guitarists to rehearsals to see how they would play together.

"During auditions they'd seen other players that were probably technically better than either Andy or me, but I think Martin picked up on what having two lead guitar players might offer," remembers Ted.

"It was very difficult deciding at that point who should replace my brother," admits Martin. "We figured, 'Why don't we investigate the possibilities of having these guys who are both good lead guitar players' – playing together and maybe establish some kind of new musical style."[2]

Andy Powell adds: "The two of us had auditioned and they couldn't decide who was going to do it, so we both got together in rehearsals. I'd been playing in soul bands, where you do a lot of arrangements for brass, so I was used to harmony. Martin had a very melodic sense and we just started to develop a sound and use the front-line guitars to create melodies".

Ted and Andy's individual playing styles complemented each other perfectly, so the search for a keyboard player was abandoned and both guitarists were asked to join the band, thus paving the way for the famous twin lead guitar sound that would become the band's trademark.

"For me it was a tremendous task getting into it," remembers Ted. "I was very inexperienced compared to the others. They'd all played in bands and they'd been playing for about five years, so for me it was a real fight. I remember the great thrill about it – having to concentrate on everything".[1]

Wishbone Ash was by no means the first band to feature the sound of twin lead guitars. Before the Ash had come Jeff Beck and Jimmy Page in the Yardbirds and a less well-known British group called Blossom Toes (who featured Jim Cregan) had also toyed with the idea. Several acts had even boasted a three guitar front-line – notably Fleetwood Mac. Wishbone Ash was, however, one of the first bands to truly explore the melodic and harmonic possibilities the twin guitar approach had to offer. As Martin Turner states: "Before that, guitarists would play against each other, which was completely ineffective." [9]

Andy Powell even remembers being in a band where there were two lead guitarists: "Just prior to joining Wishbone I was in another band which could be said to be a twin lead band. We'd just started to do some twin lead stuff, though most of it was rhythmic more than anything else."

Throughout the early seventies Wishbone were to gain the reputation of being *the* twin lead guitar band, influencing a whole later generation of rock groups including Thin Lizzy, Iron Maiden and Def Leppard. Indeed Andy and Ted gained the nick-name of "the Harmony Twins" in the British music press. Martin's fascination with harmony had in fact begun in the Empty Vessels days:

"Whether the twin lead would have developed had I stayed, I don't know," says Glenn Turner in retrospect, "but we had played some primitive instrumental stuff as a three piece, incorporating harmonies between bass guitar and myself playing twin note stuff. I think Martin did have visions of harmony lead."

With the line-up complete, the band rehearsed in the basement of Miles Copeland's home. Material from the Empty Vessels days was reworked and new material composed.

"We took about six weeks rehearsing from about eleven in the morning until eleven at night," remembers Andy Powell. "We weren't always happy with everything we did, but we knew that we were good and we knew that we had created a sound."[11]

By October 1969 Martin and Steve were sharing a bedsit in the Chalk Farm area of north-west London and Andy and Ted had moved into a flat in nearby Gloucester Avenue. At this time the four members of the embryonic Wishbone Ash were in dire straits financially. Their flats were real dives but were nevertheless useful as a source of inspiration for songs like "Lady Whiskey". Andy recalls the first time his mother came to visit him in London:

"She came up to the flat that Martin had found for Ted and myself. It was actually a condemned flat. She walked into the room and took one look at what her son was reduced to and promptly burst into tears. The first guy who knocked on our door was the rat catcher. We had literally no money and were existing on very little food. This went on for nearly a year. We used to walk over to Miles Copeland's house in St John's Wood where we had our rehearsal room. We were like waifs and strays eating the crumbs off the table. He used to toast up a load of English muffins by an open fire. We had jam and butter with them and we used to actually look forward to that, as that was all we ever ate some days."

As well as feeding his new band, Miles Copeland had already started trying to arrange gigs for them to play. But first, a new name was needed. "Wishbone Ash" was eventually chosen, in preference to Miles Copeland suggestions such as Third World War and Jesus Duck!

"I remember Miles coming in one day and saying that we must have a name as he had gigs lined up for us," recalls Martin. "We'd written down lots of names on two separate pieces of paper and to shut him up I picked two words off the lists – "Wishbone" and "Ash". It was a very flippant act on my part but in a way it gave

Blowin' Free

COUNTRY CLUB BELSIZE PARK NW3

WISHBONE ASH
RUPERTS PEOPLE

THURSDAY MAY 14 8:00   6/-

DUNSTABLE CIVIC
Monday, May 18th   In Concert

DEEP PURPLE
and their guests **WISHBONE ASH**
plus lights 'n' sounds 'n' drinks

Monday Bank Holiday | Monday, June 1st
May 25th — **CLOSED** | **FREE**

Friday, October 9th

FREE
WISHBONE ASH
15/- advance, £1 at door

SATURDAY, 2nd MAY
HEAVY JELLY
WISHBONE ASH
UNIVERSITY COLLEGE, GOWER STREET, W.C.
TICKETS 10/-

the band an identity – Wishbone for the future as in "wishing" and Ash for the past as in "ashes". They seemed to fit together well and they didn't restrict us stylistically. It meant we could go in any direction musically. If you have a name like Led Zeppelin, it's got to be heavy. "Wishbone Ash" was flexible."[2]

Miles Copeland was also managing another group at this time – Rupert's People – containing Rod Lynton amongst its members, who would go on to become Wishbone's publicist. The story goes that not having many contacts in the music business and having the task of finding work for the band, he bought a phone book from an "agent" called "Rick" through an ad in *Melody Maker*, supposedly with the numbers of hundreds of promoters and clubs all over the country. Miles even got "Rick" to work in his office at 21 Marlborough Place to start booking the gigs. It was only when Rupert's People started turning up for gigs at non-existent venues, long since closed down, that Miles and the band realised that they'd been had.

Wishbone Ash performed their first gig supporting Aynsley Dunbar's Retaliation in front of 500 people at Dunstable Civic Hall on 10 November 1969. For this they were paid the princely sum of £5. Martin also recalls one of their early London gigs – at Klook's Kleek in West Hampstead, a venue where Ten Years After had recorded an early album.

"We contacted everyone we knew in London – friends, relatives and so on and told them to be there. We told them that when you arrive you have to say to the guy on the door, 'Are Wishbone Ash really playing here tonight?' This freaked out the owner who thought that this Wishbone Ash must be a really big group. The idea was that not only would he book us again, but he'd also tell his fellow promoters who would then book us."

Despite the fact that the gigs were starting to happen, the band was still living well below the poverty line.

"We only had one place to go, and that was up," says Powell. "I was playing a home made guitar, Martin was playing a home made bass and we built our own speaker cabinets in a garage. We were existing on about £5 a week each. One flat I lived in had a gas heater that I kept going by recycling the same shilling through the coin box for a month."[11]

"Most bands tell you about when they're starving and have to scrape together enough money for fish and chips," adds Martin, "but that's the way it was. I don't regret what we did. I never felt even then that the world owed me a living, but it was good fun."[1]

Most of the autumn of 1969 was spent getting to know each other musically with the aim of finding a "sound" that would give the band an identity.

"We had nothing else to do but to rehearse all day," recounts Andy Powell. "Basically we had to get to know each other. Martin had a lot of typically Martin things that were quite different. I was used to bass players who usually kept in the background and just played, but Martin was a bass player who would do his own thing and play all over the place. I had my fairly steady blues/r'n'b background, as did Ted, so there was this 'where do we meet in the middle?' We were all very different musically and it was that fact that made us all work very hard to actually find our sound."

Wishbone Ash only managed to play a handful of gigs in 1969 but come 1970 things started to happen. They played mainly at small clubs or to students at colleges, gradually building up a following on the London club and college circuit. They opened for many of the more established acts of the day – long forgotten names such as Mighty Baby, Heavy Jelly, Boris, Flesh and Rupert's People – plus more familiar acts such as Slade, T-Rex, Taste, Ten Years After, Caravan and Smile (featuring future Queen members Brian May and Roger Taylor). Regular London venues included Kingston Polytechnic, the Temple, Imperial College, Bedford College, Connaught Hall, University College, the Marquee Club and the Speakeasy. For one gig at Bedford College, Miles Copeland managed to hype the band into a support slot for Colosseum even though they weren't booked. They just turned up played for about half an hour before the plugs were pulled.

"Miles said that we were friends of Colosseum, purely on the basis of Ted auditioning for them months earlier," recalls Martin. "In fact as he was American he bulldozed his way through local protocol to get us gigs, whereas an Englishman might have come away with nothing."

The band secured the help of a couple of friends to do the road crew duties including Chris Runciman and Mark Emery (who came to be known as "Hobbit" – a name given to him by Ted, who decided he resembled the Tolkein character). Mark had also moved up to London from the West Country and lived in the same circle of bedsits in Gloucester Avenue.

"I was a friend of the band and had a job as a photographic technician," remembers Mark. "Once they got the two guitarists in place I started as a roadie with them. They were doing rehearsals at Marlborough Place and we all got involved with building the gear. Martin and I used to paint all the cabinets white, so they had these 8x12" cabinets which were so bright to look at that they almost blinded you. The band bought a short wheel-based Transit van and I learned to drive in that. I actually passed my test in a Transit. Chris was hired by the band, but as he had tin ears I ended up taking over the sound eventually."

The Wishbone Ash live set in 1970 consisted entirely of original numbers – songs such as "Blind Eye", "Lady Whiskey", "Queen of Torture" and the set closer, "Phoenix" – all of which would make it onto the first album. Through constant gigging the band gradually began to attract more and more interest from fans and from within the music industry. During 1970 and 1971 they managed to get support slots on UK tours by Free, ELP and Mott the Hoople. Mark Emery also recalls that the DJ John Peel was an early champion of the band:

"I remember a gig in Northampton, where John Peel was the DJ for the night and he really pushed the band. This was before the first album was released, but once it was out he would always play tracks on his radio show."

On a couple of spare days in March, the band visited the West of England Sound Studios in Exeter to record a demo tape to tout around the various record companies. This would be the first experience of recording for all four members of the band. The recorded tracks would later surface on their debut album, but it "was only a trial run," Andy Powell remembers.

"It was the general opinion of the band that the studio was not up to scratch and so the session was aborted," agrees Martin.

Later, the band had the opportunity of recording in a London studio, Advision, where their friend, Phil Dunne, was a sound engineer alongside Eddie Offord (who would later find success with Yes). Martin remembers the experience well.

"Phil could get 'down time' for us late at night. So we would go in at 11.00 at night and hopefully stay 'till 12 or 1. What actually happened was that you recorded till about 3 o'clock. We had to pay about £300 for the privilege over a period of about three or four weeks. We did in fact record a whole album's worth of material. This was the tape which we later gave to Derek Lawrence, which led to our recording deal with MCA."

Another first experience for most of the band was a week-long stint in Paris. The trip ran from 27 March to 2 April, and, as Martin Turner recalls, was secured by a former college friend of Miles' from the American University in Beirut:

"She had visited Miles in London and seemed to fancy him, so we said to Miles, 'It says in your contract you will do everything in your powers to get us gigs and if that means shagging someone, then do it!' So that was how we got to visit France."

The band's introduction to overseas touring would not, however, pass without incident. On arrival in Calais, French customs officials informed the band and their manager they would need a carnet (or bond) to assure the officials that they wouldn't sell their equipment while in France – hardly likely considering most of their gear was home-made and near worthless. This resulted in Miles having to sail back to Dover to get the carnet stamped, returning some eighteen hours later to a restless group in a Calais customs shed. Even when they got Paris and found their first venue (le Bibloquet) it was not all plain sailing according to Martin:

"Le Bibloquet was a rich Arab club and perhaps a more sophisticated band would have been more suitable. We started playing and all these little Arabs started running around saying, 'Zoo loud! Zoo loud!' We only managed two or three nights there before Miles got us into 'Le Golf Drouot' and 'Le Rock 'n' Roll Circus' where Johnny Haliday hung out. We went back a couple of times and made great friends with the DJ, Jacques Chabiron."

On returning from France, Andy Powell, who had felt unwell on the return ferry crossing, was diagnosed as having pleurisy. This resulted in a month long lay-off from live work with band activity resuming in May with some more UK dates. This included a return to Dunstable Civic Hall this time supporting Deep Purple who were then riding high in the charts with their *Deep Purple In Rock* album. It was this gig that effectively launched Wishbone Ash's recording career.

As Martin Turner remembers: "During the sound check Andy was onstage playing his guitar when Ritchie Blackmore walked on and started playing. Gradually they started speaking to each other with their guitars and there was quite a little rapport going on there. Anyway, Ritchie didn't say a word to us, but afterwards he told Derek Lawrence (Deep Purple's producer) about us. Derek was looking for bands to record, so he contacted us and we gave him our demo tape. He took it to someone he knew at MCA and that was the reason they signed us."[10]

Andy Powell is eternally grateful to Ritchie Blackmore for that first break:

"I owe him so much because we did that gig and I jammed with him at the sound check. It was quite good of him to tell Derek Lawrence about us and that led to that first call."

Derek Lawrence, who had produced the first three Deep Purple albums, takes up the story:

"I was in the studio with Ritchie and he said to me, 'There's this great band that supported us last night,' and he suggested that I go and see them. I'd got to the stage then where I'd go and see bands and it would be a waste of time, so I only went on recommendation by someone whose opinion I could trust. I used to listen to so many bands then but they stood head and shoulders above the rest and so I decided to take a look at them after first hearing a tape that they sent me. So I first got to see them when they played at the Hampstead Town and Country Club. The only negative thing about them was that they were a great band who didn't have a great singer."

Indeed this question of who should sing lead vocals would haunt the band throughout their career and eventually lead to a split. Generally speaking, in the early years either Martin or Ted would sing depending on who had written the song (or at least the lyrics). Gradually Martin came to be the lead singer for most songs with Andy and Ted adding vocal harmonies. Martin Turner would stand centre stage, whilst Andy would be stage right and Ted stage left. Certainly, Martin came to be regarded as the "front-man" of the group, though not necessarily the focus of the music, which most fans perceived as residing with the guitarists.

The more the band gigged, the more they became noticed by rock fans and the music press. Notable appearances during the summer of 1970 included the Bath City Festival on 23 May, with Fleetwood Mac, Chicken Shack, Juicy Lucy and Soft Machine; supporting the Who at Dunstable Civic Hall on 25 July; consecutive support slots for Keef Hartley and Atomic Rooster at Torquay Town Hall (31 July and 1 August respectively); and an appearance at the NJF Festival at Plumpton Racecourse on 7 August. The band also recorded their first radio session for BBC Radio One. This was for the Bob Harris show and was recorded on 6 August.

While the band was busy on the road throughout the summer of 1970, Derek Lawrence, Don Shain (of MCA Records) and Miles Copeland were busy negotiating the contract that the boys had long been hoping for. MCA/Decca were not, in fact, the only record company interested in Wishbone Ash. Apparently the likes of CBS, Atlantic and Island had all sent A&R men to check out the group. However, it was with MCA that the band agreed contractual terms. This breakthrough occurred on 20 August 1970, when Wishbone Ash secured a $250,000 (£100,000) advance, five album recording contract with the American record label Decca (MCA in the UK). Derek Lawrence explains the connection:

"I had a mate in MCA USA (Decca) called Don Shain. He came with me to the Town and Country Club to see the band. We agreed that they would be worth signing so he and Miles Copeland thrashed out the deal and that was how they came to be signed to MCA."

This explains how Wishbone became a British based band with a recording contract with an American label – a deal that would work both for and against the band. Andy Powell explains:

thirty years of Wishbone Ash

Above: Early promo shot. (l-r) Andy Powell, Steve Upton, Ted Turner, Martin Turner.
Photo: Wishbone Ash Fan Club Archives

"The reason the contract was with MCA (US) was that Miles being an American and Don being an American led to the contract being drawn up in LA. Although it was probably a better deal financially, it meant that we didn't have as much rapport with the record company as we could have done. Neither did the Who or Elton John for that matter as the label was only just starting to get into rock. Mind you I don't think it would have been any different if it had been in London. They were all a bunch of suits. Very few record labels at that time could be said to be 'hip' apart from maybe Island and Chrysalis."

Recording sessions for the band's eponymous debut album took place at De Lane Lea studios, Kingsway, London during September 1970 with Martin Birch engineering and Derek Lawrence producing. Martin Turner remembers Derek fondly:

"Derek was very much the old school type of producer. His idea of producing was very much an instinctive approach. He knew when something sounded good. If we were getting a bit heavy, he would tell a few jokes, or if we weren't pulling our weight, he would crack the whip. Basically he was a Teddy boy who wore his initials on his blazer like Phil Spector."

For the sessions, Ted Turner played a Les Paul Junior whilst Andy Powell played a newly acquired Gibson SG Special (his Gibson Flying V would not appear until after the album was recorded). Martin Turner was still playing what he described as his "Mickey Mouse Special" and hired a Fender Jazz bass for the sessions. He acquired a Rickenbacker soon after the album's completion.

Andy Powell thinks the band did quite well in the sessions considering that they had been together for less than a year:

"By the time we actually got to do a recording session for real we were in pretty good shape having already gone through the experience at Advison. Mind you we were scrambling around for material. That's why there's such a wide variety of styles and sounds on that album."

Derek Lawrence explains how he went about recording the young Wishbone Ash:

"My attitude then with Wishbone Ash, as with any new band I was recording, was to try and get onto record the thing that had impressed me about them live – the atmosphere of what they had on stage. I was especially impressed with the way the two guitarists worked. Andy was the proficient guitarist whilst Ted was more of a blues guitarist. The contrast between the two of them worked very nicely. The sessions were quite straightforward – get the tracks recorded, though more time was taken on the vocals than anything else."

On 29 November the band were back in the BBC studios, recording another Radio One session for Bob Harris. Tracks for the band's BBC sessions were laid down pretty quickly, usually in one or two takes. These sessions would often be slotted in directly before a show or in the morning. The BBC allowed bands artistic freedom and, at that time, was a public body which was quite prepared to invest time and money in highlighting and promoting new talent – a far cry from its present, more corporate approach.

The eponymously titled debut album *Wishbone Ash* was released on 4 December 1970. The album, which was basically the band's live set, featured all the trademarks of the early Wishbone Ash – Andy and Ted's revolutionary twin guitar front-line, Steve Upton's impeccably tight though often jazzy drumming and Martin Turner's basswork, which was in the melodic British style typified by John Entwistle, Jack Bruce, Paul McCartney and Chris Squire.

"I tend to play in such a way as to constitute a melody," says Martin. "I think that is a very un-American way of playing. I actually believe in cultivating unorthadoxy as it tends to set you apart from everyone else."[12]

Wishbone Ash opens with "Blind Eye", an up-tempo R&B inspired number with Ted on vocals and the band's twin guitars prominent. It was recorded with Procol Harum's Matthew Fisher on piano.

"Hearing 'Blind Eye' on the radio for the first time while we were travelling to a show was very exciting. It was also the first time I heard myself sing. After that I always tried to get the others to sing!" recalls Ted.[11]

"We were all too afraid to sing for the first few years," adds Martin. "I suppose it was just a matter of confidence."[1]

"Lady Whiskey" follows – an all out rocker featuring an aggressive Andy Powell guitar solo with Martin screaming out a high-pitched lead vocal, singing a lyric inspired by Steve and Martin's landlady in Chalk Farm. "To show you what we were living in, her husband came home late one night, really out of his head and they had a fight," remembers Steve. "He knocked her through the front door and locked her out. She wasn't around for two days after that and she was eventually found in hospital."[10]

"Errors of my Way" takes the mood down and marked the band's first foray into folk-rock. Featuring harmony vocals from Martin and Andy and showcasing the typically melodic side of Ted's guitar playing, the track goes through a variety of mood changes without becoming boring or self-indulgent. The folk element would subsequently crop up on numerous occasions throughout the band's career, but was initially the influence of Andy Powell (as were the lyrics).

"I was listening to groups like Pentangle and Fairport Convention, which brought about the band's folk influence," reveals Andy.

The rocky "Queen of Torture" closes the album's first side, pushing Martin's vocal chords to their limits, as he belts out a lyric inspired by a girl the band knew.

"Her name was Sylvie," recalls Martin, "and she was into some very weird sexual trips. Ted used to sleep in this little bed which we called the trolley, and I think she used to tie him in there and rape him!"[10]

The second side of the album contains two lengthy tracks. The first of these, "Handy", had actually started life during the Empty Vessels days. Aside from a brief Martin Turner vocal towards the end, the track is pretty much instrumental, showcasing the talents of all four members of the band. Live, the song would feature a lengthy Steve Upton drum solo. The track was inspired by the jazz musician, John Handy.

The album's closing track "Phoenix" would become the climax of the band's live set for many years. During that period many groups would finish their set with a longer number designed to highlight the band's strengths and garner the best response from the audience. "Phoenix" fitted into this mould perfectly. From a peaceful beginning, with restrained soloing from Ted Turner and a Martin Turner vocal based on the legend of the Phoenix (the mythical bird said to rise from the ashes), the song builds up with Ted breaking into a lengthy and uncharacteristically aggressive guitar solo.

"I guess "Phoenix" was our masterpiece," admits Ted, "bringing a lot of attention to the band. It was just an elongated, structured jam."[11]

Andy Powell explains how the "train like" effect on the central section of "Phoenix" was played:

"Martin would damp his strings a semi-tone below the 12th fret and run the pick over the four strings to accentuate the beats. Ted would damp the strings around the 8th fret and strum in time with the drums and I would damp the strings high up on the fretboard to achieve a slight harmonic effect".

Although *Wishbone Ash* did not attract extensive attention from the music press, those who did review the album were very positive in their comments. Respected UK DJ/music critic John Peel proclaimed: "I haven't been so impressed with a relatively new band for a long time. Their music is original, exciting and beautifully played."

Thirty years on from his first recording sessions with Wishbone Ash, Derek Lawrence looks back fondly on the band's first album: "It still has that freshness today that it did then and what is excellent is that it sounds like being at a gig without the audience."

Shortly after the album's completion, Andy Powell bought his first Gibson Flying V, an instrument which would soon become his and the band's trademark, not least because of its wishbone shape. As Andy remembers:

Above: 1971, Powell shows off his trademark Flying V, the band backed by a truckload of Orange amplification. (l-r) Andy Powell, Martin Turner, Ted Turner and Steve Upton. *Photo: Wishbone Ash Fan Club Archives*

"I got word that a music store called Orange had a couple of Vs come in; we ended up using Orange amplification. There were two mid-sixties model Flying Vs there and Orange had bought them from some other dealer and they were still in their packing cases – two 1966 burgundy Flying Vs. One was already spoken for, so I strapped the other one on. I liked the way it played and how vibrant it felt even before I plugged it in, so I parted with £300 for it. That wouldn't be a great deal of money today, but for those times it was a rip-off."[7]

In December 1970 Wishbone Ash made their TV debut, performing "Queen of Torture" and "Errors of my Way" live in the studio for BBC TV's *Disco 2* programme. Martin Turner recalls: "I remember when we first started, my Gran saying to me, 'What are you going to do when you grow up?' She stopped saying that when she saw me on the telly!"[1]

By the end of 1970 Wishbone Ash had much to be thankful for. They had done the ground work necessary for success in the music business. They had played around 200 gigs throughout the length and breadth of Britain. They had secured a five album recording contract with a major record label and they had an album selling enough copies to make it into the album charts. The future looked bright.

Chapter Two

New Rising Stars

At the beginning of 1971, the Wishbone Ash bandwagon was starting to roll. All the hard work of the previous year was starting to pay off. The first album had just entered the UK album charts, peaking at a lowly 34, giving them some much needed credibility in the eyes of the record company. To keep interest in the album alive, MCA released the band's first single in February, containing two cuts off the album – "Blind Eye" backed with "Queen of Torture". Despite some airplay by the likes of John Peel and Alan Freeman, it made no impression on the charts.

Starting the year off on a high note, the band were invited back to the BBC studios in Maida Vale, London on New Year's Day, to record their third Bob Harris BBC session. Gigging continued throughout much of January and February concluding with a sold-out performance at the Roundhouse, Chalk Farm, on 21 February. This show was not only their first major headlining gig in London, but also the band's "farewell" for the time being as the following day they would depart for their first American tour. In many ways it marked the end of the first stage of Wishbone Ash's rise to the big time. It was appropriate that it took place at the Roundhouse (a former railway engine shed) a mere stone's throw from their London homes. Although the band had a recording contract and an album out, finances were far from healthy, so to save on the pennies only the band and manager would make the US trip. But Ted Turner had other ideas, as Mark Emery recalls:

"When it came to the band first going to the States, it was felt that they couldn't afford to take anybody with them to help with the equipment. It was Ted who insisted that I went. He actually stood up to the rest of the band and Miles which was nice."

The Ash were in good spirits as they flew out of Heathrow, arriving in Washington DC on 22 February, but would soon come down to earth with a bump. As Steve Upton remembers:

"The next day, while sightseeing, we ate our first MacDonalds hamburger and got stopped by police for tyre screeching near the White House and drinking beer in the car. Miles, pleading with the police officer, explaining that we were an English pop group, saved us from a premature deportation."[5]

Wishbone Ash performed their first American gig on 25 February 1971 in Austin, Texas, supporting the Guess Who, a big league band from Canada, who had peaked the previous year with their *American Woman* album and single. This was followed by appearances in San Antonio and Houston. The tour then moved West for a five night stint at Los Angeles' prestigious Whisky-a-Go-Go club, where the top brass from the band's US record company would be given a chance to check out their new signing. Such was the respect given to a visiting British band in those times that the unknown Wishbone Ash were taken from the airport to their hotel by limousine. The chauffeur is reported to have said the immortal words, "Which one of you is Mr. Ash?" before proceeding to offer the band a huge joint each. Miles Copeland was apparently not impressed and complained to MCA headquarters about how the band had been treated. Things would get stranger the longer the band stayed in LA as Steve Upton recalls:

"The third day in LA, Ted went for a walkabout in the desert with the help of a few mind expanders and local reprobates. We were very concerned when he did not return after a day, because the previous week Jeremy Spencer from Fleetwood Mac had gone missing and not come back. He had been abducted by the Jesus People and we were sure Ted was another victim. Luckily his body showed up ten minutes before we were due onstage, but his brain didn't turn up until the next day!"[5]

A bootleg cassette recording of one of the Whisky shows would later do the rounds amongst the more resourceful elements of the band's fanbase. The recording featured one unreleased track, "LA Blues", which eventually found its way onto the 1995 US fan club CD, *From The Archives*. Not a particularly outstanding track, with the band sounding out of tune and nervous at times, but nevertheless a valuable historical record of those first dates in America.

The California leg of the tour also took in several appearances at the famous Fillmore West in San Fransisco, where promoter Bill Graham had set up shop. It is rumoured that one of Wishbone Ash's performances exists somewhere on black and white cine film, as it was standard procedure for all bands to be filmed there. The tour continued with gigs in San Diego, Detroit, Chicago and St. Louis, supporting the likes of Poco, the James Gang, Elton John and Seatrain, but it was by no means a commercial success. With Wishbone Ash being virtually unknown in the States at this point, it was hardly surprising that they could not get enough gigs to fill the entire seven-week stint. Mark Emery recalls the band being holed up in a motel for several days on end:

"It was dreadful some of the time. We were actually stuck in this little motel in Wildwood, New Jersey for a couple of weeks waiting for the gigs to come. Mind you I had my first experience of drinking Bourbon there. I never touched it for twenty years after that!"

Ted Turner recalls his thoughts on that first American tour: "We treated the tour as an educational trip, which is about all you can do when you go across there for the first time. It did teach us so much."[13]

Andy Powell agrees: "Going to America for the first time was like going to an alien planet. Being a British rock 'n' roll band, they just loved us. America was and still is the land of excess, but we didn't know that, so we'd find ourselves in bizarre situations. All that you've ever read about bands touring in the United States in the seventies, we actually did. And jolly good fun it was too!"

During early US tours, both Andy Powell and Ted Turner took every opportunity to add new instruments to their collections.

"You have to understand that when Wishbone Ash first started touring the States in the early seventies, the interest in old guitars was not as great as it is now," says Powell, "so we picked up some very nice guitars at very reasonable prices. We'd buy stuff from people like Larry DiMarzio and Paul Hamer, who've since gone onto greater things. I distinctly remember Ted Turner buying a Gibson Les Paul Standard Flametop on at least three occasions, all at good prices."[14] Ted Turner adds: "It was like Christmas every day for us – you could pick them up very reasonably."

At that time the band's stage equipment was as follows. Andy Powell played his Gibson Flying V through an Orange 100-watt stack, with a reverb unit and Cry Baby wah-wah. Ted Turner played a Gibson Les Paul with three pick-ups through an Orange 100-watt stack with a reverb unit. Martin Turner played a Rickenbacker stereo bass through an Orange 200-watt amp with Orange reflector cabinet and Orange 2 x 15 cabinet. Steve Upton used a Ludwig drum kit.

Wishbone Ash returned to London on 13 April, but it wouldn't be long before they returned to the States, where they would eventually relocate. A week later the band returned to the BBC studios at Maida Vale, this time to record a session for the Stuart Henry Show. On 25 April Wishbone headlined their first major concert in central London at the Lyceum Ballroom. The bill also featured the Climax Blues Band, Wooden Horse, and Thin Lizzy whose line-up at this point was a three-piece featuring Eric Bell on guitar. It is widely held that it was after witnessing Wishbone Ash's twin guitar front-line that bassist/vocalist Phil Lynott and drummer Brian Downey decided to adopt a similar approach upon Bell's departure.

Throughout much of May the band was again touring the colleges and clubs of Great Britain, furthering their growing reputation. The band played their first headline gig at the Marquee club in London's Wardour Street (an essential venue for any up-and-coming rock band) on 4 May. Wishbone would make numerous appearances at the Marquee over the years, most notably in 1977 as a special treat to their fans just a couple of nights before playing to a sold out Wembley Empire Pool. On spare days during May and June, Wishbone returned to De Lane Lea studios to record the second album. Much of the material planned for inclusion

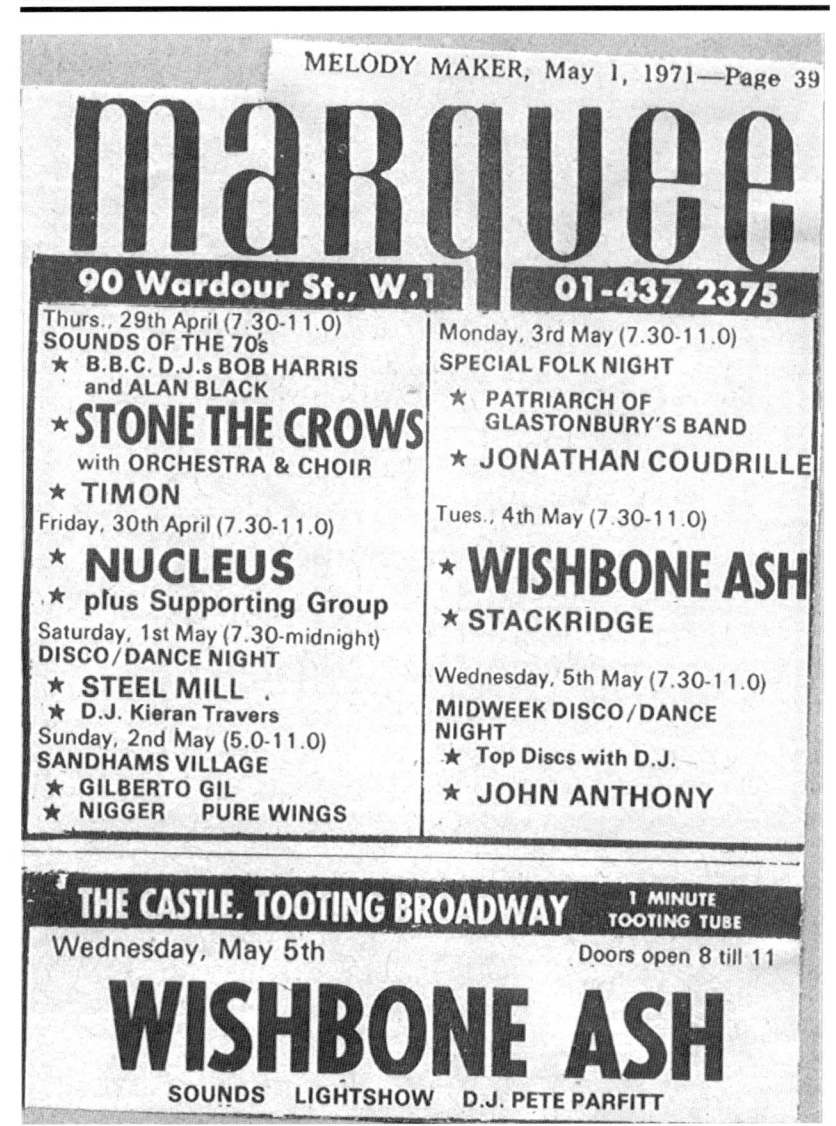

> **MELODY MAKER, May 1, 1971—Page 39**
>
> # marquee
>
> **90 Wardour St., W.1** | **01-437 2375**
>
> Thurs., 29th April (7.30-11.0)
> **SOUNDS OF THE 70s**
> ★ B.B.C. D.J.s BOB HARRIS and ALAN BLACK
> ★ **STONE THE CROWS**
> with ORCHESTRA & CHOIR
> ★ **TIMON**
>
> Friday, 30th April (7.30-11.0)
> ★ **NUCLEUS**
> ★ plus Supporting Group
>
> Saturday, 1st May (7.30-midnight)
> **DISCO/DANCE NIGHT**
> ★ **STEEL MILL**
> ★ D.J. Kieran Travers
>
> Sunday, 2nd May (5.0-11.0)
> **SANDHAMS VILLAGE**
> ★ GILBERTO GIL
> ★ NIGGER PURE WINGS
>
> Monday, 3rd May (7.30-11.0)
> **SPECIAL FOLK NIGHT**
> ★ PATRIARCH OF GLASTONBURY'S BAND
> ★ **JONATHAN COUDRILLE**
>
> Tues., 4th May (7.30-11.0)
> ★ **WISHBONE ASH**
> ★ **STACKRIDGE**
>
> Wednesday, 5th May (7.30-11.0)
> **MIDWEEK DISCO/DANCE NIGHT**
> ★ Top Discs with D.J.
> ★ **JOHN ANTHONY**
>
> ---
>
> **THE CASTLE. TOOTING BROADWAY**   1 MINUTE TOOTING TUBE
> Wednesday, May 5th   Doors open 8 till 11
> # WISHBONE ASH
> SOUNDS   LIGHTSHOW   D.J. PETE PARFITT

Above: Wishbone Ash's first headline appearance at London's Marquee club.

had been aired on recent live dates and the sessions were once again produced by Derek Lawrence and engineered by Martin Birch. One criticism that had been levelled at the first album was that the band's vocals did not match their obvious instrumental skills. Perhaps as a subconscious reaction to the critics, the second album saw the band concentrating largely on instrumental material. Derek Lawrence explains the thinking behind the second album's direction:

"With the second album, the idea was to try and grow from what we'd done on the first. We kept asking the question, 'Where should this album end up?' As with the first album, we just had to record what the band had available at the time – which was about six or seven songs."

It was sometime during the album sessions that Ted Turner, together with Wishbone's publicist and former Rupert's People frontman Rod Lynton, were invited to play on John Lennon's *Imagine* album. Rod had already done work for George Harrison and Ringo Starr and had a contact at Apple in Kevin Harrington. Kevin had worked for the Beatles since 1968 and would eventually join Wishbone's road crew. So when Lennon asked Rod to bring a guitarist along to the session, he in turn asked Ted. The Bones had been in the studio for about twelve hours and were about to call it a day, when Rod phoned to say he had a session for Ted. Ted said he was too tired but soon changed his mind when he heard who it was for and was whisked away to the studio in Lennon's white Rolls Royce. In the end Ted and Rod got to play acoustic guitars on the track "Crippled Inside". Incidentally, Andy Powell would later play sessions for both Ringo Starr and George Harrison, the latter on a song for Cilla Black. Both sessions remain unreleased to this day.

The month of June saw another milestone in Wishbone Ash's career – the first fully fledged British tour as the main act. It was a three band package bill, with Wishbone headlining over Renaissance and Stackridge. This was the first time that Wishbone were playing some of the country's major rock venues such as Newcastle City Hall and Manchester Free Trade Hall. After little more than a year, they had finally begun to move away from the club and college circuit. The tour was a complete sell out – a good omen for the future. Mind you, all seats were sold at the bargain price of 50p. The gig at Leicester's De Montfort Hall on 14 June was recorded with a view to possibly bringing out a live album sometime in the future. At the end of the tour the band made their first appearance at the Reading Festival along with Genesis and Lindisfarne – a festival they would headline more than once in years to come.

Certainly, the star of Wishbone Ash was well and truly in the ascendant in Britain, but America was another ball game. On 29 July the band returned to the States for a second US tour. This would be a six-week stint with the band headlining a number of shows as well as playing at major open air festivals. There were also support slots with the likes of the Who, Grand Funk Railroad, Black Sabbath, Leon Russell and Ten Years After. Supporting the Who – promoting their landmark *Who's Next* album – would be a daunting task for any band at the best of times but, as Andy Powell recalls, Wishbone Ash were "treated like gentlemen". For Powell however, the sight of Keith Moon bursting into his bedroom late one night brandishing a replica machine gun must have been terrifying to say the very least! Moon was in the middle of one of his japes – looking for the Who's agent, Ron Sunshine, in the belief that he had ripped off the band.

Whilst in the States, the band also made their first appearance on American TV – on the *Phil Donahue Show* – seen by millions of viewers. On 3 August, Ted Turner celebrated his 21st birthday in Wildwood, New Jersey where the band had a barbecue, followed by a jam session on a boat moored nearby. Whilst in Los Angeles, Wishbone Ash received the news that they had been voted "Best New Band" by UK music weeklies *Sounds* and *Melody Maker*, a breakthrough indeed. At the same time, more and more American fans were seeing and hearing Wish-

Wishbone concerts

WISHBONE Ash are set for their first major concert tour in June. The group, who record their second album for MCA during May, will be supported by Stackridge and Mogul Thrash.

The tour opens at Plymouth Town Hall on June 7, and continues at the Flamingo, Redruth (9), Colston Hall, Bristol (10), Southampton Guildhall (11), Oxford Town Hall (12), De Montfort Hall, Leicester (14), St George's Hall, Bradford (15), Free Trade Hall, Manchester (16), Warwick University (17), Town Hall, Birmingham (18), City Hall, Newcastle (19), City Hall, Hull (20), City Hall, Sheffield (22), City Hall, Leeds (23), Albert Hall, Nottingham (24), Caird Hall, Dundee (25), Stirling University (26), and Caley Cinema, Edinburgh (27).

In July Wishbone return to America for their second tour.

DE MONTFORT HALL
LEICESTER

THE BRICK COMPANY AND PYTHEON PRODUCTIONS PRESENT

WISHBONE ASH

Mon. June 14 at 7.30 p.m.

BALCONY 50p

A 63

TICKETS CANNOT BE EXCHANGED OR MONEY REFUNDED

Left: The band's first nationwide UK tour is announced in the music press.

Above: The gig at Leicester's De Montford Hall was recorded for selection of a live track, 'Where Were You Tomorrow' for the forthcoming album.
Courtesy of Chris Griffin.

bone Ash for the first time. On 16 August the band supported the Who at the Mississippi River Festival at Edwardsville, near St. Louis, playing before an audience of 35,000. This was followed a few weeks later by a notable appearance at the Seattle Setsop River festival, 3 September, in front of 70,000 people – one of the biggest audiences of the band's career. Such was the volume of traffic that Wishbone had to be escorted in and out of the festival site by helicopter.

There was, however, one major downer to this tour. At an open air show in Austin, Texas on 5 September tragedy struck as a store vendor selling hot dogs on the edge of the crowd was murdered by an irate punter while the band were on stage. This tragic event was later recounted in the song, "Rock 'n' Roll Widow" which appeared on the 1973 album *Wishbone Four*.

"There was a concession stand, a guy was selling hot dogs and somebody was angry that he hadn't got the right hot dog or whatever and pulled a gun and just shot the guy right there as we were standing there playing," remembers Andy Powell.

In September the second Wishbone Ash album, *Pilgrimage* was released in the UK (it had been available in the United States a month earlier). The gatefold cover featured a distinctive Storm Thorgerson design of bare tree branches in yellow and brown, whilst the inside featured several photographs taken by Storm of the band in various situations on the road. (Storm and his company Hipgnosis went on to design the covers for several more Wishbone Ash albums in the seventies and also for a whole host of other rock groups such as Pink Floyd, Led Zeppelin, Yes and Wings.)

The album featured seven cuts – six from the De Lane Lea sessions, plus a version of the band's traditional set closer "Where Were You Tomorrow" recorded live at Leicester De Montfort Hall on the June tour.

As with the first album, a diverse range of influences such as blues, jazz, R&B, folk and even reggae were clearly evident. Anyone expecting a hard rocker as the opening number would be surprised to hear instead "Vas Dis", a jazz cover which had already become a live favourite and a showcase for Martin Turner's scat-singing. Martin: "'Vas Dis' was written by a jazz musician, Jack McDuff, and we arranged it for dual lead guitars, which was not the easiest thing in the world to do. He had a live album out with that track on."[10]

"The Pilgrim", a technically brilliant guitar-based instrumental, had also been tried out on live audiences. Aside from a brief vocal chant from Martin and Andy, it is basically a highly intricate instrumental piece. The track begins with a sedate opening before changing pace and bursting into an up-tempo 7/4 section based around a Martin Turner bass riff and displaying the guitar skills of Ted Turner and Andy Powell.

"I was really into 'The Pilgrim' from the standpoint of a musical version of *Lord of the Rings*," reveals Martin Turner, "but that was probably just because I was reading the book at the same time that we were putting the tune together. That's what it meant for me, but I don't think it meant that for anyone else in the band."[10]

"Jailbait" was the album's first true vocal number. Sung by Ted Turner, the song is a natural successor to the first album's "Blind Eye", being in a similar R&B vein. With its boogie style, Wishbone would forever be unjustly labelled as a "boogie band" by certain sections of the UK music press. The song was inspired by an experience Ted had in America during the band's first US tour – "jail bait" being a reference to under-age teenage girls who would hang around backstage at gigs. It would remain a staple of Wishbone's live set for many years to come and became a popular encore number.

Martin: "Jailbait was written about a young lady called Linda who we met on our first visit to the States. She was a very beautiful girl for fifteen years old!"[10]

Closing the album's first side is "Alone", a short instrumental piece which fades in and fades out, hinting that only a segment of the recording was included. Martin Turner later revealed that this was indeed the case and that the tune had originally been part of a longer track featuring a full vocal and lyric, which he felt the record company had taken a distinct disliking to. Martin, who had been responsible for the song's lyric, felt particularly insulted by the edit at the time. He admitted that he was "pissed off that it got chopped around", but with hindsight he now regards the song as being "very limp" and is clearly embarrassed with what he describes as his "choir boy vocals". Despite this, both the edit and full version contain some beautiful, haunting playing from both guitarists. (The full, vocal version would finally surface in 1997 on the German 4CD *Distillation* compilation from Repertoire Records.)

By this time, the seeds of Martin's interest in the recording process were beginning to grow – an interest that would eventually lead to him producing several Wishbone albums. As Derek Lawrence remembers:

"By then it was obvious that Martin was becoming a strong character within the band. I remember when I went home from the studio, he would come in and remix a song and make it sound awful!"

Side Two of *Pilgrimage* opens with "Lullaby", representing Wishbone Ash at their most restrained. This largely acoustic piece, which again had been premiered live, was recorded without drums and was reminiscent of early Genesis.

"'Lullaby' was the product of getting two guitarists together, developing a chord sequence, turning it inside out and getting a tune out," reveals Andy Powell.[11]

One of the album's finest yet often overlooked cuts is undoubtedly "Valediction". Continuing the folk-rock direction of "Errors of my Way", "Valediction" added a couple of new twists in the form of an almost reggae-like middle section. The song also boasts a three-part harmony vocal – arguably the band's finest vocal work up to this point. "'Valediction' was really nice," admits Martin Turner. "Andy's solo on that was particularly good. That was a really exceptional piece of playing."[10]

The album closes with "Where Were You Tomorrow", recorded live in Leicester on the Pye mobile studio. Although perhaps the inclusion of the studio version on the album might have resulted in better continuity, the live recording – which, incidentally, is the earliest official surviving concert recording of the band – captures perfectly the excitement of an early Wishbone Ash gig. As Derek Lawrence explains:

"With 'Where Were You Tomorrow' the idea had been to do a live album, but that fell apart. But because the number sounded so good live, we decided to put it on the album and not have the studio version."

Within a few weeks of its release *Pilgrimage* had reached the respectable position of number 14 on the UK album chart (and number 9 in the *NME* chart), a much better showing than *Wishbone Ash*. *Disc and Music Echo* described the album as, "an album with a lot of ingenuity, good music and outstanding playing." The band, however, had reservations about the hurried way in which the album had been recorded.

"It took a week altogether," reveals Ted. "It was a pity we had to rush it. It was rushed simply because we wanted it to be released in America before we started the tour. In fact it came out two weeks after we arrived."[15]

The band would not make the same mistake with their third album – *Argus* – for which writing began in the autumn. The idea was that they would be fully prepared next time round.

Wishbone made their first appearance on BBC TV's *Old Grey Whistle Test* during September, performing "Jailbait" and "Vas Dis" live in the studio. The show's host, Bob Harris, became a lifelong fan and supporter over the years and has kept the faith to this day, often playing their music on his BBC radio show. The band then embarked on a lengthy UK tour running from 24 September

thirty years of Wishbone Ash

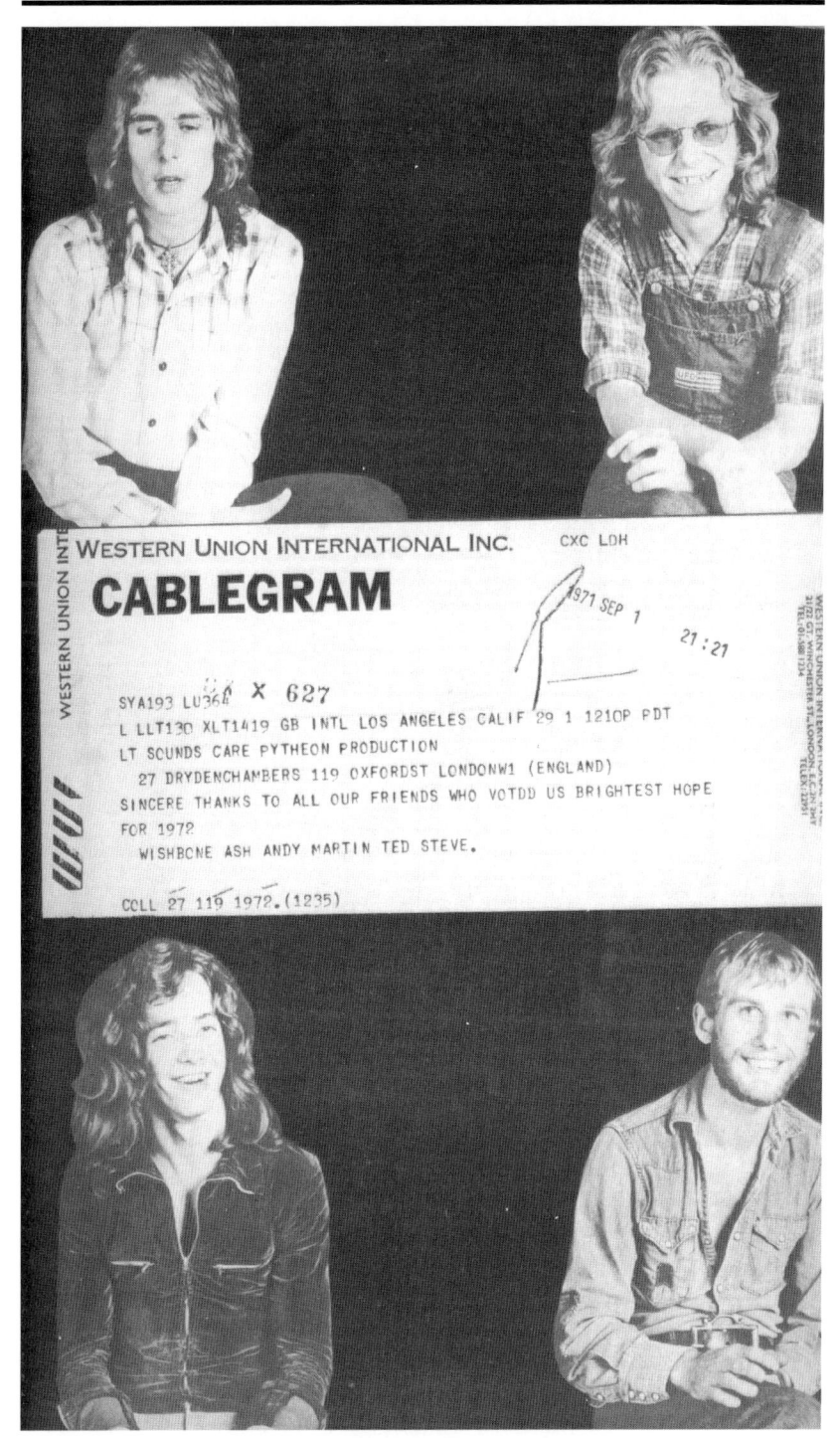

Above: Full page advert in *Sounds* congratulating the band on winning 1971's greatest hope for the coming year.

Above: Early MCA promotional advert for the release of Pilgimage.

through to 19 November, culminating with a brace of concerts at the prestigious Rainbow Theatre in London supporting American heavy rock heroes Mountain. This would be the first of many visits by the Ash to this most famous of rock venues. During a short break in the tour in early November, Wishbone headed over to the continent once again this time to record some TV shows in Belgium and Italy. The year 1971 ended with a New Year's Eve concert at London's Marquee Club to celebrate Andy Powell's stag night.

The first day of 1972 saw the entire band attending Andy Powell's wedding at Dunstable Parish Church in Bedfordshire. His bride, Pauline, had been a steady girlfriend for several years and would go on to run the fan club as well supporting Andy as he continued with the band through thick and thin in the eighties and nineties. There was not much time for a honeymoon as during most of January 1972 the band were busy recording their third album at De Lane Lea's newly opened Wembley studios, with Derek Lawrence once again handling production and Martin Birch engineering. The album was recorded on sixteen tracks, a step up from the previous two albums which were both recorded on eight tracks.

Some of the new material was premiered during a four week UK tour running from 26 January to 20 February. For this headlining tour Wishbone Ash again played and sold-out the town and city halls across the country. Many years later, Martin Turner admitted that when the *Argus* material was first played live on that tour the band were not overly encouraged by the response. "It was very new to the audience as they hadn't heard the songs before. They obviously liked them but when you haven't heard them before, they don't quite have the same impact as when you've heard them before on record. It was a bit of a slow process. There was a constantly growing recognition of the songs as we played up and down the country that year. The album [*Argus*] actually stayed in the top thirty album charts for a very long time – about six months – and that's when it was voted album of the year".

In March the band set off for their first ever tour of Germany, a country that would take Wishbone Ash to its heart, just as much as in Britain and America. Even today, thirty years later, Germany remains a hot-bed of Wishbone Ash fans, with annual tours and its own Wishbone Ash convention.

Argus, the third Wishbone Ash album, was released in the UK on 28 April 1972 and was without doubt the band's most accomplished and complete work up to this point. Whereas the previous albums had tended to sound disjointed at times, *Argus* had a solid direction. The band's songwriting had never been stronger and various references to time, history and war throughout the album hang together much better than the tracks on either *Wishbone Ash* or *Pilgrimage*. However, despite a common thread of loosely related themes running throughout the album, the band maintains that there was no deliberate attempt to record a concept album.

"I don't think there was any initial sort of conscious concept," states Andy Powell. "We'd all got into this whole frame of mind around the time of *Argus* and the songs were obviously about similar subjects and it just kept sparking us off."[10]

The band were kept busy giving countless press and radio interviews to promote the album. Certainly the press reacted very favourably to the release of *Argus*, with no bad reviews anywhere in sight. Ray Telford, reviewing the album for *Sounds*, was very positive: "They have mellowed out to an amazing degree instrumentally and the countless little flashes of brilliance in every number say pretty well that this is where Wishbone Ash really begins. *Argus* has the maturity and self-assurance of a great album – who knows where it'll end".

Similarly, Chris Welch writing in the *Melody Maker* was also upbeat about *Argus*: "The tensions and excitement generated by the soloists help to make this a satisfying set. It threatens to become a highly successful album."

James Johnson writing for *NME* had this to say: "Good though Wishbone's last two albums have been, this is the clincher. Without losing any instrumental power, added emphasis has been placed on lyrics and vocals and the result is the most complete the group have recorded so far. All in all a great album as Wishbone Ash take a giant leap forward."

It was not hard to see why the press reviews for *Argus* were so favourable. There were no dud tracks and the lyrics would strike a chord with the fans. The Storm Thorgerson/Hipgnosis designed cover of the Argus/sentry looking out over a valley added to the album's sense of mystery and foreboding. As Martin Turner emphasises:

"I think you'll agree that for an album cover it is particularly relevant to the music – it relates beautifully. Hipgnosis, who designed the cover, like to sit around for quite a while and be able to communicate and build up ideas. If I remember rightly they really got into the music, very much so, in order to interpret the album cover. Hipgnosis even went to the South of France to find a place to shoot the picture. And we had to wait for hours and hours for that flying saucer to come over! You can interpret it in many ways. In a way it sums up 'Time'."[10]

Storm Thorgerson in his book, *Walk Away Rene* (which details how Hipgnosis designed and shot their album covers), describes how the *Argus* cover came about:

"We told the band and manager that we wanted to shoot a picture of this timeless warrior at the mouth of a magnificent gorge (Gorge du Verdun in Provence, France) waiting patiently for the arrival of the space visitors."

Having convinced the band that it would be worth the expense, Hipgnosis flew out to France to shoot the scene but apparently there was a drop of about 2,000 feet which put them off shooting for fear of falling over the edge. In the end they took the shot from the roadside where it was safer. As Storm admitted:

"Going to the south of France had cost plenty and though the client was very keen on the final result, it could've been shot in the Cotswolds, or Hampstead Heath at a pinch. But we didn't tell him that!"

On the musical side there was plenty of variety ranging from hard melodic rock through to slow laid back folk music. This fusion of rock and folk was one of the factors which made *Argus* such a winner with both critics and fans alike.

The title came from Steve Upton after many disagreements as to what it should be. "It's taken from Greek mythology and it has several meanings," reveals Steve. "It means 'watchful guardian' and it's also a hundred-eyed giant that was put in a cave to protect a goddess or something – and it just seemed very appropriate."[1]

The album opens with "Time Was" – a song of two vastly differing sections, both of which would later be performed separately during concerts. The opening acoustic section starts the album in a sombre, reflective style, with Ted and Martin's vocal harmonies backed by Ted's acoustic guitar picking. In direct contrast, the second part of the song is a straightforward rock outing with a feel similar to much of the Who's early seventies work. Andy Powell would later admit that, having supported the Who on several occasions, their style had an enormous impact. "Time Was" was one of several songs on *Argus* that was written on acoustic instruments. "It wasn't until we were pretty far along that we'd pick up electric guitars and play with any volume," recalls Andy Powell.[11]

"Sometime World" opens in folky style with Ted's dreamy soloing and a fine Martin Turner vocal before breaking into a faster pace with some fine scat-singing from Martin and Andy followed by one of Andy's most fluent solos. Martin Turner gives full credit to the production team for this recording:

"The recordings of 'Sometime World' have a really good spontaneity and purity about them which I would put down to the team of Derek Lawrence and Martin Birch in the background".

With hindsight, the song should have become a live classic, yet strangely the number rarely featured in the band's live repertoire in its entirety until the late nineties. Later on in the band's career, Andy Powell would state that "Sometime World" was his favourite track from *Argus*.

Closing the album's first side, "Blowin' Free" (with its three part vocal harmonies and Ted Turner's first appearance on slide guitar) was without doubt the most commercial track the band had recorded. It would go on to become a permanent fixture of the band's live set – *the* "Ash Anthem" to many. The lyrics were written a few years earlier by Martin Turner, as a result of a gig the Empty Vessels played in Torquay.

"The lyrics to 'Blowin' Free' were about a Swedish girlfriend I had at the time," says Martin. "She was called Annalena Nordstrom and came from Gothenburg. We were playing this gig at St. Luke's Hall in Torquay and there must have been 200 Swedish girls present, who were over here on holiday. Well, to have all these girls present and only three of us blokes!... She was the complete opposite of me and loved nature and being in the open air and all that. The refrain in the song, 'You can only try', came from a reply she used to give me when I was after a certain thing! I met her a few years later in London and she hadn't changed a bit."

The famous opening riff based around the D chord is probably a mixture of two different influences. The first came from when Andy Powell was jamming in 1971 with an old musician friend, Mick Groome, later of Ducks Deluxe. As Powell remembers:

"We were trying out various chord patterns and inversions of Beatles and Who songs. One was based on the Who song 'See Me, Feel Me', I think, and this was where the opening riff to 'Blowin' Free' came from".

The second influence according to Martin Turner came from a Steve Miller Band track from 1967 called "Children of the Future": "I was trying to get Andy and Ted to play hammer on this lick from that song, but it all came out very different." Andy Powell recalls all this coming together during a soundcheck at the Whisky-a-Go-Go on Sunset Boulevard, Los Angeles during 1971.

"Blowin' Free" had a unique sound for the time, and would prove to be remarkably influential. For example, the middle section of Steely Dan's "Reeling in the Years" bears a marked similarity to the three part guitar harmony near the end of "Blowin' Free". Another example is Thin Lizzy's "The Boys Are Back in Town", where the twin lead guitar break in the middle echoes the aforementioned section of "Blowin' Free".

Looking back it is hard to understand why the record company didn't put out "Blowin' Free" as a single. It was the most commercial track on the album and received a lot of air play at the time of the *Argus* release. It was in fact later released as the B-side of the single "No Easy Road" but this was a flop (as were all Wishbone Ash singles). Even today it is Wishbone Ash's most remembered song and is ever-present in the live set.

"I think if 'Blowin' Free' had been promoted (as a single) and maybe re-mixed or whatever, it probably would have been a hit," says Andy Powell. "It's just the luck of the draw. You can't look back and say, 'What if?', but sure, it was a very commercial song."

The album's second side opens with "The King Will Come", fading in with Andy Powell's intro guitar chords which would signal the start of many a Wishbone Ash concert. This is built up against Steve Upton's military snare, overlaid with Ted Turner's wah-wah guitar, whilst Martin Turner's bass holds everything in place. The main body of the song is melodic rock at its finest, whilst the lyrical content (sung in harmony by Martin and Andy) tackles with the Biblical concept that when the end of the world comes, man will be saved.

"I did quite a lot of research for 'The King Will Come'," admits Martin, "and I can remember reading the Bible for quite a long time. The Bible's an interesting book and although I'm not a particularly religious person, I can remember getting into it as a book and being really fascinated by some of the stuff in there."[10]

Perhaps the most underrated cut on the album is "Leaf and Stream" (due largely to the band's reluctance to perform it live until some 23 years after the album's release). This is a beautiful English folk song and Steve Upton's first lyrical contribution to a Wishbone Ash album (all other lyrics on *Argus* and most of the songs were written by Martin Turner).

"It was quite a brave move for a rock band like us," states Martin. "Steve's lyric was trying to be along the lines of the lyric on 'Alone'. It sounds like a bubbling brook in places with Andy's and Ted's guitars making it a sweet piece of music."

The album's two closing tracks, "Warrior" and "Throw Down the Sword", are closely related and were usually performed together at concerts. Says Martin Turner: "Lyrically, a lot of the material on *Argus* is about time and the relationship with time, like the warrior and that classic sort of symbolism. It's written in a very historical way, but it lends itself to a number of different situations, contemporary or otherwise."[16]

"These days, you'd say that 'Warrior' was a song about fighting for your rights and not taking any crap," adds Andy Powell. "It was designed to be a very rousing concert-type song with a big ensemble ending."[11]

Certainly the opening riff based on the A-minor and E-minor chords was typical of many classic Wishbone Ash songs played in a minor key – "Phoenix", "The Way of the World" and "Living Proof" were all based on minor chords.

"Warrior" segues into the final track on the album, "Throw Down the Sword" which saw Renaissance's John Tout augmenting the band on organ. Renaissance had become good friends with Wishbone Ash, the two bands having appeared on the same bill on numerous occasions. Also, both bands were then managed by Miles Copeland. The following year, Andy Powell would return the compliment by contributing lead guitar to the title track of Renaissance's *Ashes Are Burning* album. "Throw Down the Sword" grows from a simple riff (from Andy) into a climatic finale of two guitars vying for space at the end of the song. Apparently it wasn't meant to end quite like that as Derek Lawrence admits:

"I'd made a mistake at the end of 'Throw Down The Sword' when I was remixing it leaving the two guitars coming together at the end where they cross and separate. One was meant to have been louder than the other in the mix but I thought it sounded so good that I left it."

The lyrics came from Martin's choirboy days: "It was straight out of my childhood religious singing experience and is quite hymn-like. It was conceived as an anti-war song with an ancient theme in accordance with the rest of the album. The opening guitar riff, written by Andy, was used by us as a guitar exercise to warm up the fingers."

Material from *Argus* still takes up a large proportion of the current Wishbone Ash set list almost thirty years on. While later albums certainly contained tracks of equal quality to the *Argus* material, very few of the band's subsequent albums would match its consistency. Derek Lawrence stills looks back fondly on the last Wishbone Ash album he would produce for six years:

Above: (l-r) Ted Turner, Andy Powell, Steve Upton and Martin Turner.
Photo: Wishbone Ash Fan Club Archives

"*Argus* was as far as the band could go with me. The tracks sounded wonderful. Of course the recording process was helped by the fact that the studio equipment had improved. We'd learnt about echoes and suchlike which all helped to give it that certain something which wasn't there on the other two albums."

On its release, *Argus* entered the UK album charts at number 8 before peaking at number 3. It stayed in the album charts for a total of twenty weeks, the longest ever for a Wishbone Ash album, and achieved Gold Disc status, an award the band would receive the following year. It was also voted as the best album of 1972 by the readers of *Sounds* and *Melody Maker*, defeating strong competition from the likes of Deep Purple's *Machine Head* and Jethro Tull's *Thick As A Brick*. (Incidentally the cover of *Argus* was beaten into second place by Tull's *Thick As A Brick* in the best album sleeve category.)

In May many fans were able to hear most tracks from the new album for the first time in a live setting as Wishbone performed at a two major UK festivals – first at Bickershaw, near Wigan in Lancashire and second at the Great Western Festival at Lincoln. The Bickershaw Festival, attended by about 40,000 people, was organised by, amongst others, future TV celebrity Jeremy Beadle. He is said to have made a loss of around £60,000 on the festival – but he eventually hit the jackpot by hosting practical joke based programmes on television. The festival site, situated on a bleak hillside next to a colliery in the north of England, was hardly the best area for a Pop Festival. It was also in a region of high rainfall and by the time festival headliners, the Grateful Dead, appeared on the Sunday night, the site was a mud bath. Andy Powell remembers "appalling sanitation facilities, mud and cold". Luckily for Wishbone, they appeared on the Friday night, playing second on the bill below Dr John. Steve Peacock reviewing the event for *Sounds* gave the band a rather mediocre review, claiming "Wishbone Ash proved themselves an efficient if somewhat contrived sounding band... I enjoyed them, and was occasionally excited by them, but they weren't anything particularly special."

The band's public profile in Britain was now higher than ever. They recorded an *In Concert* programme for BBC Radio One at the BBC's Paris Studios, Lower Regent Street on 25 May. This would later surface on the bootleg CD, *Fighters And Warriors*, before finally being officially released in 1991 on the Windsong label under the title *BBC Radio One Live In Concert*.

On 3 June, the Bones headed for their third US tour – another trip that would not pass without problems. Originally scheduled to run for six weeks, the tour was brought to an abrupt end when, following a concert in St. Louis on 19 June, the band's equipment truck parked outside their hotel was broken into and most of the gear stolen. Fortunately, Andy Powell's beloved Flying V was inside the hotel, as was Ted Turner's Stratocaster, but the rest of the equipment, including their Orange amplification, Ted's 1959 Les Paul, Steve Upton's drumkit and the Gibson Thunderbird bass which Martin Turner had only just acquired, was never recovered. Two days after the incident, the band returned home somewhat ahead of schedule to seek out new equipment.

"Occasionally we heard rumours that pieces of our equipment had been seen," reveals Steve Upton. "We also got a message that they would let us have it back if we paid them four thousand dollars, but we didn't bother. All our amplification then was made by Orange, which at the time wasn't very well known in America, and they couldn't get rid of it because it was too conspicuous."[17]

On arriving back in England, Wishbone made plans to record two tracks exclusively for single release but suffered a further setback when Martin Turner was rushed to hospital with appendicitis.

"Martin had been suffering from stomach pains whilst in America and put it down to seafood poisoning," remembers Steve Upton. "On our arrival in England he was diagnosed as having appendicitis and confined to bed. I remember visiting him in hospital just after the doctor told him he would have to have it out. He was horror struck!"[5]

On Martin's recovery, Wishbone entered De Lane Lea's Wembley studios to record a new number entitled "No Easy Road" as well as a new recording of "Blowin' Free", the idea being to release a single to capitalise on the success of *Argus*. The sessions marked the first without Derek Lawrence at the helm as the band had decided to produce the single themselves. A promo film was also shot to help push the single, but this has never seen the light of day. Sadly the single, which was more straightforward rock 'n' roll in style, didn't make it into the UK singles charts although in New Orleans it did make the number one position on a local radio station. One problem in England at the time was that many fans would turn up at their local record store and find that it simply wasn't in stock. Martin Turner recalls the making of the "No Easy Road" single:

"At the time we weren't in a position to think about doing another album and we thought it would be really nice to get a single together. 'No Easy Road' was light enough in mood for a single, so we recorded it for that purpose. Even though it didn't get anywhere I think it worked. We recorded it at the same time as we were trying out new equipment and I was in a right mess because I didn't have any bass guitars at all. It was about this time that I got friendly with Pete Watts from Mott the Hoople and he lent me his bass, which was a Gibson Thunderbird. In the end I forced him into selling it to me – I just had to have it. The very first T'Bird I had was picked up somewhere in America and I hadn't really had the chance to get into it before it was stolen."[10]

It was around this period that both Andy Powell and Ted Turner experimented with Gibson Firebird guitars for live performances, in order to compliment visually Martin's Thunderbird bass. As Andy Powell remembers: "Ted had a sunburst Firebird and I had a white one that ended up getting sold to Stephen Stills. I had this big thing about Firebirds, but Miles did his pieces. He figured that everybody identified me with the Flying V and so I should continue to use that."[14]

By now the band had built up such a large following of fans that it was decided to set up a fan club, which would eventually grow to over 1,500 members. The first newsletter of the newly formed "Wishbone Ash Club" appeared in July 1972 and was ably put together by Doreen Boyd who would hold down the position of club secretary for the next seven years. The newsletter was produced about four times a year with news of up-coming tours as well as bits of gossip about band members, a chance for Ash fans to find pen-pals and a useful outlet for the much in demand Ash merchandise. The first issue discussed such matters as the theft of the band's equipment in America and Martin having his appendix removed.

The band returned to the States to honour their outstanding commitments, touring from 26 July to 29 August, supporting Alice Cooper and ELP. On 21 August, the band played a live set in the studios of WMC-FM in Memphis, Tennessee. The show was broadcast live and the band's US record company, Decca, had three of the songs – "Jailbait", "The Pilgrim" and "Phoenix" – pressed up for a limited edition promotional album. The disc, entitled *Live From Memphis*, was issued to radio stations across the States but was never intended for general release. However, it soon attracted a great deal of attention from avid fans hungry for live product from the band so it quickly became a much sought after collector's item. The three tracks would eventually be released in the 1990s on CD reissues of the Wishbone Ash back catalogue. The album came packaged in a tatty black and white sleeve, whilst the sound quality was criticised heavily by the band.

"That album was a real drag and I'd rather forget about it," says Ted Turner, who has less than pleasant memories of the recording session. "It must be one of the worst recordings ever. I remember minutes before we played the set, I was in the control room soldering my guitar which had been damaged by a luggage truck at the airport. It was just one of those days – nothing went right."[18]

A further promotional album was issued by Decca around this time. *An Evening Program With Wishbone Ash* featured nothing new, being compiled entirely from the band's first three studio albums, but this too became a highly sought after collector's item.

Miles Copeland had other more unusual ideas of promoting the band during those early US tours as Kevin Harrington recalls:

"I remember that Miles wanted to get some major publicity out of one of our first shows in America, so he asked me to get hold of about a dozen live chickens which he wanted the road crew to let out into the audience. The idea was that

Above: The press campaign for *Argus* stressed the critical acclaim that the album had received from the music press.

whoever could be the first member of the audience to bring a chicken's wishbone on stage would get a free copy of the band's album! The band and the road crew all talked about it and had a good laugh. I could've got a dozen frozen ones but in the end we just didn't do it."

On 11 September Wishbone Ash filmed a performance for a one-hour show for West Country TV as guests of one of their support bands from previous tours, Stackridge. The show, entitled *Stackridge & Co.*, was not broadcast outside of the West Country region and remains a much sought after video amongst fans to this day. Once again Wishbone performed at two more major UK events – Buxton and the Oval in London. Buxton (16 and 17 September) saw Wishbone sharing the bill with Curved Air, Family, Uriah Heep and Wizzard. The band would eventually get to play at around three o'clock in the morning after extensive delays. At the *Melody Maker Poll Winners Concert* at London's Oval cricket ground a couple of weeks later, the band closed a bill featuring ELP, Genesis, Focus and Argent. It was at the *Melody Maker* event that the band was expected to receive the "Best Album" award for *Argus*.

"We played the gig, but we were late and blew out the press party," recalls Andy Powell. "We didn't realise how important all that stuff was. For the whole year there had been regular features on us every week in the papers until we inadvertently blew them out – and in return *Melody Maker* blew us out. They were most peeved we didn't turn up to collect the award – they thought it was a snub. We didn't court the press."

The gig itself did not go smoothly. Mark Emery can remember a certain amount of antagonism backstage between Wishbone and ELP, the latter being winners of the "Best Group" award.

"The audience there were very much ELP fans and it was a mistake for Wishbone to go on after them. ELP had a huge production with cannons and these creatures which showered out confetti. Wishbone insisted on going on last and they shouldn't have as ELP had the impetus at the time. The audience was bit flat when Wishbone came on and started to thin out during the set."

Yet another American tour took place during October and November – the third of the year. As ever, there were setbacks. This tour's disaster occurred in Des Moines, Iowa on 28 October. American blues artist Taj Mahal opened the show, and Martin Turner distinctly remembers the night's events:

"There really was a very strange atmosphere in the air that evening. I remember at the sound check we had so many problems and the gates ended up being opened very late. The people, who had waited for a long time, were freezing cold as the weather was so severe, and then Taj went onstage to perform and started his set with a kalimba – a little hand-held African finger piano. Most of the audience didn't realise he'd begun playing and he really lost his temper because people were ignoring him. He screamed abuse at the audience, freaked everybody out, and then we were asked to go onstage and perform immediately because everyone was getting upset. We attempted to do that – I think it was either three or four times – but the electrical feed to the building was just totally inadequate for us to be able to run the equipment we were using and the power just kept fading. It was really nerve-wracking and in the end we suggested, because the promoter obviously didn't have the facilities to promote a show there, that people should receive their money back. All we could do was apologise for not being able to perform, but the gig was a fiasco."[2]

On return from the States, Wishbone Ash closed 1972 with a triumphant 19-date sell-out UK tour, running from 17 November to 20 December, including two more dates at the Rainbow Theatre in London. On reflection, 1972 was a highly successful one for the band and could rightly be regarded as "the year of Wishbone Ash". The Bones had reached a peak in Britain and were on the rise in America – but could they stay there?

Chapter Three

Goodbye Baby, Hello Friend

At the beginning of 1973 Wishbone Ash took a well-earned break from touring and set off to the countryside to prepare for the next album. Several bands had done this before such as Deep Purple with *Fireball* and Led Zeppelin with *Led Zeppelin III*, though the intention was primarily to write new songs and not actually to record.

As Andy Powell recalls: "A lot of bands were going out to the country to write. We put everything into the back of a truck and moved to a cottage on the island of Anglesey, off the Welsh coast. All of us were stuck in a six-room cottage several miles from anywhere with no phone, no TV, no radio. There was a sign on the gate – "Pen-Y-Bonc" – that we always took to be the name of the cottage. Years later someone told us that it meant 'Please close the gate' in Welsh."[11]

Mark Emery recalls it as being a fun time:

"It was good but bloody cold. It was really isolated and I had to drive backwards and forwards getting supplies in. The band just recorded everything on demos. It was done so that the band could focus together and get away from all that was happening at the time. I thought it was a good idea."

With an album's worth of material composed, Wishbone Ash spent the months of February and March recording at Olympic and Apple Studios in London. The band decided to produce the sessions themselves. Commenting on this decision, Martin Turner says: "At the time we felt that *Argus* was probably the best thing we were going to do with Derek Lawrence, and we felt it was time for a move.[10] I think it's a big mistake for anyone to think that you don't need a producer. A producer fulfils so many functions – not just in the studio, but also when the record is finished and you have to get that sound from the tape to the plastic. I don't look back and regret the fact that we did it, because obviously we needed to do it. I think probably we would have got a better result if one of us had been the producer, rather than all of us. There's no overall continuity when there's more than one producer."[9]

On completion of the album, Wishbone Ash played two nights at London's Marquee Club on 17 and 18 March, which was recorded for BBC radio and previewed some of the newly recorded material. The band then headed for their sixth US tour, headlining a bill that also featured the Climax Blues Band and Vinegar Joe for most of the shows. The tour ran from 29 March to 29 April.

On 11 May the fourth Wishbone Ash album, simply entitled *Wishbone Four* was released. After the enormous success of *Argus*, the band had clearly made no attempt to release a follow-up in the truest sense, right down to the album's sleeve design which, as a direct contrast to *Argus*, featured a simple group portrait shot against a plain blue background (green in some territories). The material featured on the album had a distinctly looser feel than *Argus* and the emphasis was on shorter, more direct songs, with no common theme or concept. The guitar playing was as inventive as ever, but solos were, in the main, noticeably shorter.

We knew everyone was waiting for 'Son of Argus' and wondering how we were going to top *Argus*, says Martin Turner, "and for a while we were really blinded by the view that we had to surpass all previous offerings. Finally we realised the point was just to leave it at that and move onto something completely new."[1]

Wishbone Four opens with "So Many Things to Say", and from the opening few bars it is clear that the album would be far removed from *Argus*. Martin Turner's vocals were coarser than before, suiting the harder edged sound, helped by some heavier drumming from Steve Upton. There was a new instrument prominent as well. Ted Turner, who had debuted his slide guitar on "Blowin' Free", had started experimenting with a lap steel guitar purchased on an American tour. The instrument featured throughout the album and would soon become one of Ted's trademarks. Ted explains the difference in technique between lap steel and conventional "bottleneck" slide guitar:

"Playing lap steel is more natural for the hands. Some of the differences with lap steel are that you have to rely on tuning the instrument to certain chords, and it's difficult changing from major to minor. With bottleneck slide you can play guitar with a regular tuning, play chords and then a few slide licks, as the slide is usually on the little finger, as opposed to holding the slide with your left hand as is the case with lap steel."[22]

"Ballad of the Beacon", with its lyric inspired by the beacons visible from the cottage in Anglesey, represents the folkier side of Wishbone Ash, sung by both Andy Powell (verse) and Martin Turner (chorus). "No Easy Road" is a re-recording of the previous year's single, with the addition of the Bud Parks Horn Section and Glencoe's Graham Maitland on piano.

"The brass section were really good," remembers Martin, "especially Phil MacKenzie; he's a really good sax player. I saw him onstage at the Rainbow with Mick Ronson and he was also in *The Rocky Horror Show* for ages."[10]

Side One of *Wishbone Four* closes with "Everybody Needs a Friend", written mainly by Martin Turner with Andy and Ted creating the distinctive chord progressions. Later described by Martin as "a little schmaltzy", the song has a haunting feel with a particularly expressive lead vocal from the song's composer and a beautiful guitar solo from Andy Powell. It was based on Ravel's piano concerto in G-major and marked a real departure for Wishbone Ash. An extra dimension was added with session player George Nash on keyboards. The lyric is basically about friendship.

Side Two opens in rocking style with "Doctor", with Martin in particularly forceful voice. The lyric was inspired by a lady he and his brother Glenn knew from their Torquay days.

"The first time I saw her she really looked like a witch," remembers Martin, "with very straight blonde hair which she used to iron every day, heavy black eye make-up and a very tight black velvet dress right down to the floor. She was a heroin addict and she'd been registered and was receiving treatment, stepping the dose down to get her off the drug. She used to send someone round to the doctor to plead for an extra prescription because she was lying on the floor with withdrawal symptoms, which was totally untrue. When they'd eventually hustled the prescription out of the doctor they just used to fall around all over the place and everyone used to take it. She just used to hustle the doctor so she could get enough for everyone else... very heavy."[10]

"Sorrel" is another excursion into folk-rock territory with some excellent dual guitar passages, plus a lyric sung by Martin written, oddly enough, about a plant.

"'Sorrel' is about a plant that I found growing in my garden, but in the song it's personified," reveals Martin. "I cared for the plant and looked after it for a long time and then went on an American tour. When I came home it had shrivelled up and died, so I wrote a song about it!"[10]

Without a doubt the album's weakest track, "Sing Out the Song" is Wishbone Ash's attempt at country-rock. Indeed, were it not for Martin Turner's vocal, it would barely be recognisable as Wishbone Ash. In the band's defence, it certainly proved that Wishbone were willing and perfectly able to write and perform in a wide variety of musical styles.

Album closer "Rock 'n' Roll Widow", with its lyric written by Steve Upton and based around the murder of a hot dog vendor at that fateful concert in Austin two years earlier, features one of Ted Turner's finest ever vocal performances. The track is without doubt one of the highlights of *Wishbone Four* and would become a live favourite throughout 1973/74. Once again, Ted's lap steel was prominent.

Wishbone Four on its release received mostly negative reactions from both fans and press – a great shame since the album showed how the band had developed particularly as songwriters and vocalists. Certainly Martin Turner, whilst being no match for the likes of Robert Plant or Ian Gillan, had by now established himself as the voice of the band, with a distinctive tone along the lines of British bassist/vocalists such as Jack Bruce, Greg Lake and John Wetton.

Sadly, the general public had expected "Son of Argus" and this the band had refused to deliver. With hindsight it could be argued that the band had matured quicker than a large sector of its audience but at the time the band were understandably hurt by some of the reviews. As Mark Emery explains:

"They were under a lot of pressure to come up with something better than *Argus*. They weren't your average sort of rock 'n' roll guys who didn't give a fuck about anything. They were very sensitive and were very affected by what people thought. In the English sort of way they were diffused of their confidence which was a great shame."

Ironically, one of the more positive press reviews came from *Melody Maker*. Had they forgiven Wishbone's awards "snub" the previous year? The reviewer wrote: "Having been perhaps too over-concerned with getting the structure of their music right, honing its form to a fine degree, Ash are now evolving a heart with a warm pulse to beat in the solid body they've built."

On the other hand, Derek Lawrence who had produced the first three Wishbone albums was not that impressed with *Wishbone Four*: "Bands think they are better than they really are and they take a step too far. This is what I think happened with that album. It didn't impress me. Feel-wise they were much better than that, but that didn't come across on the album."

Andy Powell thinks one of the reasons for the album's poor reception was the arrangement of the vocals: "I think it was a mistake to abandon the vocal harmony sound which Martin and myself had used on tracks like 'Sometime World', 'Warrior' and 'Throw Down The Sword'. This was fast becoming a trademark of the band as much as the twin guitar harmonies and was what most people were identifying as the definitive new sound of the band."

Wishbone Four, however, was still a top ten album, peaking at number 10 on the UK chart and still selling enough copies to warrant Silver Disc status. Martin Turner in an interview for this book has his own views about *Wishbone Four*:

"There is no doubt in my mind that the engineer, Keith Harwood, as good as he was helping us to get the right atmosphere and the right feel with the music, was definitely lacking in the technical expertise department. The tapes that were recorded for those sessions just did not sound right. They ended up being cut onto record and put out but they lacked fidelity, they lacked bass at the low end and they lacked high end. That was a bit of a disappointment for us and for the audience. The material I would stand by though and say it was a good album."

On the same day that *Wishbone Four* was released in the UK, Wishbone Ash returned to the USA for the second of four visits in 1973, indicating that they were more committed than ever to breaking America. It was during visits to the States that tour boredom would inevitably creep in, not necessarily with the band themselves who had a reputation for being archetypal British gentlemen, but with the road crew. Mark Emery remembers some of the extra-curricular activities of the early US tours:

"It was great in the States in those days. If you were up for it, you just couldn't leave a gig without getting pulled. It was as easy as that. There were always loads of groupies at each gig. Some even came on the tour bus with us. Then there were the Plaster Casters! In Little Rock, Arkansas the whole crew got plaster castered. I think a couple of the band also succumbed to that temptation!" (For the uninitiated "the Plaster Casters" were a couple of girls who used to persuade members of visiting bands and their crew to have their erect members cast in plaster. They would collect these plaster casts as trophies.)

A more terrifying experience happened to Mark, fellow roadie Kevin Harrington and Ted Turner early one morning while some of the crew were relaxing after a gig in Cedar Rapids, Iowa:

"We were having a drink in this bar in Cedar Rapids when all of a sudden the place was raided for after-hours drinking. They lined everyone up at the bar and asked for ID. As we were aliens we should have had our passports with us, but we didn't, so they took us back to our hotel to get them. They searched all our rooms and seemed determined to find something incriminating. In the end Kevin and myself were arrested as they had found a bag of pot in our room. We spent the night in jail. I was freed without charge but Kevin took the blame and was deported and banned from re-entering the USA. It was a sad ending for Kevin as he had worked with the Beatles and Derek & the Dominoes and as a result he was not able to work with Wishbone again whenever they were touring in America."

In June, Wishbone made a welcome return to the UK's concert stages, their first since the release of *Wishbone Four*. The Rolling Stones' mobile studio accompanied the band to several shows, recording material for a future live album – this being prompted partly by the interest in the *Memphis* album. Meanwhile, a single from *Wishbone Four* featuring "So Many Things to Say" backed with "Rock 'n' Roll Widow" was released on 6 July. (Needless to say, it failed to make the charts.) The gigs went well with the new material fitting into the set without any problems. Most of the album was played live including "Doctor", "Rock 'n' Roll Widow", "Ballad of the Beacon" and "Everybody Needs A Friend". One unusual addition to the set was the Everly Brothers' hit, the Jimmy Reed composition "Baby What You Want Me To Do", which gave Ted a chance to play his pedal steel guitar. Some of these tracks would end up on Wishbone's first live album, *Live Dates*.

With no appearances arranged for any British festivals that year, the band were booked to play at Alexandra Palace, London for an all day event on Saturday 6 August as part of a series of concerts under the moniker "The London Music Festival". Wishbone would play the penultimate day of a ten-day event which had included bands such as Family, Black Sabbath and Ten Years After. The support bill was Vinegar Joe, the Climax Blues Band, McGuiness Flint and Bedlam and the band was augmented by a four piece horn section as well as a pianist for several songs. As Barbara Charone commented in *NME*: "It was Wishbone Ash all right, but like no one's ever seen them before. It was the Wishbone Ash of today, stronger than ever and presenting themselves as a high class, big time rock band." The Alexandra Palace event was so successful that the same venue was chosen for a Christmas party later that year.

Another shorter US tour then followed, running until 23 August. One notable appearance was at a festival in Central Park, New York along with Joe Walsh. Although it wasn't on as grand a scale as the later events staged by the likes of Simon and Garfunkel or Elton John, it nevertheless showed that Wishbone were fast becoming a major live act in the States. In fact, manager Miles Copeland took out a full-page advert in *Rolling Stone* magazine proclaiming Andy Powell and Ted

Above: Steve Upton and Ted Turner.
Photo: Nicky Masters

Turner as "the two best guitarists in the world". Andy recalls the way in which the band had to face up to the pressures of stardom in the States which differed so much from their native England:

"I think when we started to go to the States and got onto the front of all the music papers it was a bit shocking. These days they groom people. We had no grooming whatsoever. Miles was new to the business as well – and quite often he would put his foot in the wrong place at the wrong time. We were too busy doing our music and being in a band. In retrospect it was quite shocking."

Roadie Kevin Harrington recalls that with the constant pressure of touring America, tensions within the band would often surface:

"Quite often after a gig they would lock the dressing room and argue for up to an hour. Even Miles Copeland was afraid to go in and would say to me, 'Do you think it's OK to go in now Kevin?' "

Soon after returning from America the band spent a couple of days in Olympic Studios, London mixing material for the forthcoming live album. Then in October, prior to yet another American tour, Wishbone undertook a mini-tour of just six UK dates, supported by an up-and-coming British band called Home, featuring a young guitarist by the name of Laurie Wisefield.

The fourth and final US tour of the year with the Climax Blues Band supporting was a much lengthier affair than the summer visit. The tour ran from 23 October through to 2 December, with one particular highlight being a jam between the two bands at New York Academy of Music on 17 November.

December saw the release of Wishbone Ash's long awaited live album – *Live Dates* – a double set featuring songs from all four albums in addition to a recording of "Baby What You Want Me to Do" which had become a stage favourite during 1973.

Blowin' Free

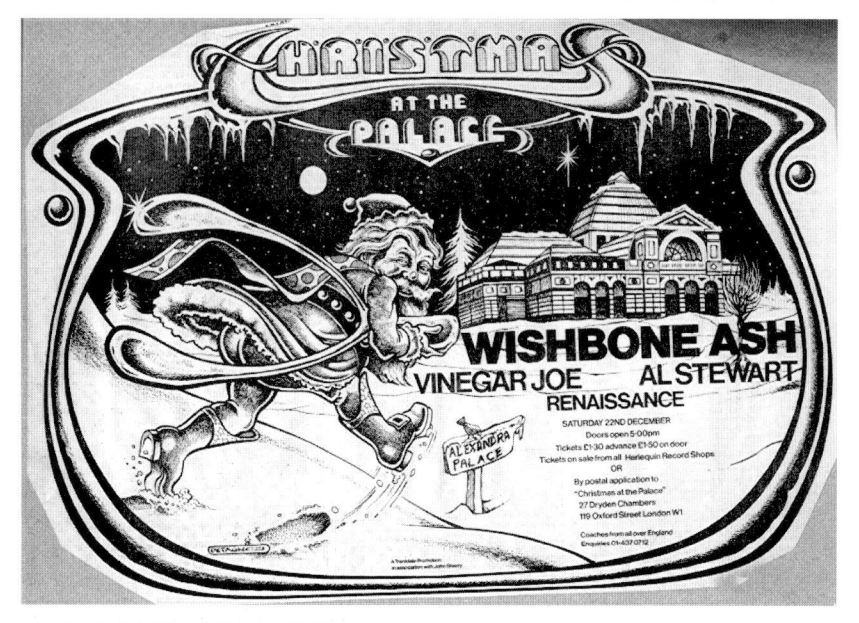

Above: Promotional poster for 1973 Christmas gig at Alexandra Palace.

Left: Early 1970s logo.

Below: Collecting their just rewards. (l-r) Martin Turner, Ted Turner, Janet Webb star of the Morecambe and Wise show, Andy Powell and Steve Upton.
Photo: Wishbone Ash Fan Club Archives

Compiled from recordings of four complete concerts from Reading University, Fairfield Halls Croydon, Portsmouth Guildhall and Newcastle City Hall, *Live Dates* is an excellent representation of Wishbone's 1973 live act. Despite being culled from four different performances, the album has the feel of a continuous performance, although five songs from the band's playlist had to be dropped due to timing restrictions and technical difficulties. (Incidentally, the four concerts recorded for *Live Dates* still exist on multi-track tape currently in Martin Turner's possession.) Most of the tracks featured on *Live Dates* are considered by many to be better than the recorded versions. A lengthy "Phoenix" was undoubtedly one of the highlights of the set. In America (where the album was packaged complete with an eight-page souvenir booklet) *Live Dates* sold 100,000 copies during its first week of release. In fact the album would go on to be the biggest selling Wishbone Ash album ever, even outselling *Argus*.

A short series of dates in France and Switzerland coincided with the live album's release and the year was rounded off with a memorable Alexandra Palace gig (supported by Vinegar Joe, Renaissance and Al Stewart) which, as with the band's August appearance at the venue, featured guest appearances from Graham Maitland on piano and the Bud Parks Horn Section for a rousing rendition of "No Easy Road". After the show Wishbone were presented with gold discs (a million copies sold world-wide) for *Argus* and silver discs (500,000 copies) for *Wishbone Four*. Somewhat curiously, the discs were presented by one Janet Webb who won her fame as the large lady who appeared at the end of the *Morecambe And Wise* comedy show on British television gushing "I love you all!".

As 1973 turned into 1974 the States beckoned once more with a three week tour in January and February. On returning, the band recorded a live concert for BBC Radio One's *In Concert* programme at London's Paris Studios. This recording would later resurface as the bootleg CD *Phoenix from the Ashes*. Then as winter turned to spring the band set up camp once again at Miles Copeland's home, writing and rehearsing new material for the next studio album. However the tension that had surfaced during the previous year's American tours continued to brew within the band. There were plans for a new UK tour in May, after which the band would record in the States for the first time. However, following a heavy touring schedule in both 1972 and 1973 and a less than satisfactory reaction to *Wishbone Four*, morale in the band was pretty low.

As Martin Turner recalls: "We had come off the road after a long time and we started to get all the ideas that had been kicking around for ages – various songs and things we had been working on – and there really wasn't a very good atmosphere. Not because anyone was getting on anyone else's case or anything, or because there was any dispute in the band, but there was just a weird kind of vibe. Negative is about the only way I can describe it."[9]

All of the recording and touring plans for 1974 suddenly came to an abrupt halt when, on 2 May, Ted Turner announced his intention to leave Wishbone Ash and temporarily quit the music industry, with plans to explore Peru.

As Andy Powell remembers: "We'd been rehearsing for a couple of months and we'd got halfway into preparing for the album. It was a very tense period because we'd been touring a lot and I think everyone was pretty down. We didn't really

Blowin' Free

Turner quits Wishbone
Wisefield replaces

Above: Ted Turner's departure makes the headlines in the British music press.

have our hearts in what we were doing and Ted, being the most spontaneous member of the group, said he wanted to leave. I think he just felt he'd been in the band for nearly five years and he really wanted a change."[10] It was quite a shock for us as he chose the most inappropriate time to leave. We were just about to go and work with one of the biggest producers in the world and really take it on to another level. It really did leave us in the lurch. It made everything go wobbly as everyone started to question what they were doing."

Ted explained the reasons for his leaving: "I was very young. I was only 24 and I just needed to grow as a person and there had to be more than just rock 'n' roll in a person's life."

Martin Turner adds: "I think the band's rise to fame or notoriety was fairly rapid and Ted was the youngest member of the band. I don't think he was ready for the severity of the kind of lifestyle we were enduring at that point. He obviously needed a rest – he needed to get away from the role of rock star, which is what he did. He went off to Peru and bought a donkey. It might have been wiser in retrospect to have actually taken a sabbatical – taken some time out to review the situation."[2]

As news of Ted Turner's departure reached the music press, rumours of a complete split in the band began to circulate. Meanwhile, Andy Powell flew to New York City to play two gigs with Renaissance at the Academy of Music. However, there was ulterior motive for Powell's excursion to New York – to sound out former Home guitarist Laurie Wisefield about the possibility of him replacing Ted in Wishbone Ash. Laurie happened to be playing as a member of Al Stewart's backing band, also playing in New York at the time of Andy's visit.

Andy Powell recalls: "It took us a few days to take Ted's decision in and think what we wanted to do. We thought, 'Shall we get a piano player in, or a vocalist even?' Then we decided to try for another guitarist. We had to make a decision really quickly. We didn't really want to go through the whole audition process. So we said, 'Let's find the guy' and Laurie Wisefield was the only serious contender. We liked his playing a lot and he didn't have any commitments at the time because Home had just split up. I was going out to New York for a few days to do a gig with Renaissance just for the fun of it. When I was out there I met Laurie and being the fall guy, I made it all happen."[10]

Laurie Wisefield adds: "Andy did the Renaissance gig and we got really friendly, but I didn't know at the time that he'd come over to suss me out. He came along and played with us on 'All Along the Watchtower' which was just an excuse to have a jam really. Anyway, we were talking and I said, 'How's Wishbone going then?' and he said, 'Well, actually, Ted's left the band'. I didn't really have any thoughts then that I'd be asked to join and the next day we were talking in the bar and he said, 'Er, what would you say if I asked you to join?' I said, 'Well, I'll give it a try and come back and see how we get on', because that's very important too, to get on with everyone personally, not just musically. When I got back from the States I was suffering from really bad jet-lag and they all phoned me up and asked me to come over. So I went over and we started talking and jamming and then it all happened from there – and we started rehearsing. I still had another gig with Al Stewart to do in London, so I went along with Andy and that was really a gas."[10]

Laurie Wisefield (born East London, 27 August 1952) began playing guitar at the age of eight, when his grandfather bought him a £6 Unicorn acoustic. He later progressed to a Watkins Rapier 33 and a Watkins Westminster amp and began to get into numerous bands with friends later playing at Butlins holiday camps where he managed to win several free holidays in talent contests. At the age of thirteen, Laurie formed his first semi-pro band, the Four Fables, who played Beatles and Shadows covers at weddings and parties. The band's main claim to fame was an appearance on the *Stubby Kaye Show*, a TV talent contest in the *Opportunity Knocks* mould. After the Four Fables split, Laurie answered a *Melody Maker* ad and went down to Tooting Bec where he met bassist, Cliff Williams (later of AC/DC). This was the beginning of Sugar (not to be confused with Andy Powell's pre-Wishbone combo the Sugarband).

After leaving school, Laurie went to art college and then began work designing jewellery in Cheapside, by which time Sugar were playing regularly at London's Speakeasy club. Laurie eventually gave up his day job although Sugar split soon after. Laurie and Cliff Williams then teamed up with Mick Stubbs, a vocalist/songwriter who had a long history of bands and writing credits behind him. With the line-up completed by drummer Mick Cook, Home was born. The band signed a record deal with CBS and their first album *Pause for a Hoarse Horse* was released in August 1971. Two further albums followed, *Home* (September 1972) and *The Alchemist* (July 1973), the latter a concept album which was particularly well received by the music press. Jim Anderson was added on keyboards and the band supported Led Zeppelin at Wembley, as well as touring with Wishbone Ash. After mainman Stubbs quit the band, the remaining members of Home were adopted as Al Stewart's backing band until Andy Powell's intervention.

Laurie Wisefield and the other members of Wishbone Ash began rehearsing together in July. Much of the material which had been prepared during Ted Turner's last days with the band was either re-worked or scrapped altogether as Laurie began to add his own musical and lyrical ideas.

"The main thing I wanted to get across was that I was playing a positive role," says Wisefield. "I sort of had to ignore the fact that I was replacing Ted Turner. I had to look at it like I was trying to actually give something to the band, not just replace someone."[19]

In August, Wishbone Ash Mark II departed for the States to record the first offering from the new line-up. Miles Copeland had instructed Leon Tsilis from MCA Records to meet to the band at Miami airport. Leon is now better known to Wishbone Ash fans as the webmaster for the US-based Wishbone Ash Internet site, but then he had the job of helping out with any new band that the label had signed or was trying to break in America. As Leon recalls, it was quite a shock to see Laurie in Ted's place:

"I got the airport to meet the band off the plane. Off comes Martin and Steve, and Miles and Andy, and some other guy who I thought was the roadie. No one had told me that Ted had left the band, so I was going round saying, 'Where's Ted then? Is he already here?' Well actually Ted had quit the band!"

After Leon recovered from the shock of Ted's departure, he spent the next few months with the band as they recorded the *There's The Rub* album at Miami's Criteria Sound Studios during August and September of 1974. The album was to be produced by Bill Szymczyk who had worked with Eric Clapton and Joe Walsh and who would later go on to produce the best selling Eagles album, *Hotel California*. Andy Powell takes up the story: "Bill Szymczyk didn't even know that Laurie had replaced Ted. It was a complete shock to him. He'd signed a deal to produce one band and he'd got this different line-up. He was quite pissed off about it really."

After Bill had come to terms with the change in the line-up, he set to work and soon managed to gain the confidence of band. As Martin Turner states, the band had faith in Szymczyk's ability: "Bill Szymczyk at the time was truly a great producer. He had at that time become very adept at recording guitars. Bill learnt a lot from us about how we constructed our guitar solos which he immediately put into practice with the Eagles on *Hotel California*. At the same time we learnt a lot from him about using the studio to its full extent."

Leon Tsilis recalls the sessions as being a particularly productive time for the new version of Wishbone Ash: "We spent the three glorious months down in Miami recording *There's The Rub*. It was great to watch them work. I don't think there'd been any official 'jamming' before then. I think the jamming started in Miami. I got to see the Mark II version of Wishbone Ash coming together. It was a great experience."

Mark Emery, who by that time was Wishbone's sound engineer, was amazed at the creative input of Bill Szymzyck and his engineer, Alan Blazey: "The technical prowess of these guys in the studio was brilliant. They were running guitar tracks like you wouldn't believe. They would play eight passes of a guitar solo. Then they would use early versions of digital switches for track changes. It would be like 'catch that lick' then 'put in that one'. So the solos were all built like that. Then Laurie and Andy would learn to play the solos that they had created. That's the way they did it with the Eagles on *Hotel California* so the band would come out with really unusual guitar phrases."

During the sessions, Bill Szymzyck tried to get Wishbone to take Joe Walsh on board. As Martin explains:

"Bill tried to get Joe Walsh to join us as he was going through a very bad patch with the break up of his marriage. But we were a complete unit and didn't need another member. So he introduced Joe to the Eagles instead and they immediately

thirty years of Wishbone Ash

Above: First Japanese press conference, 1975.
(l-r) Andy Powell, Laurie Wisefield, Martin Turner and Steve Upton.
Photo: Wishbone Ash Fan Club Archives

clicked and went on to greater things from there, recording *Hotel California* together straight after us in that studio."

With the album successfully recorded at Criteria – a studio where they would record three further albums – Wishbone returned to England refreshed and ready to hit the road for the first time with the new line-up. After several weeks rehearsing in September, Wishbone Ash's first live appearance with Laurie Wisefield was at Plymouth Guildhall on 2 October. This was to be the start of a lengthy world tour (the band's first) that would last well into the following year with dates in the UK, Europe, USA, Canada, Australia, New Zealand and Japan. In many ways Laurie was thrown into the deep end with not only a hectic schedule ahead of him but also with the inevitable "how good is he compared to Ted?" questions to contend with. In the event, many were surprised at just how well Laurie's playing suited the band. He even won over many female Ash fans with his coy nature and elf-like stature. They just wanted to cuddle him! The UK leg included an appearance at the Rainbow Theatre, London on 17 October, attended by Ted Turner.

Laurie recalls the Rainbow date: "I was a bit self-conscious because Ted was there and anyone who was anyone came and I don't really dig that bullshit – I just wanted to go on and have a good time. The northern gigs were the best, I'd say. All the gigs up north were incredible. Everyone was really positive."[10]

Mark Emery was also impressed with the way Laurie coped with his new role: "I thought Laurie was accepted by the fans pretty quickly as Ted was the pretty boy of the band and had a lot of fans. But Laurie was also cute and just got on with the job. He was always super-confident and that came across. In a way it was good news for the band. He was the best replacement they could get for sure."

Following the conclusion of the UK tour at Birmingham Odeon on 19 October, Wishbone headed for concerts in Europe commencing in Zurich, Switzerland

Above: The grave that was the inspiration for the song "Lady Jay".
Photo: Mark Chatterton

on 22 October and ending in Copenhagen, Denmark on 5 November. Throughout both the UK and European tours the new album featured prominently. Indeed, on several dates the entire album was performed – a brave move considering the work had yet to be released and audiences were unfamiliar with the music. On listening to the various bootleg tapes of those gigs one can sense a certain nervousness with some of the new material. It wasn't until well after the British dates that *There's the Rub* finally hit the stores in November 1974.

The band's first US-recorded album definitely had an American sound and feel, with even the lyrics containing certain Americanisms. Whether the album would have sounded more anglicised if it had been recorded in England is debatable, but one thing is sure – the arrival of Laurie injected a new-found vitality and energy that had been largely missing on *Wishbone Four*. The Hipgnosis designed cover portrayed a cricketer with a cricket ball that he'd just rubbed near his crotch – as cricketer's do. Eye-catching, if perhaps a little lacking in imagination. The music though was the complete opposite.

From the opening chords to "Silver Shoes" traces of Laurie Wisefield's distinctive finger picking style guitar, as perfected during his Home days, shine through. A killer guitar solo from Andy and a lyric from Steve Upton helped to make this a fine opener.

"Don't Come Back" is a typical lively rocker which showing the band's two guitarists in fine form, one minute playing in unison and the next duelling away with each other. It might have made a good single release in America but was probably passed over in view of it being too long for US radio play.

"Persephone" slows down the proceedings and features a strong chorus. The lyrics by Martin were an appreciation of Ted, although the story of "Perspehone" originates from a myth about a Greek goddess. Laurie plays the first solo and Andy plays the second one at the end.

"Hometown" is probably the least memorable track on the album but nevertheless shows some fine vocal harmonies and an impressive opening riff courtesy of Andy Powell. The Martin Turner lyric was about going home after being on the road.

"Lady Jay" was inspired by a Dartmoor folk myth. Martin Turner explains: "The story goes back a few hundred years and legend has it that a young peasant girl called Jay got mixed up with the local Lord of the Manor's son. They started having it off and she got pregnant. In those days there was no way they could be married and so she committed suicide and because sinners who commit suicide aren't allowed to be buried in holy ground, she was taken to Dartmoor and buried. After that, her lover used to travel there every day and place fresh flowers on her grave, and legend has it that when he died, fresh flowers continued to appear there every day and still do today. I went there with some friends one windy winter's night and can only describe it as being a very weird, spooky experience. It struck me as being a rather beautiful legend, though."[10]

This track with its folky mood would have not have been out of place on *Argus*. It contains a typical Wishbone riff played in dual lead style by Laurie and Andy.

Of all the tracks on *There's the Rub*, closing number "F.U.B.B." probably best displays the talents of Wishbone's new guitar twins. A lengthy, instrumental piece (featuring Cuban musician Nelson Padron on congas), the track came together as the result of several jam sessions. "F.U.B.B." starts slowly with a Martin Turner bass riff gradually moving into a funk guitar section – something quite radical for Wishbone Ash at that time. For the record, "F.U.B.B." stands for "Fucked Up Beyond Belief". Martin explains:

"We called it "Fucked Up Beyond Belief" because that probably most accurately described the condition we were in when it was recorded. Quite a bit of it we'd been playing for weeks, but it's just a jam mainly and we worked on little bits here and there."[10]

On its release *There's the Rub* attracted broadly positive reviews from the music press. The album peaked at number 16 in the UK charts, not doing as well as its predecessor in terms of sales. This may have been due to the fact that it wasn't released until after the British tour had been completed – a poor move by MCA. In the USA the album did not fare any better despite the fact that it had been released just before the band's biggest US tour up to that point, from November through to February. Despite its disappointing sales performance, many fans hold *There's the Rub* as one of the best albums to come out of the Mark II period of the band.

Chapter Four

Locked In... In New England

With the UK/European tour completed and *There's the Rub* released worldwide, Wishbone Ash headed for the US/Canadian leg of their world tour which opened in Indianapolis on 26 November 1974 running through to 7 February 1975 in Honolulu. The band spent Christmas away from home for the first time as a group, celebrating the festivities aboard a luxury yacht on the sunny Florida coast.

Leon Tsilis met up with Wishbone once again when they hit LA in mid-January to play at the Long Beach Arena. This was to be a special gig where the executives and employees of MCA would gather to meet and celebrate the previous year's successes and also see the new version of Wishbone Ash in action. What transpired was a similar scenario to the infamous *Melody Maker* awards ceremony in London a couple of years earlier. As Leon remembers:

"Every year MCA would bring the field staff out to LA, where they would be wined and dined for three or four days and get their awards, etc. It was called 'the gathering of the eagles'. Miles Copeland had set up this major gig at the Long Beach Arena with the idea of really selling the band to the MCA hierarchy. Apparently he had this meeting with the president of MCA during the day, then the big-wigs would come to the Queen Mary and have dinner with the band before they performed at the Long Beach Arena. I guess you could say that their manager Miles Copeland had turned the band against the label to some degree and that the label was a little disappointed with the sales and airplay that *There's the Rub* had garnered. What was to be the band's big breakthrough album, turned out to be a big bust. The icing on the cake was the luke-warm reception that the band and

Above: Ted Turner shortly after leaving Wishbone Ash, 1975.
Photo: Wishbone Ash Fan Club Archives

management gave to the entire promotion department that had travelled from all across the nation to attend the show. A dinner with the band had been planned before the show aboard the Queen Mary, but the band never showed leaving the higher-ups in the company a little embarrassed, to say the least. Then to add insult to injury, MCA's breakthrough band was blown off the stage by a then unknown, fire-breathing opening act named KISS. It wasn't long after that fateful night that both parties decided it would be better if Wishbone Ash moved on to a new label in the States. This might be one of the main reasons why they were dropped by MCA in America and ended up gong to Atlantic."

Meanwhile, as Wishbone toured the US sports arenas, former member Ted Turner together with his then girlfriend – a native of Louisiana by the name of Anastasia – had finally departed for Peru.

Says Steve Upton: "His intentions were to go to Peru with his girlfriend and find the Lost City of Mu. He left for Peru and our first contact that he was there came when we played New Orleans and the mother of Ted's girlfriend wrote to us at the hotel we were staying in. They had arrived and started their trek into the mountains on foot. They had brought the usual supplies and also an ass to carry the supplies. They named the ass "Wishbone" – Wishbone Ass! They had been in the mountains for a few days and then one night as they slept they were robbed. They lost everything including the ass. The letter left us even more worried and I decided to make a call to England. I remembered Miles' dad had his CIA connections – if anyone could help, he could. A week later, Ted showed up safe and sound and to this day there is still an ass walking around Peru called Wishbone. I hasten to add they never found the Lost City of Mu."[5]

Ted himself has fond memories and vivid recollections of his travels: "It was the best thing I ever did. I visited the remote regions of the Andes and met Indian tribes who had never seen a white person before. In one village they thought I was Jesus, because the only other white person they'd seen with long hair and different coloured eyes was in church. But I never stopped playing music. I bought a couple of 'Mountain Men' guitars – they're tiny ten stringed instruments. They sit up there in the Andes playing accompaniment with a flute – it's beautiful music."[2]

Ted returned to the UK in mid-1975, but eventually quit England to reside in the USA. After spells in New Orleans and Los Angeles during the late seventies, Ted returned to the UK briefly in 1981 and began working on musical projects with Martin Turner and Police drummer Stewart Copeland. However, it was not long before Ted returned to Laurel Canyon, Los Angeles where he would make his home in a geodesic dome.

Ted continued to write, record and perform music but remained largely out of the public eye, working mainly with local musicians depending on where he was living. In 1982 Ted toured with Badfinger and, in 1983, attempted to use the Wishbone Ash name for a band he'd formed in Los Angeles. The band tried to tour, performing new Ted Turner songs but little of Wishbone's back catalogue, before Ted's use of the name was prohibited by the official group. Ted also formed bands such as the Choice and the World Man Band. As far as recordings go, neither project got further than the demo stage although several songs from this period were later re-worked by Wishbone Ash, upon the eventual reformation of the original line-up in the late eighties.

Wishbone's 1974/75 World Tour finally moved on to Japan. The band received an ecstatic response from an audience ready to devour Western rock music. Indeed, such was the demand for tickets for the concerts the band played two full length shows per night. Laurie Wisefield remembers: "Japan was great really mainly because of the fans. Japan was one of these places where we actually had an image. We were put on the front pages of magazines and were like pop stars!"

Mark Emery too remembers the way the whole tour entourage was treated in Japan: "Japan was fantastic. We all had fans in Japan – even the roadies! They would all come up and give you these little dolls. The audience was nearly all young girls, most of them in school uniforms. They would just sit there all very quiet during the song and at the end of the song they would just erupt and go crazy. Then they would all go quiet again for the next song and so on. The crews were all brilliant there as well. Mal Craggs and I would set the gear up on stage, then they'd come along and measure where everything was. Once the gig was finished the gear would be broken down and it would vanish. Then when we got to the next gig it would already be set up inch-perfect! They would have driven it overnight to the next gig in open-topped vans so they couldn't store it. It was absolutely brilliant organisation."

Mark also remembers the whole crew being taken to a Geisha house by the notorious Mr Udo, who apparently would treat all visiting bands to this Japanese form of "relaxation": "That was my first experience with professional orgasms! There was nothing dirty about it at all. It was all absolutely clean and wonderful.

Above: Off for another day at the office.
(l-r) Andy Powell, Laurie Wisefield, Martin Turner and Steve Upton.
Photo: Wishbone Ash Fan Club Archives

The cold plunge was a bit scary, but the massage after it was well worth it! It was a great way to spend a couple of hours."

Whether the members of the band visited the same Geisha house, Mark neglected to say.

The Japanese leg of the World Tour was followed by the last few dates in Australia and New Zealand, the only time that the group would play these two countries. The final date in New Zealand concluded the tour with an open air concert at Western Springs Stadium, Auckland which ended with Steve Upton being arrested on leaving the stage. Throughout Wishbone's career, a regular slot in the live set was Upton's emergence from his drum rostrum – usually during a suitable break mid-set – to walk the stage with his customary towel and glass and spend a few minutes centre stage introducing the band and the following number. On this

Blowin' Free

Above and below: One of the first opportunities for British fans to see Laurie Wisefield in action at Leeds in 1974. Wishbone Ash later exiled themselves for tax reasons. *Photos: Wishbone Ash Fan Club Archives*
Opposite: The British music press accurately predicts future events.

WISHBONE TO QUIT BRITAIN

particular tour Steve would regularly introduce the song "F.U.B.B." explaining the significance of the abbreviation. In spite of the fact that he was warned that in New Zealand it was an offence to swear in public, let alone on stage, he still went ahead with his usual explanation. Most people in the audience accepted it, but apparently a woman sunbathing in her garden near the concert heard the words and rang her friend up, who happened to be the mayor. He then contacted the police and sure enough as the band left the stage at the end of their set, Steve was promptly arrested and put in jail overnight before being bailed the next morning. Luckily the band did not have any more gigs to play but because of the publicity *There's the Rub* reached number three in the New Zealand album charts. The incident even made the news back home with a short piece in the London *Evening Standard* – an eventful conclusion to a highly successful World Tour.

Incidentally, the Australian dates were backed with the release of the promo-only album entitled *Australian Tour Sampler* through the band's Australian record company MCA-Astor. This is now one of the rarest of all Wishbone Ash vinyl product with reportedly only 100 copies being pressed. It featured tracks from all six Wishbone Ash albums to this point, with extracts from an Andy Powell interview interspersed throughout.

With Wishbone spending more and more time touring as well as recording in the States it seemed inevitable that the band would one day relocate to America. As far back as August 1973 British music paper *Sounds* had run the headline, "Wishbone To Quit Britain". As the article hinted, it was Martin Turner who was least in favour of the move. In fact both he and Andy had recently bought houses in England. But following on from their experience of recording in Florida the previous summer and with the band touring the USA and Canada for ever increasing periods (plus also the high rates of UK income tax pertaining at that time) it was a logical step. As band publicist, Rod Lynton had stated in the article: "They don't want to desert England, but at the same time they must progress and America is the place to do it."

Following the decision to move, all four members eventually decided to reside in the area surrounding the rustic town of Westport, Connecticut. Situated on the north eastern seaboard, north of New York, with a similar climate to Britain, it was almost a home from home for the band. Martin Turner looks back on the decision to move to the States:

"I had reservations about going, primarily because of my concern over the group's British identity," admits Turner, "but I think the other guys in the band had been impressed by legal advice and other considerations at the time. There were also tax considerations – not that we were trying to run away from paying tax. I didn't really want to live in Connecticut at the time – to me it was like going to live in Surrey. I voted against it but was outvoted by the other guys and had to abide by the democratic decision. I personally would have rather lived in New York, which is the ultimate urban experience."

Laurie Wisefield elaborates further: "At that time in Britain the tax rate for us was about 85% and as we were working in America so much it made sense at the time to go over there."

Wishbone Ash left the UK on 7 April 1975. Steve Upton and Laurie Wisefield shared a log cabin, whilst Martin Turner, Andy Powell and their wives rented large houses. "Laurel Edge", the house rented by Martin Turner and his wife Maurn, would also double as the band's rehearsal base and provide accommodation for visiting friends and entourage. Situated away from other houses on the edge of a forest, its basement would be the setting for rehearsals and the recording of demotapes for the next few albums.

Soon after moving to the States, Wishbone Ash embarked on a spring US tour with Aerosmith, with Wishbone headlining some dates and Aerosmith others depending on which band was the bigger in each town or city. At one point they were approached by Aerosmith's management company who expressed a keen interest in representing Wishbone Ash as well. The band, however, declined this offer as Martin Turner explains:

"We were out gigging with Aerosmith – they were on the way up at the time – and we actually passed on a huge offer from their management company, who had been fans of Wishbone Ash for years. They informed us that they'd actually asked Miles Copeland if they could represent us in the States and asked if we were aware of that – which we certainly weren't. They made us an offer. They said, 'We're managing Aerosmith, we want one other artist to represent. We'll make you big stars, but it'll cost you. We'll take 50% of everything you earn.' The rest of the guys in the band were flabbergasted that they could be so cheeky to ask such a thing. My attitude was, 'Wait a minute guys – we've got a very good New York lawyer in Allen Grubman. Put him in a room with them, let them thrash it out and they'll probably come out with 40%. Then, after a year, if we're big megastars we can renegotiate.' The point I considered was because they were asking for 50%, they would have to work very hard and put a lot of time in on us, because it would have made financial sense for them. If they were only going to take 20% or something, they would have needed to sign up other acts. We passed on their offer and they settled on Ted Nugent instead. Again, this was a democratic decision which I thought was really silly especially considering it was mainly for financial reasons that we were living in the States."

Looking back on the affair Andy Powell agrees that the band could have benefited from taking up the offer: "They took Steve out in a big limousine and they made him a big offer. But we actually turned them down which in retrospect was probably a bad move. We thought we knew better. You see at that time we didn't want to be giving away 50% of what we were earning as we didn't seem to be earning that much."

During the summer of 1975 Wishbone Ash came back across the Atlantic to tour Europe in an ambitious festival package tour entitled Startruckin' '75. The brainchild of Miles Copeland, this tour played major festival and arena dates in Germany, Belgium, Holland, Spain, France, Switzerland and Austria with Wishbone Ash headlining over the likes of the Mahavishnu Orchestra, Soft Machine, Caravan, Renaissance and the Climax Blues Band. The shows gave the band the opportunity to try out four new songs penned for their next album – "Rest in Peace", "Trust in You", "Half Past Lovin" and "Bad Weather Blues".

The Startruckin' Tour, described as a "travelling festival", was a scheme designed by Miles Copeland as a ploy to break his bands in mainland Europe. The bands would be ferried across to Europe in a large transporter plane more used to carrying heavy artillery and soldiers than rock musicians and their equipment.

Lou Reed had initially been secured as the headline act and the tour ran into severe problems when he pulled out at the last minute. Promoters took advantage of Reed's non-appearance to withhold contracted fees and the tour, despite selling out at most venues, was a financial disaster resulting in Copeland being forced to liquidate all his companies and flirt with bankruptcy for the next few years.

Mark Emery recalls this extravagant tour: "I remember after this gig in Bremen in Germany we had to be down near Frankfurt the next day, so the organisers had hired about fifteen limousines for all the bands as well as some of the crew. We actually drove off the road as our chauffeur fell asleep at the wheel which was horrendous. That cost a fortune. Then there was another cock-up as they couldn't take the trucks through Switzerland to get to France one weekend as they didn't have the licences. So they had to charter a plane to move all this equipment to get to the next festival at Orange in France. Coupled with this the guy who promoted it split with all the money!"

Despite the problems with the promoter, the gig at Orange is fondly remembered as the highlight of the tour. Delays prevented Wishbone from getting on stage until about four in the morning but as the band played "Phoenix", the climax to their set, the sun started to rise above the horizon – a magical moment for Ash fans lucky enough to be there. The band's appearance at the Reading Festival a few days later was also a memorable occasion, the band playing in the UK for the first time in over six months.

On 19 September, two weeks after the Startruckin' Tour reached its conclusion in Essen, Germany, Wishbone Ash and Miles Copeland met at Laureledge to discuss their future plans. Group consensus was that band and manager should go their separate ways and Wishbone would continue with Steve Upton taking charge of the band's business affairs. Andy Powell speaks of how the band became gradually disillusioned with Copeland's services:

"Miles was great for us in the beginning, but he had a vision of building an empire, which he's since done, and we were the means for him to build his empire. He used us as a springboard, he used our money, he used our name to attract more bands. We weren't interested in his empire; we were interested in the good name of Wishbone Ash and what we could do to further our career. He was becoming less

Blowin' Free

POP GROUPS swarm into Southend Airport — and not a fan in sight.

The groups, trekking across Europe this month as part of the Startrucking '75 pop festival, broke off the tour to fly in for this weekend's Reading pop festival.

■

They included Wishbone Ash, Ike and Tina Turner, the Mahavishnu Orchestra, Soft Machine and Climax Blues.

But there were no rowdy scenes that usually accompany the pop groups on their arrival at airports.

Instead, a few airport staff waved as the groups left their specially-chartered BAF Carvair aircraft.

■

A member of the entourage said: "It wasn't well publicised that we were coming into Southend so we didn't really expect crowds of fans."

The groups will fly back to the Continent from Southend to continue their tour on Monday evening.

Above: Cutting from the *Southend Evening Echo*.
Note: Tina Turner at the front.

Left: The Startruckin' Tour, 1975.

70

interested in that and more interested in his empire. I think it would have been great if he'd given us a little more time in 1975 instead of thinking about doing massive festival tours of Europe, but in retrospect he did through those actions break Wishbone Ash in Europe in quite a big way, so it was six of one and half a dozen of the other, but overall I think he wanted a bigger playing field to play on, which is completely understandable."

Martin Turner explains further what went wrong between Wishbone Ash and Miles Copeland:

"After the Startruckin' Tour, we should have been paid a huge sum of money, about £50,000, but we never got paid. I believe his accountant grabbed the money as collateral and pretty soon afterwards Miles went bankrupt. Everyone started suing him but we chose not to as we'd started out together and were friends. We didn't really want to kick him in the balls even though it virtually put us out of business at the time. Instead we went our separate ways and started building the whole thing up again."

During the year various overseas Wishbone Ash compilation albums were released by MCA, such as *The Best of Wishbone Ash* in Germany and *Masters of Rock* and *Milestones* in Holland.

Severing ties with Miles Copeland was not Wishbone Ash's only business change during 1975, as MCA (USA) had agreed for the band to be released to Atlantic Records for a two album deal for the US market whilst continuing with MCA for Britain and the rest of the world. This came about through the band's connections with the Average White Band, also signed to Atlantic at that time.

During the Autumn of 1975 the band would be ensconced at Atlantic Studios in New York City with noted house producer Tom Dowd recording their next album. Dowd had recently done great things for artists like Rod Stewart and Lynyrd Skynyrd and Atlantic hoped he would have a similar influence over Wishbone Ash. In the event, the recording sessions proved traumatic. Wishbone's working relationship with Dowd was far from healthy and his production techniques hardly suited the Wishbone Ash style of music. Martin Turner remembers things getting off to a bad start at the pre-recording meeting with Tom Dowd:

"When we got up at the end of the meeting, I remember him saying to us, 'OK guys. Just one thing. When we go into the studio next week to make this record, I don't want anyone to be bringing in any alcohol or drugs into the studio'. We were all agog, as at that point we'd made quite a few albums and although we weren't hooligans we did like to indulge a bit. What had happened was that he'd worked with Lynyrd Skynyrd who were totally drugs and alcohol and with Eric Clapton who'd become hooked on heroin at the time. He'd had these bad experiences and so was fiercely opposed to anything like that. So we said, 'We'll do it Tom's way'."

Once the sessions started, Tom Dowd suddenly disappeared for several days as one of his friends, the drummer Al Jackson, had been shot. Then it emerged that he was going through a divorce and was being hassled by his estranged wife. In Martin's words, "He was fucked" – hardly the best working relationship. He also used to make the band sit around in a circle using tiny amplifiers to record their songs. Laurie Wisefield didn't like the studio either.

"It was flat. There was hardly a drop of echo on anything. Our mistake with Tom Dowd was that he didn't have enough knowledge of where the band came from. Nevertheless he was a lovely man and we learnt a lot from him, but at the end of the day the finished product wasn't that brilliant."

Andy Powell agrees with Laurie but puts the whole situation of the band in context: "With Dowd it was just make the best of everything – no echo, just go in the studio and plug in. That was the closest I ever came to having a nervous breakdown. We were very uncomfortable with the way we were being recorded, plus we were very uncomfortable about not having a manager to guide us. We'd lost a lot of money on the Startrucking tour and now we were now living in a foreign country. It was very scary."

Musically, the material recorded marked a distinct departure for Wishbone Ash, with a move towards a more US-flavoured soft-rock sound and the band being augmented by a group of female backing vocalists plus keyboard player Peter Wood (ex-Sutherland Brothers). In addition, things were not helped when Dowd told Martin Turner that he had nodes on his vocal chords, which meant that Martin wasn't able to sing on several of the songs.

"I absolutely destroyed my voice by singing loudly," admits Turner. "It's a direct result of the unnatural process of trying to sing against 100 watt amps. I could have a minor operation to have them removed. They have to shave the tiny nodes off the vocal chords, but they're so small that they have to do it under a microscope. I'd have visions of the guy's hand slipping and me ending up sounding like Rod Stewart."[12]

The following year, 1976, proved to be a turbulent one for Wishbone Ash. The aptly titled *Locked In* album was released in the UK on 12 March. Critics had a field day, branding the album a disaster. *Sounds'* Pete Makowski, a long-time Ash devotee, claimed: "Ash seem to be trying to take a giant step forward at the same time as if Dowd is confused as to which direction the band is heading. Somehow this album seems a drastic move and, after many listenings, it still seems to be an inconsistent effort."

Wishbone Ash had always taken a certain amount of stick from particular elements of the music press but for once even the band's loyal fans could not defend the album, with its distinctly lightweight style and lack of memorable songs. Whilst the fan club tried to be positive and upbeat about Ash's latest offering, even the latest newsletter printed the comments of one disappointed fan who considered "the vocals atrocious" and "the production thin".

Despite the fact that there hadn't been any live concerts from Wishbone in the UK for more than a year and it was now eighteen months since Wishbone's previous vinyl offering, the album only barely scraped into the top 40 album charts peaking at number 36.

One noticeable change on *Locked In* was the way in which the composer credits were listed on the sleeve. For the first time in the band's career, songwriters were credited individually for their particular contributions, whereas in the past all songs had been credited as being written by the band as a whole. Andy Powell explains:

"There were no contractual clauses stating that all songs had to be credited in a certain manner. It was by band consensus. With all the early albums, songs were credited jointly, even though writing may have been biased towards whoever initiated an idea at rehearsals. For example, the music to 'Silver Shoes' and 'Hometown' is very obviously largely Laurie's work with Martin adding lyrics, 'Valediction' was largely my work, 'Blind Eye' was Ted and me, whereas 'Doctor' and 'Handy' were largely Martin's work."

Laurie elaborates further on this subject with special reference to *Locked In*:

"It was Martin's idea as he was writing most of the songs. He thought it was unfair and said that the people who wrote the songs should get credit for what they wrote. But by the time of our next album, *New England*, this had changed back to the whole group getting the credit – possibly because Martin didn't write that much for that album."

The opening song "Rest in Peace" is a good up-tempo number which jogs along quite nicely with the effects of voice box in the guitar solo. However, the song sounds better played live. Not a bad start – but sadly the album goes downhill from there.

"No Water in the Well" marked Laurie's songwriting and vocal debut on record and was not that successful. "Moonshine" featured a typical plucked guitar riff courtesy of Laurie and was not a bad song. It even made the Top 10 in the Japanese singles chart!

The Martin Turner penned "She Was My Best Friend" was another low point on the album with dowdy vocals and a poor tune. Steve Upton had a hand in the lyrics of "It Started In Heaven", but again the song gets nowhere.

"Half Past Lovin", one of four group compositions again fails to inspire. It sounds like Wishbone Ash trying to be funky but failing. "Trust In You" lifts the spirits a little, whilst the final track, "Say Goodbye" has some nice acoustic guitar on it and is probably the strongest track on Side Two of the album.

In addition to the tracks featured on *Locked In* a further track, "Bad Weather Blues", was recorded. Why on earth "Bad Weather Blues" was left off the album is one of the biggest mysteries in the whole history of Wishbone Ash. Written largely by Andy Powell, the track would become a live favourite in the late seventies as the band's encore number. Although the song would never feature in studio format, a live version was eventually released on the B-side of the single "You See Red" in 1978. If "Bad Weather Blues" been included on the album and one or two of the weaker tracks left off, the album may have been stronger.

Locked In is considered by many to be the worst ever Wishbone Ash album, vying for that dubious honour with 1984's *Raw to the Bone*. Even the Chris Covey designed cover, with the band looking as if they were drowning beneath the waters of New York City, looked tacky. Martin Turner summed up the band's disappointment with the finished product, recalling the time the band gathered together in the control booth to listen to the album playback for the first time:

"I was very upset at the state I was in and at the state Wishbone Ash were in. At the end of the recording sessions, I ended up in a foetal position lying on the floor of the control room crying my eyes out listening to the playback of the album and thinking that I couldn't do anything about it. I really thought my career was over."

Despite the air of despondency, Wishbone duly undertook a five-week US tour in support of the album with Graham Maitland (ex-Glencoe) augmenting the touring line-up. Even onstage, the American soft-rock influence was heavily apparent – on both old and new songs alike. Some of the numbers from *Locked In* were played during the tour and one particular show appeared on the 1999 Receiver Records release *The King Will Come*, which is still an interesting showcase of the band's live set from this period.

Despite making their best efforts to promote *Locked In*, the band knew that the album was a failure in both commercial and artistic terms. Certainly it was the lowest point of the seventies for Wishbone Ash and an experience which would galvanise the band into positive action in the future.

Says Steve Upton: "We'd left our record company, had no management and we were working on a record with Tom Dowd. That was not a particularly healthy time to make a record. That whole time was probably the roughest of the lot. We just had no solid foundation any more. Musically we were taking a detour. I don't think *Locked In* turned out to be Wishbone Ash playing Wishbone Ash music. The title is more apt than I thought at the time. We were locked into a heavy situation. We were very cramped. We were just like blotting paper. We were that vulnerable."[20]

"We lost track of everything," says Andy Powell. "We couldn't focus on where we should be going and we put too much faith and responsibility on other people. We were looking for guidance – we didn't realise we should be taking the lead. It disillusioned us, it got pretty miserable. It was being married to a very stable person, Pauline my wife, that got me through all this in the end."

Another US promo album surfaced during the *Locked In* period. *Nightbird and Co* was a two-album set featuring an entire radio programme (complete with adverts). One side featured Andy and Laurie being interviewed plus several tracks from the *Locked In* album. The other three sides featured music and conversation from Jethro Tull and the Don Harrison Band.

With the US tour complete, Wishbone Ash abandoned promotion for *Locked In*. For the first time there were no dates booked for the UK. In Europe there were just three festivals in Germany to play. Instead, the band wisely took a serious look at their situation and began writing the material which would mark a return to the style of music which had made the band successful. American producers Ron and Howard Albert were recruited – they suggested recording at Criteria, Miami where they were house producers, having worked with artists such as the Bee Gees and Joe Walsh. Wishbone, however, were not keen, since the recording of *Locked In* had put the band off using a professional recording studio for the time being at least. The band had agreed that for the next album they would bring in mobile recording equipment and record largely in a makeshift studio assembled in the massive basement of Laurel Edge in an attempt to capture some of the excitement and spontaneity of their rehearsal sessions. Mark Emery had the job of sound engineer and a mobile 24-track recording studio was installed. Criteria was used only for vocals and final overdubs. The recording process would take four months, being interrupted only for the German festivals booked for June.

"When it came to recording the album, we just realised that we didn't want to face traipsing over to New York every day like we had for *Locked In*," recalls Laurie Wisefield. "We really wanted to record our music in the loose atmosphere that we'd written and rehearsed it in. The album was recorded in one room with us all standing around in a circle with just a few simple screens behind us. We wanted to relax and enjoy what we were doing and it worked well."[19]

"Recording at the house was a brave move for us," continues Martin Turner. "It was almost like recording live. The whole thing was one big jam session and most of the time we were hardly aware that the stuff we were playing was being recorded. I really enjoyed working that way, but you obviously lose some of the technical quality that you get from a studio."[21]

The new material was debuted on Wishbone Ash's second Japanese tour which took place in October. The band were surprised to find on arrival in Tokyo that *Locked In* number "Moonshine" was in the top ten singles chart. Indeed it was only in Japan that *Locked In* had achieved any real degree of critical or public acclaim. A promo album, *Special DJ Copy*, was issued to radio stations to help promote the shows.

Having been residents of Connecticut for well over a year, Wishbone decided to dedicate their new album to the area in which they lived, thus titling the set *New England*. It was rush-released in October 1976 to coincide with their return to the UK's concert stages from which, save for the Reading 1975 performance, they'd been absent for two years. They had taken steps to repair the relationship with the UK Music Press arranging for Barbara Charone from *Sounds* to stay at Laurel Edge during the *New England* sessions. Such was the thirst for Wishbone Ash product that the tour completely sold out and the album fared much better than its predecessor. The cover was once again designed by Storm Thorgerson/ Hipgnosis, showing three shirtless males standing together, with the middle one sharpening a wooden stake with a knife, implying a brave new world. The inner cover had black and white pictures of the four band members, also shirtless, at the lake near Laurel Edge. According to Laurie, Storm Thorgerson made them get up at five o'clock in the morning for the photo shoot only for them to be bitten to shreds by mosquitoes.

Musically the album contains a much better mix of songs (both rockers and ballads) than *Locked In*. The opening track "Mother of Pearl" with its brash guitar riff, shows that Wishbone had once again found the winning formula.

This is followed by "(In All Of My Dreams) You Rescue Me" – a dreamy ballad with laid-back guitar in stark contrast to the previous and following tracks. Andy Powell's wife Pauline contributed heavily to the song's lyrics. As the song ends the crickets in the evening air of Laurel Edge can be heard.

Next up comes another rocker in the form of "Runaway", with a killer of a riff from Andy. This was the set opener on the *New England* tour. Side One finishes with "Lorelei", another slow number featuring some blistering guitar work from Laurie Wisefield. The song tells the story of the rock by the side of the River Rhine in Germany where Wishbone would a few years later play at the annual music festival.

WISHBONE FANS GET THEIR WISH

By ROSIE HORIDE

WISHBONE ASH were firing on all cylinders. The capacity audience were loving it. And then the trouble started.

Minutes after the gig at Sheffield's City Hall, bass-player Martin Turner said:

"*It was insane. One minute everything was fine and the next minute rows of people were collapsing like dominoes.*"

Waiting

"No band likes a quiet gig, but this one went a bit far. Twenty people were injured, and one chap got a broken ankle.

"*We knew we were back in England.*"

Thousands of Wishbone Ash fans have waited patiently for two years for this tour. There have been only the odd album, a few reports from far-off corners of the world, and one appearance at the last Reading Festival, to keep them interested.

Martin, 29, said: "I'm afraid we have been neglecting Britain. But we are one of the few bands who have been lucky enough to build up a following in most parts of the world."

Touring

"We didn't plan to be away for two years. We just started touring. And when people wanted to see us in various countries, we went there. We covered America and Europe and then the Pacific area—Australia, New Zealand and Japan.

"When we finally fitted in a British tour, we were all worried. Rock fans are fickle and two years is a long time."

The band need not have worried. Britain had not forgotten them.

The 20-date tour sold out within days of tickets being available. Tonight's concert at the Hammersmith Odeon, London, puts them halfway through their tour, and they have not played to an empty seat.

The other members of Wishbone Ash are the two lead guitarists, Andy Powell, 27, and Laurie Wisefield, 24, and drummer Steve Upton, 29.

Unlike most bands Wishbone Ash enjoy touring. Which is probably why they do so much of it. Rock musicians usually want to tell you about the loneliness of life on the road.

Martin Turner has a more romantic approach.

He said: "I treat every tour as an adventure.

"We never have much advance knowledge of where we will be or what we will be doing. And that's great."

Martin is an unlikely-looking adventurer—pale and frail in the way that rock stars are expected to be.

He grinned as he made the sort of confession that few rock musicians would admit to.

Agree

He said: "I'm always getting told off by the others for being a bit sloppy about my playing. They tell me I don't practise enough.

"But I am not convinced that a couple of bum notes played on stage are all that important. The atmosphere and the amount of excitement and enjoyment you can generate are much more important.

"I suppose every band needs at least one person like me. It stops the others taking themselves too seriously."

Martin is married. He and his 26-year-old wife Maureen live in Barnes, London, when they are not touring.

"For Maureen is one of the few rock wives who tours with her husband. And Martin says she enjoys it as much as he does.

"She loves it all," he said. "And the one thing all adventurers need is a good woman to look after them. That's where Dr Livingstone went wrong, or something . . .

"I really agree with the sentiments of that new single by Robert Palmer. It's called Man Smart, Woman Smarter.

"I'll drink to that!"

THE HAPPY BAND of travellers . . . Wishbone Ash, from left, Martin Turner, Steve Upton (top), Laurie Wisefield and Andy Powell. PICTURE BY ROGER BAMBER

THEY SOUND GREAT!

■ WISHBONE ASH — New England (MCA): Wishbone Ash fans will go for this high-class rock album in a big way. All self-penned stuff, with the performances as tight as ever. Laurie Wisefield has fitted into the band beautifully.

Above: An idication of the success of Wishbone Ash in the mainstream "Pop" world. A full-page spread in *The Sun* newspaper, 5 November 1976.

Side Two opener "Outward Bound" must rank as one of the best Wishbone Ash instrumentals. Certainly the record company thought so and released it as a single backed with "Lorelei", but as with all Wishbone Ash singles, it failed to make the charts.

The next three tracks, "Prelude", "When You Know Love" and "Lonely Island" all had their moments, but it was the final track – "Candlelight", another instrumental, which attracted most attention. It marked Ted Turner's first songwriting contribution to a Wishbone Ash album since his departure, with some of his earlier ideas being incorporated into the track credited to Powell/Upton/Wisefield/Turner/Turner.

"I wanted to include 'Candlelight' since it was a piece that Ted and I worked on previously and I felt it only right that he be credited, even though he had no idea that we would eventually include the tune on a later album," says Andy Powell.

The success of *New England* meant that Wishbone Ash were once again in the top 30, with the album peaking at number 22 on the UK album chart. Not a bad achievement considering the band's profile in the UK had dropped over the previous two years through lack of live shows, plus the first stirrings of the punk rock phenomenon were starting to appear. The album was widely recognised as a return to form for the band, with many UK music papers citing the album as being Wishbone's finest offering since *Argus*. *Sounds*' Barbara Charone proclaimed: "There is nothing ordinary about *New England*. Wishbone Ash expose a mature musical self-portrait that easily places them back on top of the rock 'n' roll hierarchy."

The UK tour marked a triumphant return home and saw the band playing to packed houses across the country. The Edinburgh and Glasgow shows (18 and 19 November) were recorded for the US radio programme "King Biscuit Flour Hour". The tapes, mixed by Martin Turner, were also aired by John Peel on his BBC Radio One show. The Liverpool Empire gig of 15 November was also recorded via a four track feed from the sound desk, and later surfaced as the bootlegs *Live Vol.1* and *Mother of Pearl Live*. The track "Lorelei" from the Liverpool show would later be included on the US release *The Best of Wishbone Ash* in 1997.

The UK dates were followed by a lengthy European stint, re-establishing the group's identity with fans on the continent – taking in dates in Germany, Austria, France and, for the first time, Yugoslavia. One particular highlight of the European tour was the concert at Cologne Sporthalle on 1 December 1976 which was filmed by ZDF television for the Rockpalast series and broadcast throughout Europe. At the end of the series viewers were invited to vote for their favourite show to be broadcast again – Wishbone Ash coming out on top. In recent years, the concert has been shown on the Satellite/Cable network. The tour ended in Holland a week before Christmas, with Wishbone taking a well-earned Christmas break having been on the road continually for the previous three months. The period 1975 to 1976 had seen some important changes: the departure of Miles Copeland, a lousy album release and the band rediscovering themselves with a triumphant world tour backed by arguably one of their finest album since *Argus*.

Chapter Five

Everybody's Talking Front Page News

Back in Connecticut during the months of January through to May 1977, Wishbone were once again writing and rehearsing material for a new album. Meanwhile, to fill the gap between releases, MCA-UK issued a compilation album entitled *Classic Ash* in May. It featured one cut apiece from each of the band's albums up to that point (*Locked In* excepted) plus some amusing sleeve notes from John Peel. From the album, a three-track single was culled featuring the original versions of "Blowin' Free", "Jailbait" and "Phoenix". Two budget-priced compilation albums were released in Germany that year, namely *That's Wishbone Ash* and *The Original Wishbone Ash*.

1977 also saw changes to the band's management with John Sherry, their long-time booking agent taking over as manager – a position he would hold down for the ensuing eight years. Martin Turner recounts the events that led to Sherry being offered the position of manager:

"We had tax problems in the UK. We owed the Inland Revenue some money – not a huge amount. We were flying in from the States to do a tour and John phoned telling us that we would be arrested as soon as we got off the plane, because we hadn't paid this tax. We got John to negotiate with them, and sort it all out. I was immensely grateful to him for that. It was a messy period. John had always been our agent, but after handling this tax incident, John had got more involved and had demonstrated that he could actually manage the band, maybe not quite as creatively as Miles had in the early days, but certainly in a very good, solid way. I certainly trusted him and thought he was the right man for the job at the time."

Above: Laurie Wisefield. *Photo: Nicky Masters*

In May, Wishbone entered Miami's Criteria Sound Studios with producers Ron and Howie Albert to record their eighth album, *Front Page News*. The sessions would run through to the end of July. During their stay in Miami they rented a large house from the Bee Gees and were joined by their families for some of the time. Although the setting may have been idyllic there was tension within the band, as Laurie Wisefield recalls: "I remember there was a bit of friction at that time between Steve and Martin. They had a bit of a bust up. It lasted for quite a while. I think Martin wrote 'Surface to Air' partly through that."

The emerging songs were a mix of group collaborations and individual compositions from Martin Turner and Laurie Wisefield. Overall, the music has a rather laid back feel reflecting the summer heat of Florida, featuring strings (arranged by Mike Lewis) on several tracks.

"I believe the string players were regular session players at Criteria," recalls Andy Powell. "They were probably the same players who appeared on various Bee Gees hits, since most of *Saturday Night Fever* was prepared there."

The album's producers, "the Fat Alberts" as their company was called, continued to work their magic with the band. Laurie recalls how they worked:

"They would work in shifts with one of them starting at seven and finishing about eleven. Then the other one would start at eleven and work with us through the rest of the night".

Midway through recording sessions, Wishbone broke off to make an appearance at the Pinkpop Festival in Geleen, Holland on 11 June. The concert was recorded by Dutch radio and marked the band's largest crowd as a headline act, performing in front of 30,000 fans. In September the band undertook a month long European tour to promote *Front Page News*, taking in shows in Germany, Switzerland, France, and Holland.

The album was released in October receiving mixed reactions from press and fans alike. An overall American feel was evident both in the music and the sleeve design (again by Hipgnosis). The album featured a generous helping of laid back numbers in addition to a handful of all-out rock tracks. Also noticeable was a greater use of vocal harmonies compared with the previous few Wishbone albums.

The title track and opening number on the album, "Front Page News" refers to the band's triumphant return to the UK in 1976 to play their first tour in two years. Musically the track is very much in the style of the original Fleetwood Mac featuring key and time changes and a gentle guitar introduction setting the scene for much of the album.

"Midnight Dancer", although slightly rockier, features more harmony vocals and a softer Martin Turner vocal lead. Laurie seized the chance to redeem himself after his vocal efforts on *Locked In* with one of his better compositions, "Goodbye Baby Hello Friend". A gentle acoustic guitar starts the track and then the refrain kicks in. This track was chosen as one of two single releases from the album and according to Mark Emery was the nearest the band ever came to having a hit single in Britain.

One of Wishbone's more unusual compositions follows next with the song "Surface To Air", resplendent with its stepped vocal harmonies from the band's three vocalists, giving the song a truly unique identity. This was the last song of the album to be recorded, being written at the eleventh hour by Martin Turner.

The Laurie Wisefield instrumental "714" follows complete with strings. Listening to it one could almost be on Miami Beach. The title comes from a number found on the in-drug of that time, sleeping pills called Quaaludes, which made the user relaxed and sleepy – like the music.

Side Two opens with the Martin Turner rocker "Come In From the Rain". The title refers to the sudden downpours in Miami during recording. "Right Or Wrong" and "Heart Beat" are two more Martin Turner songs that fit nicely together whilst the group composition "The Day I Found Your Love", takes the mood down a little featuring saxophone as well as some of Martin Turner's finest ever vocal work. The album ends with a real gem, the often forgotten "Diamond Jack" featuring some nifty duelling guitar work and yet more vocal harmonies.

Although by no means the band's most consistent album release, *Front Page News* remains, perhaps, Wishbone Ash's most musically varied album.

By the time the UK leg of the *Front Page News* tour got underway at Newcastle City Hall on 16 October, the whole Punk scene had taken over in a big way in Britain. The Sex Pistols, the Stranglers and the Clash were now at the forefront of the British music scene. Many of the bigger "dinosaur" bands like Yes, Led Zeppelin and Pink Floyd were looked on with disdain by the new order of young musicians who had gone back to basics with short and simple two or three minute songs. Nevertheless the tour (which took in thirteen dates in principal cities, culminating with two London shows at the Marquee, and Wembley Empire Pool) was still a sell out.

One surprising aspect of the tour was how little of the new album featured in the live set. Only three new songs "Front Page News", "Goodbye Baby Hello Friend" and "Come In From the Rain" made the set with older favourites such as "Phoenix", "Lady Whiskey", "Blind Eye" and "Jailbait" making a welcome return.

"We decided to play a lot of old songs that we hadn't done in ages, rather than play the whole of the new album," says Martin Turner. "We'd done that in the past, but it's very ambitious if people don't know the material, and the album's quite studio orientated with orchestrations on some tracks."[21]

Many of the *Front Page News* dates were recorded. The Glasgow and Wembley shows were taped for BBC and Capitol Radio respectively, while the concerts in Newcastle, Sheffield and the Marquee Club London were also recorded for future use. The Marquee show was a particular tour highlight. Four years after their last appearance at the club, Wishbone made a back to basics appearance just two days before a sold out concert at the 8,000 seat Wembley Empire Pool. Demand for Marquee tickets, priced £1.50, was overwhelming but it meant that only the most dedicated fans (who had queued up overnight) were able to see the band in a small venue – although it was alleged that on that night the promoter allowed in twice the venue's official capacity.

Despite playing predominately larger venues on the UK tour, Wishbone Ash made a point of keeping in touch with their fans, spending time after each show chatting and signing autographs – something they had always done in the past and still do to this day. Says Martin Turner:

"I think it's important to keep in touch with 'normal' people, and it's amazing how much you can learn from them. It probably breaks up the stardom thing a bit when people see what you're like. People come up and tell you how much a particular song has meant to them, because of what was happening to them at that time, and I love that. It's really spontaneous."[21]

MCA took out a full page advert in the music papers featuring a picture of Andy and Martin belting out at number at the Marquee show with the caption "Why did 40,000 people pay good money to see four boring old farts?" Underneath the photo were all the dates of the tour stamped over with "sold out" followed by the words, "Here's ten good reasons" with all ten Wishbone albums pictured. Presumably this was published not just as a marketing ploy, but also as a reaction to the punk movement which had taken over the pages of the established music papers. Wishbone Ash remained a force to be reckoned with. Also from that tour came a special Wishbone Ash newspaper called "Wishbone News/Evening Argus" which contained fictitious yet amusing stories and pictures about the band, such as

Blowin' Free

Above: Full page music press advert taken out by MCA Records as a reaction to their punk-obsessed critics view that bands like Wishbone Ash were redundant.

Martin Turner being called up for jury service on the day of the concert at Wembley.

The UK dates were followed by an American tour throughout November and December 1977 which would be the last for the band as US residents. In 1978 Wishbone Ash ended their three-year "exile" and returned to the UK. Martin Turner looks back:

"We lived in the States for a couple of years and that made a fairly heavy impression on us. I don't really think it's a great thing musically for any group. I wouldn't say it was to our detriment but, musically, I think we were a very English group and we started to become Americanised. I don't like to knock America, because we certainly benefited a lot from working there. I don't like to sound negative about the place, but we sat down and knew something was happening to us – we had to move on. John Sherry was very much of the opinion that we should be based in the UK and I really pushed for that to be the case. I think Andy was very reluctant to come back – Steve and Laurie too maybe – but we did come back and John Sherry set about really trying to revitalise the band's business affairs and straighten out the mess that had been created through being managerless for a couple of years."

Steve Upton looks back positively on the band's time spent in America: "Life in America is like plugging into a whole advanced technological society and I had to adapt to the lifestyle. I feel I've been touched by living in America – it opens you up a lot."[3]

Likewise, Andy Powell feels that the American experience sowed the seeds for the band to become more self-dependent and more personally accountable, both strong American tenets. "It had the effect of exposing our strengths and weaknesses and in addition, for me, it allowed me a time to grow and fostered a relationship with the country later destined to become my home."

For the first few months of 1978, Wishbone once again got into the routine of writing and rehearsing material for the next album, planning to record in England for the first time since *Wishbone Four*. There was now a greater stability in the band than ever before and with the luxury of a one-album-a-year contract the band was able to rehearse, record and tour with clockwork regularity. There was, of course, the danger was that they could get stale, but with the challenge from the New Wave scene in Britain, Wishbone were kept on their toes.

Recording for the *No Smoke Without Fire* album took place between 29 June and 13 August at the Music Centre, Wembley (formerly De Lane Lea Mk 2) and led to a reunion with former producer Derek Lawrence. Derek takes up the story:

"John Sherry came to me (which was very hard for him to do) and said the band had never got anywhere near the brilliance of *Argus* with their albums since then – and would I produce the next album as I was the one person who can get that sound? I said 'OK!'"

The band members themselves were quite happy to be working again with Derek as much water had passed under the bridge since *Argus*.

"We were far enough from *Argus* and the earlier albums to think in terms of working with Derek again," elaborates Martin Turner. "Derek's a great guy, I always got on well with him."

Trying to recreate something from the past was never going to be an easy ride and, as both parties would testify, the sessions did not always run that smoothly.

"Going back to Wembley, where *Argus* had been recorded, was a bit strange," says Martin Turner. "It had basically stayed the same, although the whole business had moved on leaps and bounds. It was a very dead, old fashioned sounding room and it was quite hard to record there in 1978. I wasn't thrilled with the outcome. I thought the album could have sounded a lot better."

Derek Lawrence had this to say about the *No Smoke* sessions: "The first few days were good, then Mart decided he knew better than anyone and I began to lose interest. Soundwise, the band had become a bit 'West Coast'. There were three tracks that I spent a lot of time on that actually didn't sound American and these hopefully make the group sound like an English band again. The problem was that they'd never really broken America not having a great vocalist. They'd been trying for about five years to get that American sound and lost their Englishness on the way. Hopefully *No Smoke* got some of that English sound back again."

Whilst Derek Lawrence may not have seen eye to eye with Martin, working with Laurie Wisefield for the first time did pay dividends resulting in a more thoughtful approach to Laurie's playing and songwriting. As Laurie remembers:

"Derek said to me, 'You play really well, but the next step for you is to really think about what you play'. Before then I'd just plug in and see what came out. That really made an impression on me. I always remember that and I'm grateful to Derek. After that I started to think more about what I wanted to hear. Forethought is everything in music, especially with songwriting."

The recording of *No Smoke Without Fire* coincided with the peak of the Punk/New Wave explosion which had been sweeping the UK for well over a year. While the New Wave scene did not have a direct influence over Wishbone Ash's approach to songwriting or performance, Martin Turner admits that, unlike many of their contemporaries, Wishbone could certainly relate to the new culture.

"I don't think it affected us consciously, but we were certainly in contact with bands from that scene. My brother Kim was working with the Police as sound engineer and road manager – not that the Police were a punk band, but they were certainly around at that time. I became friends with Gene October from the band Chelsea, Jools Holland had just got going with Squeeze who Miles Copeland was also involved with. It was a good time. There was a shot in the arm for music. Everything had become a little over sophisticated and overblown and we'd kind of got associated with that whole trip. Having said that, when Wishbone Ash first started out we were very much a bunch of 'young punks' pumping out a lot of energy, so we could very much identify with the kids who were picking up cheap amps and guitars and getting up onstage and just doing it. It was very reminiscent of the late Sixties, so we could relate to it."

Laurie Wisefield also remembers being impressed by the energy of the New Wave acts: "I remember going down to the Marquee one night and the Boomtown Rats were on there. I kind of enjoyed the whole excitement of it, although I wasn't particularly into the music that much. But I thought the energy was good."

Songwriting for *No Smoke Without Fire* saw the emergence of Laurie Wisefield as a strong songwriting force within Wishbone Ash with the album featuring, in the main, songs written by him and Martin Turner individually. The general direction of the material was a deliberate move towards a harder-edged British rock sound after the altogether more laid back feel of *Front Page News*. The album cover was once again designed by the Hipgnosis team and the title came from a line in the track "Anger in Harmony".

thirty years of Wishbone Ash

Above: Andy Powell, 1978. *Photo: Phil Matthews*

The opening number "You See Red", was penned by Wisefield and was chosen as the album's single release. A highly melodic tune, the track features Laurie on lead vocal together with some fine three-part vocal harmonies.

"It was around that time that Laurie really did start to come of age and write some really good songs," says Martin Turner. "'You See Red' was certainly one of the best songs he wrote."

Laurie recalls the story behind the song: "I remember when I moved back to the UK, I was staying with my folks and I had this Revox tape machine. I remember writing and demo-ing a lot of the *No Smoke Without Fire* songs on that and presenting them to the band. We spent a lot of time recording 'You See Red' but I thought a lot of the life got kicked out of it. Lyrically, it was inspired partly by an American girl I was living with for a few years. She was very much rooted in America and we'd got engaged, then we came back to England and it was difficult to keep the relationship going."

"Baby the Angels are Here" was written by Martin Turner. Musically the song is a fairly straightforward rock number with Martin on lead vocal. Lyrically it deals with an encounter he'd had with an old flame the previous year.

"I'd been in love with a girl in the sixties who's dad thought I was a horrible, smelly reprobate, and was not good enough for his daughter," says Martin. "He put up all kinds of barriers and actually packed her off on a round the world trip. I was outraged, but I had my music and career to get on with, and we ended up drifting apart for about ten years, until I walked into Bristol Colston Hall in about 1977 to do a gig and there she was, standing there. It was a big emotional experience for me and, to cut a long story short, I ended up having an affair with her. She was married, so was I; she had a couple of kids. It got very messy and in the end I bottled out and told her to go back to her husband. I got very depressed about the whole thing – it was an awful mess. I ended up staying at a friend's flat and I remember he had a caseful of shotguns. I was so desperate that I actually did think about blowing my brains out. I'm not naturally that way, but I was so low at that point that it did flash through my head. His wife had a bunch of books there, one of which was the Bible. I was sitting in this flat really manic for hours on end, and I picked up this Bible and read some stuff which was highly appropriate and that got me through. I actually mention in the song something about a Bible and a gun. It's a very emotive song for me."

Laurie Wisefield's "Ships in the Sky" brings the mood down a shade. This atmospheric piece dealt with Laurie's fascination with the world of the unexplained.

"I'd been to see *Close Encounters*, which was around at the time," recalls Laurie. "Also, I read a book called *Communion*, which was about a guy who got taken away by green men – alien abductions. I like stuff like that. It was probably a mixture of all sorts of subconscious things. There's a girl called Tracey mentioned in the song – she was the little daughter of some friends of mine. She had a spooky experience and it all kind of tied in."

"I think 'Ships in the Sky' is an absolutely beautiful song," adds Martin Turner. "It has a lovely, airy, magical quality about it. I think Laurie was really going through a hot patch when he put some of these songs together. It's a lovely piece of music."

"Stand and Deliver" was another of Laurie Wisefield's compositions. The most aggressive track on the album, the track was a fine vehicle for the guitar duelling of Powell and Wisefield. However, the song was less than popular with Martin Turner who was distinctly uncomfortable about singing the lyric – which could be interpreted as being about forced sex.

"I used to find his lyrics a bit chauvinistic," admits Turner. "I really was not happy about singing 'Stand and Deliver', and when I did condescend to sing it I didn't want it to go on the album because I didn't want people thinking that was what I had to say. I can't believe that I allowed myself to sing it. I really didn't think the vocal would get used, because I couldn't sing it with any conviction."

"Stand and Deliver" was always going to attract controversy. Indeed, one music paper upon reviewing the track insisted on informing the band that "it is not clever to boast about rape". However, in fairness to Laurie, some of the lyrics are based around the classic English poem *The Highwayman* by Alfred Noyes, in which the Highwayman falls in love with the landlord's daughter – but she is captured and tied-up by the King's soldiers. The only way she can warn the Highwayman is by killing herself with the gun to which she is tied so that he can escape. Fleetwood Mac also covered this touching story in the song and video entitled "Everywhere" from the 1987 album *Tango In The Night*.

"Anger in Harmony", the only co-written song on *No Smoke Without Fire*, was composed by Andy Powell, Laurie Wisefield and Martin Turner, with Martin being responsible for the lyrics.

"It was trying to be commercial, but I think it lacks a certain grittiness which it was intended to have," says Turner. "That is something Wishbone Ash has always struggled with – the ability to create the live energy the band has on stage in the studio. It should have been there on that song, but it wasn't. The song sounds a bit limp and half-baked. I wasn't terribly fond of the way it ended up."

"Like a Child" was another Martin Turner composition inspired by his ill-fated relationship the previous year. "It was the first time in my life I'd got involved with children, because she had two lovely little children," recalls Martin. "At that point in my life I had no children and for the first time I found myself really liking children, liking their energy, their honesty and their view of the world and their whole spontaneity. It kind of reawakened something in me and the song was an attempt to talk about that and deal with it. It's a bit of a sweet song, probably bordering on the sentimental."

"The Way of the World" which closes Side Two was a lengthy epic in two parts. Written by Laurie Wisefield (although with much input from the other band members for the second, largely instrumental, section), the song was penned with stage performance very much in mind.

As Laurie recalls: "'The Way of the World' started off with the slow section, although I also had the section with the strange timing, which I'd been playing for months. We kind of glued them together. It was written as an epic. We'd been playing "Phoenix" for a long time and it felt like it was about time to write something else in that style – kind of like "Phoenix Part Two". On all the stuff around that time, I was trying to write in a rocky, English style that had the flavour of the earlier Wishbone Ash material – slightly folky, but with a modern edge of the time, which was more towards hard rock."

Wishbone Ash had recorded more than enough material for the album and three tracks were left unmixed and consigned to the vaults. "Fire Sign" was a Martin Turner composition which he had offered to Wishbone on numerous occasions.

Above: Laurie Wisefield, 1978. *Photo: Phil Matthews*

"'Fire Sign' was written in 1967," says Martin. "I actually tried to record it with Wishbone a couple of times, but it didn't sit right. It's a song about reincarnation – and I know that Steve Upton just used to fall off his stool every time I sang certain lyrics such as 'I hope I'm not a dog or maybe a monkey.' Steve just used to fall about laughing – he thought it was hilarious. Steve was a guy who used to see everyone as an animal. He'd tag you a badger or a fox or whatever and make up stories about you. He's got a great sense of humour in that area: it's a bit obtuse but quite funny. I always liked that song, and it's an important part of how I became what I became. It was either Andy or Steve – when I wrote songs, they'd say, 'Listen, Mart, if you crapped on the floor you'd think it constituted art,' and I would say, 'Yeah, kind of'. What they meant was, 'Just because you've written a song, doesn't mean to say it's good – it might be a bunch of crud'. I don't think that way, personally. Creativity is such a precious, magical, special thing and I don't think you should be that negative with it. You should just let it flow. That song for me – maybe someone could turn around and say, 'That's a crap song', but if I'd said that at the time I wrote it, then I'd probably never have written all the Wishbone material that I did. I would have said, 'Oh well, you're not really a songwriter Martin, why don't you get a day job'. It's not the greatest song in the world, but neither are most of the other songs that I've written, but they have a certain something and people enjoy them... sometimes!"

"Fire Sign" would later surface as a bonus track on the 1998 CD reissue of the *No Smoke Without Fire* album. A Martin Turner solo version, recorded in 1982, would also see the light of day on Martin's 1996 solo collection *Walking the Reeperbahn*.

A further Martin Turner song entitled "Time and Space" was arguably one of the true highlights from the *No Smoke Without Fire* sessions and, with hindsight, would have probably merited a place on the album in preference to some of the eventual inclusions. Again it was added to the album's CD reissue, whilst an alternative mix appeared on the 1997 4CD collection *Distillation*.

"'Time and Space' was a mini-epic," says Martin. "It was a number I'd written and we'd put in a lot of time on it. It was shoved – it was given the Spanish Archer – 'El Bow'. It was felt that the balance of material on the album overall was too much towards material I had written. It was also quite similar to 'Like a Child' stylistically – it was unpopular and it was shoved. The opening line of 'Time and Space' contains the words 'nuclear bombs' and it was considered a little heavy and awkward. Listening to it from today's perspective, it's a really good song and certainly deserved to go on the album."

The final track was a Laurie Wisefield ballad entitled "Hard on You". This, however, was soon abandoned and recording didn't get beyond the instrumental backing track.

Once the album was completed, the band members concentrated on domestic matters. Andy Powell's wife, Pauline, became the first "Wishbone wife" to give birth to the first "Wishbone baby" – a boy named Richard Lester born on 22 August. The other three members of the band all moved into new homes as they settled back in England. Laurie chose a sixteenth century house in Saffron Waldon, Essex, while Martin chose a large town house in East Sheen in South West London. Steve, meanwhile, settled into a farmhouse near Woking, Surrey.

Throughout the Summer there had been rumours in the music press that Wishbone Ash would play at the 1978 Reading Festival, headlining as they had in 1975, but with the various domestic commitments this did not come to fruition. However, on 9 September the band premiered new material at a festival appearance in Stuttgart (other acts on the bill included Status Quo, Uriah Heep and the Climax Blues Band).

No Smoke Without Fire was released on 6 October and a limited quantity of copies were presented together with a free live seven inch single featuring "Lorelei" (recorded at Glasgow Apollo, 1976) and "Come In From the Rain" (recorded at Sheffield City Hall, 1977). The tracks were selected from a considerable number of tapes with a view to releasing a second live album. Although the live single was seen by many as a marketing ploy, Martin Turner claims the decision to release live material was made as much for artistic reasons:

"Wishbone suffered from a lack of 'liveness' in the recording studio and that was particularly evident on *No Smoke Without Fire*. What better way to counter balance that than put out a couple of live tracks – there was an element of that in our thinking. I wouldn't call it just a marketing ploy."

A single from the album, featuring "You See Red" was also released (in both seven and twelve inch formats) backed by a version of the band's stage encore "Bad Weather Blues", also taped in Sheffield 1977. The number had previously been recorded during the *Locked In* sessions and had remained unreleased despite being a live favourite. Fan pressure led to its eventual release on vinyl.

To coincide with the release of *No Smoke Without Fire,* Wishbone Ash embarked on a major UK tour starting at the Ipswich Gaumont on 6 October. Despite a lack of media interest in both the album and tour, Wishbone managed to retain their status as one of the UK's top concert attractions, drawing sell out crowds throughout the 22 date UK tour. The album, however, would only stay for three weeks in the charts, peaking at a lowly 43. Robin Smith in *Sounds* had this to say about *No Smoke Without Fire,* "This is Ash with the Miami suntan stripped away".

The set list for the *No Smoke Without Fire* tour was a long one, as Wishbone chose to perform without a support act enabling them to play many of the songs which had been overlooked on recent tours. The choice of back catalogue material went as far back as songs from the first album such as "Errors of my Way" and "Queen of Torture", both being played for the first time since 1971.

Mobile recording equipment accompanied the band to several shows, with further recording for the planned second live album taking place in Bournemouth and Bristol. The Hammersmith concert of 25 October was aired by both BBC Radio One and London's Capital Radio. During a break in the tour, Steve Upton married American Nancy Davis in Surrey, with Martin acting as a witness.

For overseas fans the *No Smoke Without Fire* tour was a short one, the UK leg being followed with only a short series of dates in Japan. Although the band played just three concerts in Japan – two in Tokyo and one in Osaka – they were kept busy with appearances on several TV and radio shows. They also had time to visit the ancient Japanese capital of Kyoto and met up with one of Japan's top singers, Asanawa, who gave each member of the band a silk "happy" coat as a present.

The Tokyo dates on 10 and 15 November were taped for a live album exclusive to the Japanese market. *Live In Tokyo* was produced by Martin Turner and released in April 1979. The album soon attracted considerable interest from avid UK and US fans hungry for live material (the planned second *Live Dates* album having been put on ice), making its way into the import racks at particularly high prices. *Live in Tokyo* is an excellently recorded set capturing the band on top form throughout. It would later resurface on the CD *In America and Over Japan,* a bootleg that also featured the *Live In Memphis* set.

Chapter Six

Leaving Is A Sin They Say

Following the Japanese leg of the *No Smoke Without Fire* tour in November 1978, the four members of Wishbone Ash went their separate ways to spend time with their families and pursue outside interests. Andy Powell, in particular, took the opportunity to follow musical projects away from the band and had struck up a songwriting partnership with Ian Harris, a long-time friend, musician and artist. Indeed, during an experimental session at London's Majestic Studios in January 1979 Wishbone Ash attempted to record two Powell/Harris compositions entitled "Baby Don't Mind" and "Give It Up". Powell also collaborated with Harris on a "novelty" track entitled "Just a Little Mod", released under the moniker of Terry Tonik. Powell contributed guitar and produced the single, which would later become a collector's item.

Ian Harris recalls recording the single: "The songs were written about ten years before they were recorded in 1979. We taped them in a morning at Gooseberry Studios in Gerrard St in central London. I designed the logo and did the artwork as well as writing and producing the fanzine that was sold with the record, titled "Talkin' 'Bout My Generation". I personally went round record shops trying to flog them! Virgin bought a box of 50 and it got playlisted on Pennine Radio. We had about 2,000 pressed up, so if you're lucky enough to have got one it's worth about £100 now!"[23]

1979 saw Wishbone Ash taking a well-deserved break from live work, concentrating solely on songwriting and recording. The early months were spent working on new ideas before entering Surrey Sound Studios, Leatherhead in March to record the tenth studio album *Just Testing*.

The band discovered Surrey Sound through Kim Turner (Martin's younger brother) who was working as sound engineer/road manager for the Police (managed by Miles Copeland), who had used the studio to record their first two albums. Having worked with some of the most respected producers in the business, with varying degrees of success, the band elected to produce the sessions themselves with principal songwriter Martin Turner and manager John Sherry firmly in control.

Despite being armed with some particularly fine material, composed mainly by Martin Turner, morale within the band was low and recording took the best part of six months – the longest Wishbone Ash had ever spent on an album. As Martin Turner remembers:

"It was like pushing a truck up a hill – it was really hard work. I think the band was old and tired. We all needed a bloody good holiday, but we'd gone back into the studio, perhaps a bit reluctantly, and I think everyone's approach was a bit, 'Here we go again.' We were all fatigued with the process, which was a great shame because I personally felt that I was really getting into a flow with songwriting. We were getting paid very respectable money for what we were doing, but everyone was being perhaps a bit reluctant."

"Martin was certainly getting into the flow," states Andy Powell, "but at the expense of the band spirit of old. He was very fired up about our move back to the UK, but the rest of us weren't so sure."

Another problem was isolation. Having lived in America for so long they'd lost contact with several friends and contacts in the music business. Being stuck in a studio for months on end didn't help matters – a point that Laurie thinks affected the band at the time:

"We were very much in our own little world with people running around doing everything for us. It was all very isolated and secretive for the band then. It was like that for many bands in the seventies. Even when I was in Home it was like that to a certain extent. It wasn't until I left the band that I could see this image that people build up of you; that you're untouchable or you're not approachable. It took a while to get rid of that really."

As an example of the general lack of motivation within the band at this point, Martin Turner recalls an incident that happened at Surrey Sound during the recording of a new composition entitled "Haunting Me":

"I'd played bass, Steve had done the drums, I'd put a rough vocal down and had even played guitar. Laurie had come in that morning and fallen asleep. I was stuck, I didn't know what to do next, so I gave Laurie a prod. I think he was a bit pissed off about being woken up. I said, 'Laurie, have a listen to this song and see what you think it needs next'. So he sat there while I played it and at the end he said, 'It sounds like a pile of shit to me,' at which point I went totally berserk. Here I was, I'd written this song, I'm asking a guitar player for some input, because there was only one of them around, and all he's got to say is, 'It sounds like a pile of shit'. I was pissed off. I screamed at him that there were a bunch of guys out there who would give their right arm to be where he was; that he was being advanced a large sum of money from a record company to make a record; that he was a lazy bastard; and I didn't like his attitude. I stomped out of the studio, walked up the road, bought some cigarettes and came back half an hour later. As I walked down the corridor at Surrey Sound, 'Haunting Me' was playing and Laurie was playing a guitar solo. I stopped in my tracks and thought, 'That sounds good.' I went back into the control room. I'd stunned Laurie into action: he'd got his guitar out and was playing this corking lead guitar work which exists to this day in the form of the guitar solo on 'Haunting Me'. I was bowled over. I thought what he did was phenomenal and, somewhat sheepishly, I told him so."

By his own admission, during recording sessions Martin Turner would constantly strive for what he believed to be right in terms of sound, performance, and especially production. As Laurie Wisefield admitted:

"Mart, at that time, could be very argumentative. He can be stubborn when he wants to be – bless his cotton socks – but we've all been responsible for being pricks at different times, myself included."

By the time summer came, the recording process was taking much longer than anticipated and a release date before the end of the year was looking more and more unlikely. To compensate for the long gap, Wishbone decided to release a single. Featuring two exclusive tracks not subsequently included on the album, the single hit the stores on 17 August 1979. The A-side was an unusual cover of the Chuck Berry classic "Come On", which had started out life late one night in the studio as a jam session.

"I think 'Come On' was my idea," recalls Martin Turner. "I really like Chuck Berry's lyric, but I wanted to do it as a 'commercial' single for Wishbone Ash. That was my intention. I think the recording is quite interesting. It's got a nice, moody pace to it. The feel is also quite loose for Wishbone Ash; it has a nice 'party' spirit. I think it's nice to get that spirit into the music from time to time – it stops the music from being too studied, stiff and clinical, which is something I think Wishbone Ash has had a tendency to suffer from on occasion. I felt 'Come On' worked very well, but it wasn't a great success as a single."

Andy Powell agrees with Martin. "For my money, 'Come On' is one of the best covers of a Chuck Berry song ever and really represented probably the closest we came to cracking the singles format. It also shows us really playing as a band in the studio."

"Come On" was backed with a new group composition entitled "Fast Johnny" which features some blistering guitar work by both Laurie and Andy. "'Fast Johnny' was never really intended as a particularly serious piece of music," admits Turner. "It's basically about a car chase. It's fairly lighthearted and I think it was appropriate for a B-side at the time." Both tracks were later added to the MCA 1998 CD release of *Just Testing*.

One issue that particularly concerned Martin during the Surrey Sound sessions was the band's inability, in the past, to recapture their live energy in a studio environment.

"John Sherry was acting as anchorman," recalls Martin, "sitting there on occasion to give feedback when he felt things weren't going in the right direction. I had a chat with John about Wishbone Ash's inability to create live energy in the studio. I said, 'John, we've got to do something – can we have a photo of the front row of the audience and stick it on the wall or something?' We experimented with trying

Above: Martin Turner, 1978. *Photo: Phil Matthews*

to 'bully' the band into playing with total commitment, as we do onstage. John had also become involved with managing Claire Hamill and I noticed that when he brought her down to the studio one day – as soon as there was a female presence in the studio – all of a sudden everyone started to play with a bit of attitude, which put a whole different slant on things."

Claire Hamill was a 25 year old singer/songwriter with a brace of solo albums to her credit, dating back to the early seventies. When her previous manager, Tony Diamitriades, dropped her to move to America to manage Tom Petty, John Sherry took her under his wing. As a result of her connections with John Sherry, she was eventually asked to sing on several songs on the album. By her own admission, Claire thought at the time that she was "a funny choice for a band member". Nevertheless her contribution to Wishbone Ash would be an important one lasting for two albums as well as a whole tour. On *Just Testing* her most important contribution was as co-writer of the album's opening track, "Living Proof", with Laurie Wisefield. This song would become one of the all-time favourite Wishbone Ash songs among fans. Laurie had originally demoed the backing track complete with the "oh, oh" chorus hook and Claire subsequently wrote the lyrics. Laurie takes up the story:

"Claire and I struck up a friendship in more ways than one. I had this place out in Essex, in the country, and had a little studio set up. Claire came over and I played her this idea I had and she wrote some lyrics for it. It's basically about looking for proof in a relationship."

"'Living Proof' is definitely my favourite Laurie Wisefield song," adds Martin Turner. "I kind of made it my song too. It fits like a glove. It was a really nice song to sing. I'm immensely fond of that particular recording. You can shoot holes in it from every which way – you can say the bass is crap, the drum beat is too slow, the vocals are out of tune. You can shoot holes in it forever, but I still think it's one of the best Wishbone Ash recordings ever and I'm very fond of it. Laurie's solo work on the song is phenomenal."

The aforementioned Martin Turner composition "Haunting Me" follows and was lyrically inspired by the same encounter that had inspired "Baby the Angels are Here" on the previous *No Smoke Without Fire* album. Says Martin: "When I walked into Bristol Colston Hall and saw that girl standing in front of me, my knees went weak. It was so great to see her – I loved that girl passionately. I wanted to know if I'd been in her head the way she'd been in mine for the last ten years and, yes, I had. It had been the same for both of us – 'You've haunted me for all these years,' is what she said."

"Insomnia", one of Martin's more obtuse contributions to Wishbone Ash followed, and was influenced partly by his meeting with David Bowie a few years earlier. Indeed, several critics were keen to point out the vocal similarities between Martin on this track and prime time Bowie, something Martin himself does not deny: "I do have a tendency to sound that way. I've been using very similar effects to those that David uses since the *Wishbone Four/Argus* days." Lyrically "Insomnia" is self-explanatory. "It's obviously about not being able to sleep at night – something I've always suffered from," says Martin. "One particular night, I went downstairs to my music room and wrote the song during the night. In fact, most of the creative work I've done has been late at night or early in the morning. It's a strange song, but I'm quite fond of it."

These first three tracks all feature distinctive and extraordinary guitar work by both Andy Powell and Laurie Wisefield. Martin Turner is quick to praise both guitarists' work on the album:

"I thought Andy's guitar playing on it ['Insomnia'] was brave and unique. I had to constantly encourage both him and Laurie to be adventurous. Sometimes you've got to put yourself on the line and be prepared to do something original. I think Andy really got into that spirit on 'Insomnia' and 'Haunting Me'. We spent a lot of time in the studio experimenting with various gizmos to get the ultimate guitar sounds. The solo Andy did on 'Insomnia' sounds like a synthesiser, but it's Andy playing guitar. Also, the stuff he did at the start of 'Haunting Me', which sounds like violins, was all guitar."

The second single release from the album, "Helpless", was the only track on the album not written within the band; it was credited to the unknown P. Kendrick.

"The record label was looking for a song that was 'radio friendly' and 'Helpless' fitted the bill," recalls Andy Powell. "John Sherry used to get songs via the house writers of various publishing companies. He found us two songs at Rondor Music in London. I remember reviewing the first song, penned by an unknown writer by the name of Bryan Adams! It was great, but we decided to go with 'Helpless' – it was a bit heavier."

"Helpless", incidentally, was also the only track on the album not recorded at Surrey Sound. It was instead recorded at Ian Gillan's Kingsway Recorders (formerly the original De Lane Lea studios). Martin Turner was not particularly keen on the choice of "Helpless". "Although it's a good song, you find yourself by the end of the song going 'What was that called again?' For me, it was kind of trying a bit too hard. I found it a little repetitive and it's my least favourite recording on the album – but it does have its moments and I think John's suggestion was very well intentioned."

In direct contrast to the experimental nature of much of Martin Turner's contributions to the album, "Pay the Price" has a more commercial rock feel and a great set of lyrics. Pay the Price" is about the price you have to pay for being with a female," reveals Martin, "but I don't think the lyrics need to be taken too literally."

"New Rising Star" is a moody, atmospheric Martin Turner song once again featuring some heavily processed guitar work. Lyrically, the song was inspired by a woman Martin and his wife Maurn had met in the days when they lived in East Sheen. Martin remembers: "She ran a pine shop in Barnes. When we first met her she was very shy and lacking in confidence. When we went off to live in America in 1975, my wife and I offered her and her partner our house to live in. The guy she was living with turned out to be a drunken bully and from time to time we would hear all these stories about how he used to beat her up. We encouraged her to get rid of him, and eventually she did, and she continued to live in our house for quite some time. We became really friendly with her and over a period of time I saw her emerge, almost like a butterfly from a cocoon, from someone who was difficult to gain access to, to a really confident person with real beauty."

Despite the high quality of the song material, not all of the band members were totally convinced that things were moving in the right direction. Says Laurie Wisefield:

"I seem to remember Andy being a little lost in terms of direction on that album. I don't think he could get his teeth into some of the stuff. Mart had a lot of songs we were recording and I just remember Andy being a bit low because he wasn't coming up with much. I think guitar-wise I was probably more dominant then."

"Andy, on this particular album, was finding it quite hard at times to get to the studio," adds Martin Turner. "He was the first member of the band to have children and of all of us, that time was most difficult for him. There was quite a bit of time where he wasn't involved – often it was just Laurie, Steve and myself in the studio."

Andy Powell explains his side of the story on this issue: "I think the band dynamics were shifting a lot during this period. There was the Turner/Sherry alliance which Martin drew a lot of strength from, and there was this whole Bowieesque vocal style coming out which I really wasn't into. Everything became a bit camp and self-obsessed," says Powell.

Andy Powell did, however, compose one of the album's true highlights. "Master of Disguise" marked Andy's debut sole songwriting credit on a Wishbone Ash album. The song has a folky feel to it, reminiscent of material from *Argus*, with a beautiful blend of electric and acoustic instruments and a closing vocal duet between Martin Turner and Claire Hamill. Ian Kew played organ on the track.

"It was composed on the acoustic guitar and we decided to keep it like that on the recording," says Andy. "The lyric comes from the feeling of alienation that I first had when the band settled in America in 1975 and the shock of living in a new culture."

"At that stage Andy was not particularly confident in singing in the studio," reveals Martin Turner, who ended up singing Powell's composition. "He'd written something which was quite tricky to sing. It's a really nice song and it contains some lovely guitar picking. Claire Hamill's contribution was really different for Wishbone Ash as a band and, vocally, I really enjoyed having a member of the opposite sex to sing with."

'Lifeline', the final song on *Just Testing*, was also the last number written and the only track jointly credited to all four band members. As with "F.U.B.B." the music evolved out of jamming in the studio and, as with many classic Ash numbers, minor chords are heavily featured. Martin Turner provided the lyrics from his little black book, in which he would write down lines and poems that might be suitable for future Wishbone songs.

"I didn't feel I had any suitable lyrics," remembers Martin. "But Laurie said, 'Get your little book out and find something.' I opened the book up and read some lines I'd written about my Gran dying. She'd always said that when she died she would 'touch' everyone she cared about. I was asleep one night and suddenly woke up at 2 in the morning. I sat bolt upright and I could see her at the end of my bed. I could feel like a rushing wind, even though the air in the room was still, and I had a sickly sweet taste in my mouth. I felt a very powerful energy coming from her and I just knew she was going. The following morning I rang my parents and, sure enough, she'd died during the night. It was a really powerful psychic experience that I'll never forget. I'd written all this down and that's what I ended up singing over the music. It was really quite spooky how it fitted together. It's quite an impressive piece of music. We've done quite a few epics over the years, but I think 'Lifeline' has a nice balance and it's a shame we didn't perform it more often on stage."

With the album completed, attention once again turned to domestic matters. On 28 August 1979, Martin Turner's wife, Maurn, gave birth to their first child, a girl called Jessica Siobhan. Wishbone made an appearance at the UNICEF Year of the Child Benefit concert at Wembley Empire Pool on 22 November. Although restricted to a short, four-song set, the show was simultaneously broadcast by BBC radio and television and gave Wishbone the opportunity to premier two new songs, "Helpless" and "Living Proof", in front of a live audience, not to mention the vast number of TV viewers and radio listeners. ("Blowin' Free" and "Bad Weather Blues" were the other two songs performed that night.) Throughout the set, both Andy Powell and Martin Turner jokingly referred to the show as "The Year of the Gig", in reference to the fact that this performance happened to be Wishbone Ash's sole concert appearance of 1979.

"We went on quite early and out of habit came offstage and had a drink," recalls Martin Turner, "but because we went on so early it was about 8.30 in the evening when we started drinking. There were so many people coming backstage to say hello that evening that we were still having a drink at eleven o'clock. I was pissed as a rat!"

The Wembley gig also marked the retirement of Doreen Boyd from her post as fan club secretary. After conscientiously producing over thirty newsletters in seven years she had decided to step down. After the gig she was presented with a specially engraved gold watch in appreciation of her services to the Wishbone Ash cause. Her place as fan club secretary was taken over by Penny Gibbons, who would later help the band out on the road in the early eighties. When Penny stepped down, Andy Powell's wife, Pauline, took over the reins until the original fan club folded at the end of 1985.

Whilst 1979 might have been a quiet year for Wishbone Ash, 1980 would prove to be a memorable one for the band in many ways. The tour that started in January was promoted as the tenth anniversary tour. On 4 January "Living Proof" was released as a single, backed with a live version of "Jailbait" from the *Live in Tokyo* album. This was followed by the release of the tenth Wishbone Ash studio album, *Just Testing*, on 18 January. The album spent four weeks on the UK chart, peaking at number 41. The title of the album was already familiar to many fans as it had previously appeared as "vinyl graffiti" on the play-out grooves of *There's the Rub* back in 1974. The phrase had been coined by Laurie Wisefield during recording sessions for that album. Whenever he made a mistake in the studio, he would say, "Just testing!" The album cover depicted the band in some sort of testing chamber looking at a Flying V going through its paces. To be fair to Laurie, the back cover featured a Stratocaster (Laurie's main choice of guitar) undergoing a similar inspection.

On the same day as *Just Testing* was released, Wishbone Ash embarked on the UK/Eire leg of their tenth anniversary tour, starting off at Hanley Victoria Hall. The tour would be a lengthy one, taking in thirty shows including first time visits to Belfast and Dublin.

As had now become customary, several of the shows were recorded and it was revealed that 1980 would see the long awaited release of the second *Live Dates* album. The shows in Sheffield, Newcastle and Bristol were all recorded using the Manor Mobile, whilst the BBC also recorded the second Hammersmith show on 2 February for Radio One's *In Concert* series. This show would later surface on one of the better quality Wishbone bootleg CDs: *Super Golden Radio Shows – Live in London*. Following the UK tour, Wishbone undertook a five-week tour of Europe which included dates in Sweden, Austria, Belgium, Holland, Germany, France and Italy. The concert in Vienna on 27 March was filmed for a German TV broadcast.

May saw the release of a double A-side 10th anniversary live single coupling two tracks recorded on the UK tour – "Helpless" (Newcastle City Hall) and "Blowin'

Free" (Bristol Colston Hall). This release coincided with a twelve date mini-tour of the UK, entitled the "Blowin' Free" tour which saw the band performing in smaller regional venues. This was a John Sherry idea partly to "warm-up" the band before playing the festival circuit later that summer and also to enable fans in smaller provincial towns to see the band. Most of the venues had the seats removed to accommodate more fans. The tour, which opened in Bracknell on 24 May (Steve Upton's 34th birthday), saw Wishbone Ash performing two brand new Martin Turner songs, "Lookin' for a Reason" and "I Need People", while the encore, at Steve's suggestion, often featured Wishbone's cover of Chuck Berry's "Too Much Monkey Business". Other show highlights included the first live performances since 1974 of "The Pilgrim". The shows in Hull and Wolverhampton were recorded for the forthcoming live album.

There was the usual array of summer festival appearances during 1980, most notably the Loch Lomond festival at the Cameron Bear Park in Scotland in June. The first day of the festival showcased New Wave acts including Stiff Little Fingers and The Jam. Wishbone headlined the second day above the likes of Wild Horses, Ian Gillan, Lindisfarne and Saxon. Wishbone's planned publicity stunt for the day was to have a large hot air balloon (which had appeared in the Martini commercials) bearing the group's name fly over the festival site as the band took to the stage. However, as the show was running behind schedule, the balloon actually ended up flying over the crowd during Denny Laine's set.

The summer months were spent listening to and subsequently mixing the second *Live Dates* album at Wembley Music Centre. Martin Turner was chiefly responsible for assembling the album. John Sherry located every available Wishbone Ash live recording since 1976 to ensure the widest choice of material. In addition to the numerous recordings of the band on tour, various radio recordings made by the BBC, Capital Radio and the King Biscuit Flour Hour were also included in his "haul". The intention was to provide a montage of the band's live performances over the previous four years although perennial favourites included on the first *Live Dates* album would not be duplicated.

The tail end of August and September saw Wishbone playing further festivals in Europe, including one in a bull ring at Santander, Spain and the Golden Summer Night Festival at Nuenkirchen, Germany with Saxon, Johnny Winter, Judas Priest, Molly Hatchet and Ian Gillan (who played for just ten minutes before throwing his monitors from the stage in disgust at the poor sound). The next day the same line-up (except for Judas Priest) played at the Lorelei festival in a large amphitheatre by the River Rhine. It was announced in the music press that the band would play the Reading Festival – but the date had not been confirmed and band were already contracted to play at the German festivals the same weekend. Wishbone then culminated their touring schedule with a headline appearance at the Colmar Festival in France on 20 September, headlining over UFO, Electric Sun and Magna Carta. Little did the fans know but this show would mark the final appearance of Wishbone Ash in its Mark II format.

With touring now over for the year, the band began to think about what direction they should take for the next album. Despite *Just Testing* being regarded by some Wishbone Ash fans as the band's most consistent effort since 1976's *New*

England album, there were internal divisions regarding future direction – causing something of a rift between Martin Turner and his colleagues.

According to Andy Powell: "Following the release of *Just Testing*, there wasn't a significant increase in record sales, which was, after all, what everyone wanted. Decision making was becoming increasingly bogged down and I think it would be true to say that everyone felt that a change of some sort was needed."

At a meeting at Martin Turner's house, Andy Powell, Laurie Wisefield and Steve Upton expressed their desire to make changes within the band. Single success was largely what they were aiming for and they felt this could only be achieved with the introduction of a "proper" lead singer/frontperson. Martin Turner strongly opposed this point of view, arguing that for a band that had peaked commercially in 1972, Wishbone Ash circa 1980 were still doing well on both a musical and business level. Says Martin:

"I received a phone call from the other members of the band who wanted to have a "meeting" with me. They came over to my house and told me that they had decided that they wanted to get a singer in, as the band was not doing as well as it could commercially. They felt the way to fix this little problem was to get a singer in. My reaction was to say, 'How the hell are we going to go on stage and sing "Blowin' Free" and "Warrior" with a singer? I mean what's he going to do? I disagree with your analysis of the band's career at this point. I think we're on the threshold of doing some really good things; breaking new ground, etc. I think you're creating a problem in your own heads, dreaming up some stupid solution to a problem that doesn't exist and I completely disagree with everything you say.'

"They were like, 'Well, we knew you were going to say that. We're telling you what to do, so you can lump it or leave it.' So I was put in a position where I had to say, 'OK, if that's what you really want to do, then you can fucking well do it without me!' I was seething. I was really, really desperately upset about that bullshit because it was absolutely wrong. *Just Testing* was an extremely difficult album to record and I felt really exhausted after making that album. However, looking at it from today's perspective, I think *Just Testing* is one of the best albums Wishbone Ash ever recorded. Maybe it lacks a commercial element, but there are things on there I really like. I think it's a great shame the band didn't carry on in the way it was going musically and in every other respect, but instead, the band felt they needed to change things, which I felt was wrong at the time and was proven to be wrong. What did they do? They went and got John Wetton in the band. Within a matter of a couple of months, he came to the same conclusion that I did – 'These guy's don't know what the fuck they're talking about', and he left the band."

The meeting was a stormy affair and feeling unable to go along with his fellow members' recipe for future success or relinquish his lead vocalist duties, Martin Turner eventually decided that he had no option but to resign from Wishbone Ash. Andy Powell recalls the meeting and the events leading up to it:

"We were finding at that time that we had a lot of problems – not just on the music side, but also on the business side. Every single thing that we would want to do, the three of us would find ourselves disagreeing with Martin. On most issues it got to be the three of us plus John Sherry. It got so bad that we called a meeting at Martin's house. 'Look, we've got this problem… we want to try this… we don't like this…' and so on. He just got so outraged that he said, 'You can fuck off now!' It was basically assumed then that 'Martin's left'. Basically everybody was growing up and becoming their own men. Martin had his own studio in his house and I guess he had his own ideas. The band was ceasing to become a band. It was fragmenting. So he just basically left."

Laurie Wisefield also has given his views on those events: "I think everyone was tired of the direction we were going in and looking for another area that we could try. I think Martin wasn't up for this. I remember we were looking for a front singer. Not necessarily someone who had to play bass. I remember John Sherry putting forward John Sloman (Uriah Heep, Lone Star) as a possible candidate. He had a great voice and was a good looking guy. He had both a Robert Plant side to his voice as well as a soulful side."

This decision shocked the band's following – Martin Turner was irreplaceable in the eyes of the faithful. Indeed, the ensuing years saw an uphill struggle to effectively replace Martin's definitive bass, vocals and songwriting talents. Ironically, in view of the majority decision that prompted his departure, the band never recruited a permanent front-person (although Claire Hamill would join the band briefly as "fifth member" for touring and recording purposes).

Following his split with Wishbone Ash, Martin Turner pursued his love of studio and production work developing his home recording set-up which he eventually moved to the basement of Miles Copeland's offices in Portobello Road, London. During this period Martin produced a diverse range of artists, but continued writing and recording demos of his own material with a view to a solo project.

The first song written by Martin Turner after leaving Wishbone Ash was "The Naked Truth", a track which lyrically was largely inspired by his departure from the band.

"It deals with belonging to something – whether it's a marriage, a band or whatever – and then all of a sudden it doesn't exist anymore and you feel very naked, very on your own," reveals Martin. "I'm not saying I don't like feeling that way, because I do like being naked, but that's what the song is about."

Other songs written during this period included titles such as "Where Will I Go When I Die", "Change Your Mind", "Broken Down House", "Kelly's Away With the Fairies", "You" and "My Brother", all proving that Martin Turner, even without Wishbone Ash, could still be creatively strong. Martin also experimented with synthesisers, but one of his first sessions following the split from Wishbone Ash was a 1981 studio project involving Ted Turner, (who had briefly returned to the UK), Gene October (of Chelsea), Stewart Copeland (the Police) and Jools Holland (Squeeze). The sessions were never released. By 1982, Martin Turner had formed a new band, Martin Turner's Wolf Gang, which consisted initially of Scottish musicians Stewart MacKenzie on guitar and Ray Weston on drums, with Welsh keyboard player Eryl Price-Davies. The band entered the studios for the first time in November 1982, re-recording the songs Martin had demoed as well as resurrecting "Fire Sign" from the *No Smoke Without Fire* days. Martin was also keen to break the band in live – so the new outfit began to perform club dates. Eventually Ray Weston was replaced by Tim Broughton.

Above: Martin Turner's Wolf Gang, 1984. (l-r) Tim Broughton, Eryl Price-Davies, Martin Turner, Stewart MacKenzie.
Photo: Martin Turner personal archive.

Further recording and live work continued and the new material flowed. Songs such as "Hot Surrender", "Walk on Water", "Passion", and "Strangers" were as strong as any of Martin's past work and revealed a musician who, unlike many of his contemporaries, was totally in touch with the changing face of the UK's music scene. However, while Martin Turner was eager to progress musically, attempting to persuade his contacts within the music industry to take his new direction seriously would prove difficult. This was not helped by the fact that at live shows, Martin was reluctant to represent his back catalogue and, of his Wishbone Ash material, only an unusual synth-domniated rendition of "Doctor" featured in Wolf Gang's live set.

"I was really just dipping my toe in the water to see if anything was going to happen," admits Martin. "John Sherry, bless his heart, came to see us a couple of times. Although he liked the band he was adamant that I was trying to do something which I couldn't do. He said, 'If you're going to go out and play onstage, there has got to be two guitarists, and you've got to play Wishbone Ash songs.' I said to him, 'That's not what I want to do, I'm trying to move forwards, not backwards.' He couldn't quite see how I was trying to reinvent myself. It was kind of like a Tears For Fears or Mike and the Mechanics type of sound, using synths within a rock band, but it was still a vehicle for my creativity. The people at the gigs were enthusiastic, but I couldn't seem to get record companies, agents and managers involved. I thought it was a really good band. However, it soon became obvious that it was never going to take off. Everyone was telling me it was too modern." Somewhat disillusioned by the lack of support, Martin Turner disbanded the Wolf Gang during 1984, consigning the band's legacy of unfinished and unmixed recordings to the vaults.

Following Martin Turner's departure from Wishbone Ash, his former cohorts wasted little time in finding a replacement, appointing the services of veteran British bassist John Wetton (ex-Family, King Crimson, Roxy Music, Uriah Heep, UK), who began rehearsing with the band on 16 October 1980. Wetton's first contact with Wishbone Ash dated back to one of his earlier bands, Mogul Thrash.

"We happened to be with the same agency who booked Wishbone Ash," recalls Wetton. "John Sherry was my contact there. I didn't know the guys from Wishbone Ash too well, but I knew them to nod to. It was only much later, when ten years had passed and Martin left the band that our paths crossed again. I got a phone call from John Sherry telling me what had happened with the Wishbone Ash guys, about how Martin had left the band and that they were looking for 'a replacement' and he asked, 'Did I want to go down and see if it would work out?' At that point I thought he meant a replacement for Martin as a singing and writing bass player. So that's what I thought I was signing up for. We had several meetings and a couple of jam sessions and it was quite exciting."

John Wetton's involvement with Wishbone Ash coincided with the release of his debut solo album *Caught in the Crossfire*, on which he was joined by noted musicians such as Simon Kirke (Free/Bad Company) and Martin Barre (Jethro Tull). As Wishbone Ash broke in their new bassist and prepared for the recording of their new album, MCA released *Live Dates Volume II*, as planned, on 20 October 1980. Ironically, just as *Live Dates Volume I* was released prior to Ted Turner leaving the band, so *Live Dates Volume II* was released at the time of Martin Turner's departure. It was a fitting tribute to the Mark II line-up. With numbers recorded from tours stretching from 1976 to 1980, it gave the fans a chance to relive what many see as the best live period of the band with some outstanding guitar solos on tracks such as "Living Proof", "The Way Of The Word", "F.U.B.B." and "No Easy Road". The album reached number 40 in the album charts.

Colin Elgie's sleeve design took the themes displayed on the first *Live Dates* album design a stage further. The front cover featured the inside of a theatre, similar in style to London's Rainbow Theatre, and perfectly captured the moments immediately before the band's arrival onstage from the audience's standpoint. Indeed, the band members can be seen waiting in the wings to take the stage. Meanwhile, the inner gatefold sleeve showed a dressing room scene with Andy's Flying V nestled amongst the crisps and Jack Daniels on the dressing room table. In all, *Live Dates Volume II* is one of Wishbone Ash's most attractively packaged albums. The first 25,000 copies were a double album set with a gatefold sleeve after which the second disc was deleted and the set reverted to a single album. In Germany, the second bonus disc was issued as an album in its own right entitled *Live Dates II: Additional Material*.

Live Dates Volume II was not issued in the US. American fans were served with the release of *Hot Ash* instead. This release came about largely through the efforts of Leon Tsilis, who was still working for MCA in the States, gathering together selected tracks from the double set plus several live single recordings which had not been given a US release. Also in America, recording for the new album began towards the end of November with the sessions taking place largely at Criteria Sound, Miami with additional work at Surrey Sound. Nigel Gray (who had played an enormous part in helping shape the Police's studio sound) was enlisted as producer and Claire Hamill was brought in to contribute backing vocals. Of the new producer Claire remembers him as "not very commanding."

"He was a nice enough guy, but if he'd been more together I don't think the album would have taken so long to make. Perhaps he should have been more snappy and less easy-going."

As for new bassist John Wetton, it soon became apparent that his role on the album would be more as a "session" bassist rather than the more central role Martin Turner had played. Says Wetton: "It wasn't a full-time offer of, 'Martin's left, will you take over his duties as lead singer and principal songwriter?' What was offered was more tentative than that. There was the feeling that I was a new boy – even though I was a seasoned professional."

Wetton was also keen to introduce his own material, which met with a less than favourable reaction from his new colleagues.

"Whilst John's playing was a perfect substitute for Martin's and he was a dream to play with, he was already writing material in the Asia vein," says Andy Powell. "His material just didn't gel with ours, mostly I think because he wrote on the piano and we obviously constructed our songs from a guitar standpoint. It was a classic case of misrepresentation – we'd already rehearsed and demoed the bulk of the album and were wanting to get to a more band orientated feel. We just assumed John Wetton would fit into this. I think John Sherry had probably sold John another concept which was that of becoming our frontman. Our manager had gone along with the concept that we had become the backing band for Martin and now we would become the backing band for the new guy – a stupid assumption! We were never stronger than when we were a unified band."

In the end just two of John Wetton's songs were recorded – "Now or Never" and "That's That". Of these, only the latter made the album. With hindsight, Wishbone could have perhaps benefited from being receptive to Wetton's musical ideas, as the bassist himself reveals:

"I offered a couple of songs while we were in Miami which didn't get picked up on. No one seemed to be interested in them, but the songs later turned up on the first Asia record which sold nine million copies. It would have been in Wishbone's interest to pick up on those songs, but that didn't happen."

Another sticking point for Wetton was Andy Powell and Laurie Wisefield's decision to sing the bulk of the lead vocals on the album.

"I would like to have done all the lead vocals on that album," admits John. "I think Andy had designs on being the lead singer. I'm not saying this in a conceited way, but I do have a very recognisable voice. It's not that Andy's a bad vocalist at all, it's just that some people have signature voices. I think if I'd been allowed to write and sing to the fullest extent of my capability, then it would have been a really good album. Maybe because of the experience they'd had with Martin, they didn't want to give anyone that much power within the group. The feeling I had at the time was that they didn't want anyone to take over where Martin left off."

Andy Powell defends: "What Laurie, Steve and I did when Martin left was to continue writing music. Whoever decided to sing it would sing it. It wasn't that we were going to try and be "the lead vocalist". It became an issue when we pulled

Above: John Wetton. *Photo: Jill Douglas.*

John Wetton in as I think John Sherry had told John that he was coming into the band as "the lead vocalist". Laurie and I had already written most of the songs and were singing them and John was in the studio at Criteria writing all these ballads on the piano. It was all this sort of drippy kind of Asia stuff. I never thought that John had that great a voice or anything and we were quite oblivious to the fact that John Sherry had told him that he was going to be the singer. So he was probably wondering all the time, 'When am I going to get a chance to sing?' So that's where I think a lot of the bitterness comes from."

John Wetton, however, maintains that he feels no bitterness towards the other members of Wishbone Ash: "This is not being bitter at all. I'm just explaining what happened. Looking back on it I have no bad feelings at all but I feel frustrated because I think I could have done more. I didn't want to be what I had been in Roxy Music – just the bassist. Playing bass is just one of a thousand things that I do. Most people know what I bring to the party and it's in their interest to make the most of that. In Wishbone Ash's case, they didn't seem to want to do that."

Although he had never formally "joined" Wishbone Ash, John Wetton's involvement would not last beyond the album sessions with the bassist making no concert appearances with the band.

"I had already decided that, because they didn't want my full involvement, I wouldn't stick around," says Wetton. "I think it was understood by then that I wouldn't be taking it any further with the band. My time in Miami was not wasted however, although I thought there was a lot of time-wasting going on in the sessions. I was formulating in my mind what I was going to do. What I wanted to do next was Asia, though at the time I didn't know it. Wishbone were stuttering in America by then and that album, *Number the Brave,* did not give them the hit that they needed."

Laurie Wisefield takes up the case for the other three members of Wishbone: "I liked John a lot and tried to make him feel a part of it, but the band was established and things take time to develop. He came up with a couple of ideas which we liked, but Andy and him didn't get on. We'd already written most of the songs by the time he came and knew the direction we wanted to go. I don't think John was prepared to go along with the things that we had in mind for him."

Following his departure from Wishbone Ash, John Wetton formed Asia with Carl Palmer (ex-ELP) and Yes men Steve Howe and Geoff Downes (formerly of Buggles). Wetton had more freedom to express himself as a singer/songwriter, contributing to the albums *Asia, Alpha, Astra, Then & Now, Live in Moscow* and *Live in Nottingham*. Asia became one of the biggest rock acts of the eighties in America and around the world, though in their native Britain they were largely ignored. In 1986 Wetton collaborated with Phil Manzanera and also contributed vocals to the *Phenomena II* project the following year. Various ventures followed before Wetton made a concerted effort to establish himself as a solo artist with the release of the acclaimed *Battle Lines* album in 1994 followed by the live releases *Chasing the Dragon* and *Akustika*. 1997 saw the release of his third solo studio album *ArkAngel*.

Chapter Seven

The Streets Of Shame

Nothing would be heard from Wishbone Ash in the opening months of 1981. Then on 27 March the silence was broken by the release of a single featuring "Underground", an anti-nuclear song taken from the forthcoming album, backed with a non-album track "My Mind Is Made Up". As with all previous Wishbone Ash singles it failed to make any impact on the charts.

The release of *Number the Brave*, Wishbone Ash's eleventh studio album, followed soon after on 10 April. The cover, designed by Cream, shows hundreds of bayonets held high ready for battle – a nod back to *Argus* perhaps? With Martin gone, the album obviously marked a change of direction. However, there was certainly no shortage of fresh ideas and the melodic qualities that had characterised the Wishbone sound were still very much in evidence.

"Loaded" opens the album with a distinctive riff from Laurie Wisefield, who also provided the lead vocal. Claire Hamill also made a notable contribution revealing a vastly different sounding Wishbone Ash to the one which had made *Just Testing*. On this track in particular, the music had a definite funk-rock flavour.

"I think part of the reason they wanted me to play on *Number the Brave* was that they had made a decision to go in a slightly different direction," says John Wetton. "I know Laurie Wisefield particularly wanted the band to go that way, with the bass being ever-so-slightly funk orientated – you know, white guys play funk."

Lyrically, the song was inspired by a party Laurie had attended, where one party-goer kept asking, "Anyone wanna get loaded?"

"Where Is the Love" follows, with Andy Powell on vocals for a straight forward, no-nonsense boogie number which was played live on the *Number the Brave* tour.

"Underground", the album's first single release, is undoubtedly one of the finest moments and was probably the first time that Wishbone had made such a strong political statement. The "underground" in the lyric referred to the anti-nuclear movement being forced underground, a fear that was ever-present from the seventies until the end of the cold war in the eighties. Musically, "Underground" featured some fine melodic guitar picking and a superb twin lead playout. Laurie Wisefield played the rhythm part with the echo effect being suggested by producer Nigel Gray. The song was also notable for some of Andy Powell's finest ever vocal work, whilst Claire Hamill's contributions were both tasteful and stylish.

"Kicks on the Street" is a workmanlike hard rock number with Andy once again taking the lead vocal, while "Open Road" is probably Wishbone's most successful venture into funk-rock. Powell once again took the lead vocal and there is a distinct similarity between Steve Upton's drum intro to that on the unreleased Martin Turner number "I Need People".

Side Two opens with "Get Ready", a cover of the Smokey Robinson number sung by Andy Powell, which was in many ways a return to Andy's days with the Sugarband with its soul/R&B sound. Despite going down less than favourably with many Ash purists, it was a valid, if unsuccessful, attempt at chart success.

"Rainstorm" is a mid-paced melodic rock number, let down by rather weak vocals from Laurie Wisefield, while "That's That" is John Wetton's sole songwriting contribution to the album – and as such is more in the vein of his former group Uriah Heep rather than Wishbone Ash. Having said this John did, in fact, have a hand in the composition of some of the other songs. For instance, the distinctive bass riff in "Underground" was certainly his input.

"If I had been a fully paid up one quarter of the group, then you would have seen my name on there and I would have been responsible for one quarter of the composing of that album," says Wetton. "As I didn't join, they just put my name after the song that I was principally responsible for. If I'd been offered the job of singer/songwriter/bass player within the band, I would probably have taken it and you would have seen everything as a four way split. There are parts of my songwriting on songs other than 'That's That'. To keep things clean, whoever helped with writing on 'That's That' sacrificed their credit on the track and I sacrificed my credit on everything else."

"Rollercoaster" reverts to Laurie's much favoured funk-rock style. But again, weak vocals spoil the overall effect and the song becomes extremely repetitive. "Number the Brave" closes the album in fine style with a power and drive that seems to be missing from much of the rest of the album. Whereas many of the other songs have weaknesses in certain areas, here all the elements come together and the band manage to successfully merge Wishbone's classic melodic hallmarks with a fresh sound for the eighties. Andy Powell's voice is perfectly suited, whilst John Wetton's keyboards help to create a bigger sound.

"The song was written in a hotel room in Surrey," recalls Andy. "I had the music and the idea for the lyric was inspired by a Stephen King book I'd just read called *The Stand*. I had some lines and scraps, and together with Steve Upton's help, it was bashed into shape. He hadn't actually read the book, but got quite inspired by my account of it."

Incidentally, in addition to the aforementioned "My Mind is Made Up", a further two songs were recorded for *Number The Brave* – John Wetton's "Now or Never", which musically was rather similar to "That's That", and Laurie Wisefield's "Hard on You", a number which had first seen the light of day during the *No Smoke Without Fire* sessions. These two recordings remain unreleased, though may be considered for inclusion on a future CD reissue of the album, although in the case of "Now or Never", John Wetton says, "I would want to hear it first, as it was never finished. I remember only a rough vocal being put down."

Number the Brave peaked at number 61, the lowest chart position yet for a Wishbone album. *Record Mirror* claimed: "Powell has easily slipped into the pilot's chair vacated by Turner and he can more than handle the pace. This album represents another Ash re-birth and Gray has been responsible for bringing out a new range of dynamics."

Some fans were not so easily convinced. For them Martin Turner's input was naturally missed and, likewise, many were disappointed by the lack of input from John Wetton. General opinion was that the album was a reasonable, but far from spectacular, attempt to keep the Wishbone Ash flag flying. It would be the last the band would record for MCA as the label decided not to renew their contract.

With John Wetton out of the frame, Wishbone Ash had spent the early months of 1981 auditioning bassists, having advertised in *Melody Maker* for possible candidates. Powell, Upton and Wisefield finally settled on former David Bowie/Uriah Heep man Trevor Bolder (ironically, it had been Bolder who had replaced Wetton in Uriah Heep back in 1976). Bolder officially joined Wishbone Ash on 14 April 1981.

"At the time I was very despondent with Heep and I saw an advert in *Melody Maker* that said, 'Top band requires bass player'," remembers Bolder. "I decided to give them a call and spoke to a guy who turned out to be their manager. I said, 'Who's the band?' and he said, 'I can't tell you until you tell me who you are'. We went on like this for a while and in the end I gave in and told him who I was and he said it was Wishbone. I'd been a fan of Wishbone Ash from the very early days seeing them as far back as 1970 when they first played the Hull area, supporting Savoy Brown. The last time I'd seen them was just before I joined Bowie in 1971."

Trevor was asked to audition but he didn't realise how great the competition was. "The audition was a massive affair with about 60 bass players being auditioned and the whole thing took four days. I was asked to come back for a second audition and ended up getting the job."

As to the question of whether Trevor found it daunting to follow in the footsteps of two well respected bass players, Trevor had this to say: "I wasn't scared of replacing Martin Turner or John Wetton. I'd replaced John in Heep. They were both great players and good singers, but it didn't bother me at all."

Trevor Bolder made his first live appearance with Wishbone Ash just two months later on 16 May at Manchester University, the start of a major UK tour, which would take in eighteen shows in all, including two university dates.

Immediately prior to the tour, rumours in the music press suggested that Wishbone would be augmented by a fifth member, possibly a keyboard player. However, many long-time fans were surprised when the band chose to add Claire

Above: The 'new look' Ash at Hammersmith Odeon 1981
(l-r) Andy Powell, Claire Hamill, Steve Upton, Trevor Bolder and Laurie Wisefield.
Photo: Wishbone Ash Fan Club Archives

Hamill to the touring line-up. The reason for this was that the band had been impressed with her vocal contributions on *Just Testing* and *Number the Brave*, and thought that her presence on stage would add to the overall live sound.

When asked about whether he found it strange being in a traditional four-piece rock band with a female singer, Trevor Bolder didn't have any qualms: "With Claire Hamill I just accepted that she was a member of the band although it was different for Ash being a five-piece. She had a song called 'Danny Don't Go to Ireland', that the band played on stage. I thought it was great."

Many criticised Hamill's onstage contribution, with Claire herself thinking that "the fans preferred an all-male group". With hindsight it was a bold move and a credible attempt to add a new slant to their live show. However, while the collaboration worked perfectly on live renditions of new numbers such as "Underground", the band did have a tendency to sound somewhat uncomfortable on some of the earlier Wishbone Ash material.

The Hammersmith show on 2 June was recorded by the BBC for the *In Concert* programme, whilst the show at Brighton Dome on 5 June was recorded for possible future use, although the tapes remain unmixed to this day. The BBC show later came out as the bootlegs, *Playing Free and Lady Whiskey*.

Following the UK dates, the tour continued with gigs in France followed by a festival in Macroom, Ireland where Wishbone appeared on a bill also featuring Paul Brady, the Undertones and the Q-Tips, the latter fronted by future solo star

Paul Young and also boasting members of Andy Powell's early outfit, the Sugarband, in their line-up.

A further single from *Number the Brave* was released showcasing an alternative mix of "Get Ready" featuring Claire Hamill (she hadn't featured on the album version) backed with "Kicks on the Street". Early pressings of the single included a free Wishbone Ash patch, which was destined to become a collector's item. At this time a German TV appearance was recorded to promote the single – the only known filmed document of the band featuring Claire Hamill. As the band attempted valiantly to reinvent itself with its new line-up, the band's Japanese record company, MCA/Victor, released a lavishly packaged double anthology of the band's first decade of music, simply entitled *Wishbone Ash*.

The five-piece line-up proved to be an experiment that only partly worked and by July/August 1981, when the band played their first US dates since 1977, Wishbone Ash had parted company with Claire Hamill and had reverted to their standard four-piece format.

"It was at the beginning of the US tour that she decided to quit the band," reveals Andy Powell. "We were in New York and she had just got married to her then husband Nick Austin, the owner of Beggars Banquet Records. He was acting as her manager and wanted a bigger profile for Claire, which didn't gel with what we were doing at that time."

Claire, in an interview for this book, revealed more fully the reason why her stay with Wishbone Ash came to an end: "They didn't ask me to join the band as a permanent member but wanted to pay me per gig. However, they were only intending to pay me half of what I had previously been paid. Also relations between me and Penny Gibbons (the band's tour manager) were rather strained and I had just got married. So I agreed to do just the New York gigs with them. When we got to New England for the warm up gigs, I found out that they'd dropped my only solo song, 'Danny Don't Go To Ireland'. I was really disappointed and moaned to my husband Nick on the phone back in England. He jumped onto a plane immediately and flew over to New York. When he got to the hotel he had a serious argument with Steve Upton where they nearly came to blows. Nick told me to pack my bags as we were leaving! Looking back it was a terrible thing to do to the band and I was so ashamed that I didn't speak to them for fifteen years. Thank God they've forgiven me, but I hate myself for my more plaintive ways sometimes. By the way it was nice to see Penny Gibbons at the 30th anniversary show rehearsals. When you're older you realise how petty your negative vibes were. We got on so well that night."

When Claire Hamill finally met up again with Andy Powell in 1997 at the annual Wishbone Ash Convention in Mansfield, she admitted certain regrets about not continuing with the band. According to Andy Powell: "She shared with me, that in retrospect, it hadn't been a very smart move and things could have worked out better for all of us if a little more patience had been used. She and Nick are no longer married, so 'C'est La Vie!'"

The US tour continued with the band once again a four-piece outfit. One memorable gig was in Chicago where the band played as headliners to a 10,000 festival crowd, the stage being moored out in Lake Michigan. As the band played

"Phoenix" fireworks and a fantastic laser show could be seen behind the band. Following the completion of the US tour, Wishbone came back to the UK for a return to the Reading Festival stage, where they once again headlined as they had done in 1975. "The Reading Festival went really well," recalls Trevor Bolder. "Although there were several New Wave Of Heavy Metal bands there like Samson and Iron Maiden, we still went down very well. The weather was perfect, sunny, and it was a really good gig."

In the Autumn some scheduled German dates had to be cancelled when Trevor Bolder went down with gastro-enteritis. However he was fit enough to play a handful of UK college dates before Wishbone Ash embarked on what was to be a pioneering move by the band – their first tour of India. Wishbone, who were only the third Western rock band to perform in India (the previous two being Kraftwerk and the Police), performed two open-air concerts in Bombay and a further show in Madras. This visit to India marked the start of an adventurous side to Wishbone's travels. In the eighties the band would tour several countries rarely visited by western rock bands, including Russia, South Africa and Brazil. Laurie Wisefield recalls why the band agreed to go to India and what it was like when they first got there: "The offer came up and we thought, 'India – let's go for the crack – see what India's like'. When we got to Bombay we went from the airport to the hotel through these shanty towns. It was completely mind-blowing. We only took a couple of guitars and some cymbals. There were about two Marshall amps in the whole of India! There were no spares! I think we played to about 20,000 people in Bombay. They just went apeshit! The people were great. It was a really great experience except that at some point nearly everyone got ill."

Steve Upton too enjoyed the Indian experience: "The Police had been to India earlier in the year and had left their PA system in Bombay as a contribution to Third World Rock," remembers Upton. "We were using their PA system and playing the same venue. The audience was as baffled by loud rock music as we were about India. There were about 5,000 people inside the venue and 10,000 outside dancing in the streets. By the time it came for us to leave India we had all grown to love it, despite obvious cultural differences, and were talking about returning to play more shows."[5]

Trevor Bolder has fond memories of India, citing their visit to Madras as one of his highlights: "In Madras we stayed at this hotel where the rooms were beach huts looking out onto the sea. We watched the sun come up over the horizon which was quite magical."

"The lighting rig in Bombay was just a light bulb covered by coloured plastic bags like you get in a Tesco supermarket" Bolder continues. "Penny Gibbons (the bands PR officer, who was by now also running the fan club) came out on the road with us and was doing the lighting from a desk at the side of the stage. I noticed during the gig that she seemed to be bopping about a lot, so after the gig I said to her, 'You seemed to enjoy the gig tonight with all your dancing'. She told me that she hadn't actually been dancing but each time she had to move the knobs on the lighting desk, she got an electric shock!"

After a well-earned Christmas break, 1982 started off actively for Wishbone Ash with a short series of UK dates, after which the band began writing material for

Above Bolder, Upton and Powell. Reading Festival, 1981.
Photo: Wishbone Ash Fan Club Archives

their next album at Steve Upton's Surrey home. Demo sessions took place at Surrey Sound with Nigel Gray at the controls once again. In May Wishbone began to test this new music on live audiences during a ten-date UK tour. Four new songs were aired – "Streets of Shame", "No More Lonely Nights", "Engine Overheat" and "Cat and Dog Fight".

Meanwhile, MCA UK issued *The Best of Wishbone Ash*. The album featured tracks chosen by the band from their output to date and came complete with liner notes from Steve Upton. The album largely duplicated material featured on MCA's previous compilation *Classic Ash* and ironically comprised only material recorded prior to Martin Turner's departure, with *Number the Brave* totally overlooked.

Recording sessions for the new album took place at the Sol Studio, Cookham, Berkshire. Owned by Jimmy Page, the studios were originally remodelled for use by Led Zeppelin, having been previously owned by Elton John producer Gus Dudgeon. The sessions were produced by Ashley Howe (an associate of Trevor Bolder from his Uriah Heep days) with assistance from Stuart Epps and ran from June through to August. Trevor Bolder explains about why there two producers on the album:

"Ashley Howe started as producer of the album but as he had commitments elsewhere the second half was finished by the engineer Stuart Epps. I heard that Ashley Howe now lives in America and has won Grammies for film scores he has written for organisations like Disney and CBS/NBC."

A short break in mid-July in the recording process allowed the band to make an appearance at the Lisdoonvarna Music Festival in County Clare, Ireland. Meanwhile, Andy Powell and Laurie Wisefield were reunited briefly with Martin Turner at a star studded party thrown by Police drummer Stewart Copeland on 16 July. Celebrating his marriage to Sonja Christina (the former Curved Air vocalist) on the same day as his birthday, Copeland threw a party in the grounds of his large Buckinghamshire home. A stage was set up and various musicians jammed with Copeland and friends throughout the evening. These included Jools Holland, Andy Summers, Sting and Wishbone's guitar duo of Powell and Wisefield. Martin Turner was also there with his bass and took turns at the mike with Sting and Gene October (ex-Chelsea).

After an American tour throughout July and August, the new Wishbone Ash album, *Twin Barrels Burning*, was released in September 1982 through AVM Records, a label that John Sherry had set up. The catalogue number for the album was "ASH 1". The cover, depicting a fast car accelerating, was designed by Ian Harris, a friend of Andy Powell who had also designed the "Blowin' Free" single cover and tour merchandise stand two years earlier. If *Number the Brave* had introduced new influences to the band's sound, then *Twin Barrels Burning* marked a drastic change with its overall heavier rock direction. The album's release coincided with the New Wave of British Heavy Metal movement which was then sweeping the UK and had spawned the likes of Iron Maiden, Saxon and Def Leppard. Cynics would say that Wishbone Ash appeared to be jumping on the bandwagon in a contrived attempt to attract a younger audience, but after the commercial failure of *Number the Brave* the band seriously needed to win over new fans as well as keep the old ones. As Andy Powell said at the time: "We've got to move on and hopefully take the kids with us."[24] Certainly *Twin Barrels Burning* was the band's heaviest sounding album yet, containing a lot of aggression both in the music and in the vocals which were largely shared by Andy and Laurie.

Perhaps somewhat unfairly, Trevor Bolder took much of the blame for the change of musical direction, largely due to his Uriah Heep pedigree.

"Trevor's playing made the band a lot heavier," says Andy Powell. "He really fattened out the bottom end. He's a very orthodox player – there was less wild experimentation. Martin's bass playing was very much like our guitar playing – he just dived in at the deep end. He wasn't what you'd call an orthodox player and, in some ways, that was what gave us our unusual sound."[25]

Bolder himself elaborates: "There was no deliberate attempt from me to change the sound of the band, although I do accept that my bass playing may have been heavier than previous Wishbone Ash albums. I think at the time Laurie was edging the band towards heavier rock along the lines of AC/DC or ZZ Top. He was very much into ZZ Top and I think you can hear that influence on the album."

The guitar playing on *Twin Barrels Burning* was, as always, admirable and Trevor Bolder proved to be a worthy successor to Turner and Wetton in the bass department. Vocally, however, some would argue that Andy and Laurie's voices were not suited to the heavy rock numbers which comprised *Twin Barrels Burning*, with both vocalists sounding strained at times. Musically, the album lacked the usual melody and subtlety of a Wishbone Ash album. Instead, the overall sound was mainstream heavy rock, bordering on metal. Certainly every heavy metal cliché in the book was dragged out with references aplenty to fast cars and chicks! For the true Wishbone Ash connoisseur, *Twin Barrels Burning* was a great disappointment and sits uncomfortably amidst the rest of the band's back catalogue.

The opener is the hard rocking "Engine Overheat", featuring a strong riff and echoey drums. It sets the style for the rest of the album. With chord changes that could have come straight from the AC/DC guitar book, the lyrics are of the macho male chauvinist variety.

Laurie also takes the lead vocal on "Can't Fight Love", a song which was has a fairly similar sentiment to "Engine Overheat". It also features one of the all time great Laurie riffs half way through, which is also used during the opening sequence of the *Live at the Marquee* video, and one of the few moments on *Twin Barrels Burning* to contain the hallmarks of the Ash of old.

"Genevieve" sees Andy Powell taking his turn on the lead vocals next to Laurie Wisefield, while lyrically "Me and My Guitar" was inspired partly by an abortive appearance on a TV talent contest Wisefield had made during his adolescence. "It all stemmed from this thing he did when he was fourteen," explains Andy Powell. "He went on this TV show and sung with an outsize guitar and apparently it just didn't happen. As a result all his schoolmates laughed at him and it actually put the mockers on him singing for a long time."[24]

The more laid back and commercial sounding "Hold On", like all the songs on *Twin Barrels Burning,* was credited jointly to Wisefield/Upton/Powell. The song, however, was actually written entirely by Trevor Bolder who had also had a hand in many of the album's other tracks. Trevor explains why his name was left off the credits: "The reason I am not credited is at the time I was still signed to my publishing company from my time with Uriah Heep. I didn't think I was getting a very good deal from them so I decided to take my name off the album so they wouldn't know I'd been writing. I didn't want them getting any royalties because they owed me money. Thankfully all that has now been sorted out."

"'Hold On' was written one night in a drunken stupor," Bolder contines. "It's about that feeling after a gig when you're on tour and you want some sanity in your life away from all the tour madness. You try ringing home to speak to your wife but she's not there. You keep calling but you can't get through. That song was written totally by me. I took the lead vocals on it and backing vocals on the other tracks."

"Streets of Shame" is one of the better received songs on the album and the lyrics, written by Steve Upton, recall the band's experiences on their visit to India in 1981 and some of the more exotic sights that they saw in the red light district of Bombay. Laurie explains:

"We'd hardly got out of the car before we were swamped by it all. There were people hanging out of doorways ranging from about five to about ninety-five. It was really bizarre. If you got out of the car people would come over to you and start pinching you and chasing you."

"No More Lonely Nights", one of the album's more melodic moments, is memorable for the opening riff which Laurie had formulated whilst the band were rehearsing for the album. Apparently the track was composed first with Laurie providing the title line, "No More Lonely Nights" as something that just came into his head in the studio. Steve Upton then went home and wrote some lyrics for it.

"Angels Have Mercy" again had similarities to AC/DC, and featured Andy on lead vocal. The final track, "Wind Up" does actually feature a little twin lead guitar! Again Laurie screams out the vocals sounding uncomfortable at times.

Two further songs were recorded during the sessions, namely "Go For Gold" and "Cat and Dog Fight". These numbers remain (officially) unheard to this day. Two singles were lifted from *Twin Barrels Burning* – "Engine Overheat"/"Genevieve" and "No More Lonely Nights"/"Streets of Shame".

The change of musical direction on *Twin Barrels Burning* did not stop the album from achieving Wishbone's highest chart placing since *New England*, peaking at number 22 on the UK chart. Certain elements of the press gave the album rave reviews. UK heavy metal magazine *Kerrang* described the album as "a particularly good record, containing material that is far more poignant than some of the earlier songs". However, while the album may have initially seemed a success, the band's new direction alienated many long-time supporters who would approach future releases with great caution. The fact that *Twin Barrels Burning* would mark Wishbone Ash's final UK chart placing was possibly more than coincidental.

With a schedule running through to mid-December, extensive UK and European tours followed the album's release. The tour began with a series of seventeen English dates, the majority at city halls and theatres, marking a return to the venues in which the band was always most comfortable. Martin Turner turned up to watch their London gig at the Dominion Theatre in Tottenham Court Road while the final date of the tour was a charity show on 11 October at Norwich's Theatre Royal in aid of the SOS Children's appeal. During the afternoon of the show, the band filmed a slot for Anglia TV which was broadcast later in the day. Andy Powell was interviewed briefly before the band mimed to "Engine Overheat".

The European section got off to a hectic start on 18 October in Ljubljana, Yugoslavia, when fans began to climb the front barrier to avoid being crushed by the 8,000 strong crowd which surged forwards. Andy Powell and Trevor Bolder leapt from the stage, guitars in hand, to tackle security stewards who had started attacking fans. Andy used his Flying V to knock security men off the fans, while Trevor deserted his bass to haul them to safety. The band then found themselves the target of the bouncers, at which point the road crew intervened. The remainder of the tour continued more peacefully with dates in Switzerland, France, Spain and Germany. The show in Pforzheim, Germany on 20 November was broadcast by German radio. 1982 drew to a close with a return to Wembley Arena for a support slot to Ian Gillan on 17 December.

In January 1983, Wishbone fans in the US were confused and dismayed when they turned up at gigs in Texas expecting to see the band perform their first US dates since the Summer of 1981. In fact the "Wishbone Ash" they came to see turned out to be none other than Ted Turner with three other musicians using the "Wishbone Ash" name. At one gig in Dallas, the whole front row reportedly walked out in disgust! Naturally when the real Wishbone Ash found out about the gigs the legal eagles sprang into action. Andy Powell takes up the story:

"Steve and I were trying to put together some dates in Texas and one of the clubs, Cardis in Houston, told us that the band had just played there! It had consisted of Ted, together with Joey Mulland from Badfinger, I believe. Apparently, it had not been a good night. Steve had a lawyer put a 'cease and desist order' out to Ted, since it was a bit naughty of him to do that. He'd previously quit the band, you see. It subsequently made it difficult for us to go back into the venues he'd played."

Business concerns were also to the fore in February when Wishbone and their manager John Sherry parted company. AVM Records had been set up with money from the band. When AVM subsequently lost money, John Sherry suggested to the band that they should all declare themselves bankrupt. Sherry also advised Martin Turner that it would be in his interests to resign as a director of the band's company, a position he had maintained since his departure. While Martin took Sherry's advice, the band were not prepared to file for bankruptcy. Laurie Wisefield takes up the story:

"Basically the band had financed the album themselves as John was very sure that we'd get a record deal. So we actually borrowed a lot of money from the bank. We made the record and when we didn't get what we wanted in terms of financial return, we were in debt. John's idea from a businessman's point of view was, "Let's pay money to the small people that we owe money to and worry about the bigger people later". The bank made a deal with us to pay off the bigger people and as a result the band had to basically go out on the road to make the money to pay off the debt. From a businessman's point of view you could've just shut up shop as far as that company went and start up again, but the band, and especially Steve had the attitude of paying people on time and if you didn't have the money, get it through hard work and then pay them. In the end it took us about two years to do this, but we managed it."

The second visit to India took place in February which took the band further afield than the first, to outlying places such as Poona and Bangalore, where again there were thousands of fans both inside and outside the venues. On return from India, Wishbone played two concerts at London's Marquee Club on 22 and 23 February, the second of which was filmed. A patchy performance by Wishbone's standards, the set had been plagued by technical problems including a total power failure. However, almost an hour of footage was salvaged for a UK Channel 4 TV broadcast which marked the Marquee's 25th anniversary. The programme was also issued on video and has appeared under various different titles (*Wishbone Ash In Concert*, *The King Will Come* and, most commonly, *Phoenix*) and is a useful document of this particular incarnation of Wishbone Ash in a live setting.

The Marquee shows were followed by return visits to Dublin and Belfast. A repeat of the infamous 1972 St. Louis scenario almost occurred in Dublin when the band arrived early on the morning of the concert only to find that the crew truck containing all their equipment had been stolen. Fortunately police found the truck abandoned several hours later with all the equipment still on board. Touring continued throughout Europe in March and April and the concert in Vaal, Holland on 17 April 1983 marked Trevor Bolder's final appearance with the band. Speaking about his two-year association, Trevor has mainly happy memo-

Blowin' Free

Above: Trevor Bolder returned to Uriah Heep in 1983.
Photo: Wishbone Ash Fan Club Archives

ries of his time with Wishbone Ash: "I decided to leave mainly because Mick Box asked me to go back to Heep," says Bolder. "Quite by chance out of the blue, he rang me up and asked me to rejoin. All the management problems had been sorted out and they had a tour of stadiums in America with Def Leppard already booked. My heart was more with Heep than it was with Wishbone and as it was a quick decision that needed to be made. So I decided to leave Wishbone and rejoin Uriah Heep. I missed the friendship side of Heep – we were like a family. I really enjoyed playing with Wishbone Ash. They were dedicated musicians and were always looking for different types of music to play. The problem was that after two years with the band I felt that I was never really a member. Quite often I was not involved in the decision making and gradually I lost interest. Ash weren't sure what direction they wanted to go in and the management wasn't that good. To me, they didn't have a real leader in the band – a great vocalist or someone who writes great songs – and I'm sure that's why it started to fall apart. We had a bit of a bad break up when I left, which was hard, but we're all good friends now. Looking back I think it was the right decision as I've been with Heep ever since."

Trevor Bolder's departure came just as Wishbone were preparing for a six week US tour. The band began an emergency search for a new bassist and held auditions in London. The successful candidate was the largely unknown Mervyn "Spam" Spence, who joined on 25 April. He was a twenty five year old bassist/vocalist/songwriter born in Larne, County Antrim, Northern Ireland, where he qualified as an engineer at University before moving to England in 1980. Taking up residence in the Staffordshire area, he began playing with local bands such as Jury and Big Daisy. An offer from local musician Mel Galley to join Trapeze followed. Although never hitting the major league, Trapeze were a respected outfit who had, at various times, boasted such notables as Judas Priest's Dave Holland, Deep Purple's Glenn Hughes and Uriah Heep's Peter Goalby in its line-up. Spence toured with the band and recorded an album's worth of material, although this remains unreleased. The band broke up shortly after, with Galley accepting an offer to join Whitesnake. Spam, who, legend has it, acquired his nickname following a bet as to how much of the canned meat he could eat, then spent several months writing and demoing songs in his home studio, before being contacted to audition for Wishbone Ash.

Mervyn recalls that: "It was Andy who made contact. I was informed by a friend connected to Trapeze that Wishbone Ash were after a bass player and I should call their management. There was an urgency in replacing Trevor Bolder and I went to London the following day. I was a fan of the band, so I knew their music anyway. I went over "Blowin' Free" with the band and put in a third harmony which they loved. I then did a fast blues track where I had the opportunity to let my voice go. This I believe, was what sealed my joining the band. If I had relied on my bass playing I would never have got the job! My bass playing at the time was very basic and not at all in the same league as Martin or Trevor. But I knew this was not my first instrument. My voice was."

Such was the urgency in finding a bass player in time for the US tour that Mervyn got a call from Andy Powell offering him the job in the middle of the night! "I got home about 9 p.m. My wife and I went out to see some friends, I told them what had happened during the day and that I didn't really expect to hear from them. At 2 a.m. the next morning the call came through that I'd got the job, another list of songs to learn and, 'Oh, by the way, we leave for a US tour next Tuesday,' with just one rehearsal before departure."

The band departed for the US on 3 May and the six week tour covered mainly the East Coast and Mid-West states. Although on this tour Mervyn Spence only handled bass and backing vocal duties, on subsequent tours he would assume the position of lead vocalist. In addition, the young and good looking Spence proved to be a charismatic frontman providing the visual spark that had been missing since Martin Turner's departure. At first Spam was cautious on stage, but as he gained more confidence he was able to take on more responsibility. "That first American tour was really enjoyable as I could concentrate on improving my playing. I think the overall idea was to put me up front on vocals as they felt the band needed some new blood and I was prepared to embrace this. I'm definitely a performer and would really go for it when we were onstage. I think the nice thing about the band was they all felt the same way. If you enjoy yourself onstage then that comes across and the people actually get into it as well."

To coincide with the US tour, the *Twin Barrels Burning* album, which had not yet been given a Stateside release, finally appeared on the Fantasy label. The album was packaged with an alternative sleeve design and was re-mixed with American radio airplay in mind. Trevor Bolder, in particular, was disappointed with the remix.

"I don't like the remix at all," states Trevor. "I heard that the son of the guy who owned the record company decided for some reason that he didn't like our mix. He took the multi-track tapes back to America and re-mixed it in their studio. That to me was crazy; there was nobody from the band there. He didn't know what we wanted the album to sound and feel like. He took lots of stuff off that he shouldn't have and just stripped it down to the bare bones. I'd left by the time it got re-mixed, but I don't know why they let him do it. The first I knew of it was when I was at Steve's house one day and he gave me a copy of it. Even the cover's naff!"

After the American tour had finished the band members had some spare time on their hands as the date sheet was fairly quiet for the rest of the year. Andy Powell produced and played guitar on a single by a new band called Jeunesse, while Laurie Wisefield contributed guitar to Claire Hamill's *Touchpaper* album. The band also started writing and rehearsing material for their next album, despite the lack of a record company to release it. The year ended with a European tour throughout November and December, but no British dates. In fact the strange thing about Mervyn Spence joining Wishbone was that the majority of British fans wouldn't get to see him play until two years later.

Chapter Eight

There's No Longer Magic In Your Eyes

Armed with a batch of new songs written by all four members, Wishbone Ash once again entered Surrey Sound Studios in Leatherhead in January 1984 with engineer Jim Ebdon (a long-time friend of Martin Turner, who would later become the band's live sound engineer) to lay down demo recordings to tout around record companies with the aim of securing a new recording contract. Six songs were recorded; "People in Motion", "Dreams (Searching for an Answer)", "She's Still Alive", "Perfect Timing", "Long Live the Night" and "Don't You Mess". The music continued the heavier rock direction of *Twin Barrels Burning*, but benefited greatly from the addition of Mervyn Spence's superior vocal and songwriting talents and an altogether greater emphasis on melody.

The actual album sessions would take place during the spring and summer of 1984, when Wishbone Ash returned to Surrey Sound with *Number the Brave* producer Nigel Gray at the helm. The sessions would be interrupted for a handful of European dates during July, including appearances in Poland and East Germany for the first time. The band also appeared at the Wakefield Music Festival on 25 August and toured France during October. With the band lacking a UK recording contract, *Raw to the Bone*, as the new album was titled, was initially released in Germany in November 1984 through the Metronome label (who had also released *Twin Barrels Burning*). There were also German TV appearances at this time to promote the German single release of "People in Motion".

Despite being far removed from Wishbone Ash's classic style and a tendency for some of its songs to sound too similar, *Raw to the Bone* contained some fine material firmly rooted in the melodic hard rock vein, albeit with a more commercial

Above: *Raw to the Bone* vocalist/bassist Mervyn Spence (centre) pictured with originals Andy Powell (l) and Ted Turner (r) in Birmingham, 1992.
Photo: Gary Carter

sound. However, despite being a particularly well-crafted album in its field, many purist Ash fans clearly resented the band's continuing move away from their original style.

"The fact that *Raw to the Bone* leaned more towards mainstream hard rock was very much a product of Mervyn Spence's influence," reveals Andy Powell. "With vocal chords like his, we needed music that was energised. Also, as with all the albums we've made, *Raw to the Bone* was very much a product of the times – in this instance, the mid-eighties. Mervyn was particularly inspired on that album, since it was a debut of sorts for him, and he brought a lot of music to the table. Mervyn played a big part in the change of direction for the band on *Raw to the Bone*."

The album opens with "Cell of Fame", a medium-paced rocker about the pitfalls of fame, and was released as a single in Spain only. The catchy Steve Upton penned chorus showed Spam's unique vocals off to the fans and featured some nice guitar work from Andy and Laurie together with some great bass playing by session man Brad Lang.

The next track, "People in Motion" was released as a single in Germany and continues where the opening track left off with a catchy hook.

"Don't Cry" begins with synthesisers rather in the style of the Human League and is hard edged pop-rock in style. "Love Is Blue" has a similar feel with a slow build up to a memorable chorus. "Long Live the Night" is a more laid back song and, with its moody feel and strong vocal melody, is one of the stronger numbers on the album.

"Rocket in my Pocket" is the only non-Wishbone track on the album. A cover of the Lowell George song, it takes the Little Feat groove into more of a rock feel. "It's Only Love" sounds like it could have come from the *Twin Barrels Burning* sessions with its heavy riffing guitar sound, but was a good showcase for the sheer quality and range of Spam's voice.

"Don't You Mess" features a promising finger picking opening guitar from Laurie but highlights one of the album's main weaknesses – a tendency for many of its songs to rely too heavily on over repeated hooks and chorus lines, rather than the imaginative arrangements for which the band were known. "Dreams" is similarly catchy but, again, lacks the true Wishbone Ash hallmarks. "Perfect Timing" starts out with another distinctive heavy metal-type riff from Andy Powell, and features a screamed vocal from Mervyn, but like many of the tracks on *Raw to the Bone* was a fairly average song.

Surprisingly, the track "She's Still Alive" which had been demoed, was not actually included on the album – a great pity, since it was a superior composition to just about any of the album's chosen tracks, with a style and sound that successfully merged the band's new, commercially orientated sound, with the classic Wishbone Ash ideals. It would later surface on the *Distillation* 4CD box set. Mervyn is unsure about how it ended up on the box set, but put forward an interesting reason as to why it was left off the album:

"I have no idea how that song got out and even got onto a CD. I think everyone felt the lyrical content a bit morbid. That's why it never went any further." Andy Powell remembers himself adding a chord sequence and Steve Upton adding some more lyrics to make the song into what it is today.

In retrospect, despite its imperfections, *Raw to the Bone* still sounds quite palatable as an album. It was well produced, expertly played and featured some of the strongest vocal work ever to grace a Wishbone Ash album. While criticism can be levelled at many of the album's tracks, most of them stand head and shoulders above the product issued by the myriad of other bands who were working within the same genre of commercially orientated hard rock at the time. But, in reality, it was not the album the majority of Wishbone Ash fans wanted to hear. Laurie Wisefield admits that at this time he and Andy did deliberately try and move away from the harmony twin-lead guitar sound that was part of the Wishbone Ash trademark:

"I think we'd got to the stage where we said, 'Let's not put it in just for the sake of putting it in'. I suppose with the influence of Spam being in the band the weight went onto the vocals and less emphasis went onto the harmony guitars. Don't forget that at that time we'd been playing harmony guitars for God knows how many years. You've done something for so long, so you're not inspired to keep doing it."

Another aspect to the album was the inclusion of several session musicians in the credits. Andrew Bown and Simon Butt added keyboards and Brad Lang bass guitar. According to Spam, this was due to the influence of Nigel Gray:

"This was a Nigel Gray decision and we went along with it as we wanted to experiment with a new direction. They only played on a couple of tracks each which was fine and really worked."

With the album out in Germany, the early part of 1985 was spent negotiating for that elusive UK record deal. Tapes of the album and recent publicity shots were presented to former manager Miles Copeland, who since parting company with Wishbone Ash had achieved enormous success as manager and guiding light of the Police and was now co-managing the solo career of Sting with Kim Turner. At this point Copeland decided that he would be embarrassed to be associated with Wishbone Ash again. Two years later he would change his mind.

Raw to the Bone was finally released in the UK by the independent heavy metal label Neat Records on 31 May, and was repackaged with a different sleeve. Andy Powell: "Mervyn directly influenced the theme of the UK album cover (which people seem to either love or hate), by introducing us to Ian Lowe, the artist."

Mervyn had indeed showed the rest of the band examples of Ian's work which they liked, so Ian was given the job of designing the album cover. It was pretty gruesome with a stone-age woman eating the raw flesh off a bone. It was certainly eye-catching if nothing else.

The UK release of *Raw to the Bone* was backed up in June 1985 with Wishbone Ash's first full UK tour in nearly two and a half years. Apart from an end of tour appearance at Hammersmith Odeon, it was noticeable that the band were no longer playing the city halls of England but instead had moved down a notch into the clubs. It was unfortunate that the tour coincided with a troubled period at Neat which resulted in little backing for either the album or the tour. Despite this, the tour was a reasonable success and even those fans who had been unconvinced by the new line-up's recorded output were forced to comment on how well Spam had integrated with Wishbone in a live setting. As Laurie recalls:

"It was a mixed reaction really. There were those fans who thought he was a good singer and had a good voice and some others who weren't that keen". Founder member Martin Turner attended the Hammersmith Odeon show: "I always found it strange watching the band after I'd left, but on this occasion, I really was quite impressed, particularly by Spam. I thought he had a great voice – very high, kind of like Jon Anderson in Yes – and I thought he was great for the band. They played a lot of stuff that I'd originally played – songs like "Don't Come Back" and "F.U.B.B." – and those are not the easiest basslines to get your head around, but I thought Spam did really well. Years later, after I'd rejoined the band, I was surprised when Andy told me that he thought Spam wasn't much of bassist."

Meanwhile, the album received some quite promising reviews in the rock press. For example *Kerrang*'s Derek Oliver claimed: "Once written off, Ash have now re-merged with a new sense of purpose. Everything on the record is damn near perfect. It's fresh, it's futuristic, it's certified live and it's hot wired with brilliant variations on the mainstream dream and the best vocal work Ash have ever produced."

In July, Wishbone recorded their first BBC studio session since the early seventies, performing four songs for Tommy Vance's *Friday Rock Show* at London's Maida Vale studios. This same month also saw the band undertaking a European tour. Also, Andy and Mervyn made a personal appearance at the British Music Fair at London's Olympia Exhibition Centre, and Laurie and Andy filmed an interview for Sky TV. Added to this, there was the usual array of European festivals during 1985, one notable appearance being at the Metal Hammer Festival in Lorelei, Germany, where Wishbone appeared on an ill-suited bill comprising thrash/metal bands. With their considerably more melodic approach to rock music, Wishbone Ash appeared uncomfortable, as can be seen on the video compilation *Metal Hammer Vol.1*, which features "The King Will Come" alongside tracks by the other acts on the bill. The footage by no means does justice to the live capabilities of the Powell/Upton/Wisefield/Spence line-up. As Spam admits: "It was a bit strange being up there with Metallica and those sort of acts."

In December the band played a handful of UK dates prior to embarking on their third Indian tour. Recordings were made on this jaunt with a possible live album in mind. Instead fans seeking a souvenir of Wishbone during this period have had to put up with two poorly recorded bootlegs of their performance at the Lorelei Festival, which emanate from an unmixed soundboard tape, namely the vinyl album *Lorelive Date* and the CD *No More Lonely Nights*. The Indian tour wasn't without incident, the entire band being struck by illness (guess what).

"I really thought I was coming home in a wooden box," says Mervyn Spence. "I felt terrible, I could only just crawl to the bathroom. Steve called into my room and I was lying on the floor feeling just awful. He just looked at me, burst out laughing, and left me there. I managed to shower and clean myself up a bit and went down to meet the rest of the band. I must have looked dreadful, everybody pointed at me as I walked in. I sat down with the band just as Steve started to show the first symptoms. There's justice for you. I had to laugh."

The Indian tour proved to be Laurie Wisefield's final stage appearances with Wishbone Ash and on 30 December 1985, just days before a scheduled European tour, the guitarist announced his decision to quit the band via a phone call to Steve Upton. Laurie explains his reasons for leaving:

"I'd put so much into Wishbone Ash for ten years. I was pretty much exhausted both musically and with the way the band was going. I think people were drifting apart on who wanted to do what. Something had to give basically and it was me! I hadn't really planned it. It was the end of the year and I was sitting down one night with my wife and thought, 'Next year I need to do *something* else. I don't want to do another year of this,' because for the last two years before that we had been slaving away just paying off debts. I'd done two years of that without getting too much reward out of it, so it was fairly uninspiring as well. I just felt it was time to do something else, though I didn't really know what I was going to do. So I called Steve and told him what I'd decided."

Although Laurie's departure came as a great shock to fans of the band, it had been noticed by the other members of Wishbone Ash that Laurie's interest in group activity was waning. "It was not the surprise of him leaving, but the surprise of him finally doing it," says Steve Upton. "He had acted in a very negative way for a long period up to that phone call."[5]

Having quit Wishbone Ash after eleven years with the band, Laurie Wisefield went on to pursue a varied career, recording and touring with major artists such as Tina Turner and Joe Cocker. Prior to joining Tina Turner's band he even auditioned for Duran Duran! Laurie also recorded with Luxembourg vocalist Jimmy Martin (Jimmy Martin had previously recorded a solo album which had been pro-

Above: Laurie Wisefield, who announced his departure from Wishbone Ash in December 1985.
Photo: Wishbone Ash Fan Club Archives.

duced by Martin Turner). In 1992 Laurie also played guitar and co-wrote several songs on former Family frontman Roger Chapman's *Under No Obligation* album and has appeared as a member of Chapman's live band, the Shortlist, on several tours since. In 1993 he toured with members of Status Quo in the covers band Four Bills and a Ben, raising funds for the Starlight Foundation, which grants wishes for children with terminal illnesses and in 1995 Laurie formed the Little Devils with vocalist/songwriter Johnny Warman. The band recorded some tracks for an album in the mid-nineties but nothing ever came of the session apart from a few low-key gigs. In addition, Laurie has toured major venues in Europe as part of the *Night of the Proms* – an annual televised event where leading rock and pop performers are backed by both a resident rock band as well as a symphony orchestra. The event has, to date, featured such names as Andrea Bocelli, Tony Hadley and Lisa Stansfield. Laurie also regularly appears with the SAS Band, an all star line-up formed by Queen keyboardsman Spike Edney.

To this day, many fans still cite the original Wishbone Ash line-up as the definitive incarnation of the band. However, there can be no denying the importance of the Mark II line-up with Laurie's contribution helping to create a tighter knit sound both live and on record. Certainly with this line-up the band were bigger in America and other territories than they had ever been. Likewise, Wishbone Ash had an enormous impact on Laurie, as Andy Powell is keen to stress:

"When Laurie joined the band he was very much a rhythmic player," recalls Andy. "He really did want to be in a full blown concert-style band, and I think he got a lot out of that. Likewise, I think we benefited from his playing. On a musical level there was an equal trading of influences and ideas. I think it would be true to say that we influenced him and he influenced us. Laurie didn't really come from a blues background as much as a country-rock background. He was into fingerpicking, a very rhythmic player. He's a much heavier, bluesier player now than then."[2]

Despite Laurie Wisefield's departure, surviving original members Andy Powell and Steve Upton remained undeterred and had no intentions of dissolving the band. "Steve and I were very much a unit at that point," says Powell. "We were pretty tight and we'd weathered being told we should go bankrupt. Steve very stoically said, 'I don't think we should go bankrupt,' and I agreed. We'd fought for several years to claw ourselves back from the brink, so we'd gone through all of that and achieved a great deal and pulled ourselves back through sheer hard work. So, after you've gone through those kind of things, you don't think just because someone leaves you should call it a day."

Laurie Wisefield's place in Wishbone Ash was filled by Jamie Crompton (ex-Radio Stars, New Hearts, Blue Meanies and Suzi Quatro). Crompton had, in fact, already performed one show with Wishbone Ash, back in the Autumn of 1985, as a temporary stand-in for Laurie at a gig in Basel, Switzerland – a show that was arranged at short notice while Laurie was several thousand miles away on holiday in Hawaii. "Phil Griggs, the guy that was doing the sound for Suzi Quatro got offered a tour doing the sound for Wishbone Ash," remembers Jamie. "It was through him that I was put in touch with Andy Powell. He came round to my house and we got on very well. I'd always been a big fan of Andy and Wishbone since the early seventies. I can remember having a poster of him in *Sounds* on my wall when I was a teenager! They asked me to do one gig with them in Basel, Switzerland. It was going to be a one-off, standing in for Laurie. Andy left me some tapes to learn the songs and then I remember we did the first rehearsal in the dressing room before the show. The only problem was that I'd learnt several of the songs in the wrong tunings due to the tape not playing at the right speed! But the gig went really well and Andy then asked me to do a few more dates in Europe. I was really pleased as it's great fun playing guitar in a band like Wishbone Ash, doing all the harmony stuff."

At the start of 1986 a short, 11-date European tour began in Tuttlengen, Germany. The Powell/Upton/Spence/Crompton line-up would, however, be short-lived, playing its final show in Stockholm on 25 January after less than a month together. After two and a half years with the band, Mervyn Spence had decided to leave. Mervyn explains the decision behind his departure from Wishbone Ash:

"There were a lot of problems within the band and I feel that something had to give. When Laurie told me he was going I also felt maybe it was the best thing for me as well. I also had a new baby in my life and the thought of going off on the road for months did not appeal. I felt terrible about it. I'd had probably the best time of my life with Wishbone Ash, but I had so many other things I wanted to do."

Andy Powell had this to say about Mervyn Spence's time with Wishbone Ash: "I liked Mervyn Spence a lot but I never thought he was particularly right for the band. I admire his musicality a lot. He's got a hell of a voice. A lot of *Raw To The Bone* isn't bad but at that time it was very difficult time for the band and this is reflected in the music on that album."

After his departure from Wishbone Ash, Mervyn Spence moved towards a solo career, but was never short of offers from some of the industry's biggest names: "When I left Wishbone Ash, I wanted to get more into writing and taking a more positive step towards being a solo artist. With Wishbone Ash it was four people doing everything collectively. We didn't always agree, so things were running stale by the end of it. I gave up touring and worked on a project with Carl Palmer and Don Airey but nothing came of it. I worked with Mike Oldfield on his *Islands* album and I was approached to join Black Sabbath, but I was never really into the heavy metal thing. I was always getting approached by people to play in their bands. The main one was Yes. Jon Anderson had just left the band and I had a call asking if I'd be interested, but as it turned out Trevor Rabin handled the vocals so it wasn't to be. I've done quite a lot of film and TV scores, one in particular was for a film called *The Gnostics*, which was shown on Channel 4. I did that with Anthony Phillips, the original Genesis guitarist. I also did the music for a film on Africa called *They Shall be Kings*."

In 1988 Mervyn released an album under the band name of Silent Witness, recorded with songwriter/collaborator Dieter Petereit. 1992 saw Mervyn playing bass on *Phenomena III: Inner Vision*, an all-star collaboration featuring musicians including Scott Gorham and Brian May. 1993 saw the release of *Something Strong*, Mervyn's debut solo album released under the moniker of O'Ryan. This, again, was a collaboration with Dieter Petereit. In 1994 Mervyn linked up with a new collaborator Jason Fillingham, the first fruits of this partnership being the second O'Ryan album entitled *Initiate*, which was released in 1995 in Japan, where the project has been met with considerable critical acclaim. He has also established a new company called Creative World Entertainment, involved in both music and video production that now takes up most of his time.

Mervyn Spence was replaced in Wishbone Ash by bassist Andy Pyle, a veteran of the UK music scene who had toured and recorded with some of the most respected names in the business in a career pre-dating Wishbone Ash itself – McGregor's Engine, Blodwyn Pig, Savoy Brown, Rod Stewart, Juicy Lucy, Alvin Lee, The Kinks, Sutherland Bros, Gary Moore, and Chicken Shack. Andy Pyle remembers how he got the call from Andy Powell:

"I had bumped into the band about two or three times over the years, the first time being in America. I remember that Andy lived quite near me and I recall that I used to go round to his studio and do different things. When Mervyn left, Andy called me up. I wasn't that familiar with their music so I had to learn it all. They did try and get me to sing, but I forewarned them that this was not a good move! With Mervyn going, Andy had to do all the vocals."

The new line-up rehearsed throughout February and March before embarking on a two month US tour. For many Wishbone Ash fans, this period in the band's history represented an all time low. Live performances were becoming increasingly erratic. For instance, the band's trademark dual lead guitar sound was by now largely redundant, as Jamie Crompton's role in the band was more that of a rhythm guitarist than a true guitar twin. The band was faced with the dilemma of being on the road promoting an album (*Raw to the Bone*) that had been recorded with a 50% different line-up. Andy Powell was uneasy singing Spence's vocal parts and, understandably, many of the *Raw to the Bone* numbers had to be rearranged to accommodate his voice. Gradually, this material would be phased out of the set altogether.

Touring continued throughout 1986 and for a brief period the band experimented with using guitarist Phil Palmer (ex-Joan Armatrading, Eric Clapton, Tina Turner and later of Dire Straits) in place of Jamie Crompton who was now living in Los Angeles and was not able to fly to Europe for some of the dates that year. By this time, UK performances had become increasingly sporadic, but the Palmer line-up performed a handful of dates during the latter half of 1986, including a headline appearance at a Live Aid style event in Folkestone in the summer, some East German dates in December followed by two Marquee shows on 17 and 18 December. After this period of touring, Jamie Crompton returned to the fold.

Although no albums were released featuring either the Palmer or Crompton line-ups, a number of new songs were written and demoed at Surrey Sound Studios. "We had some rough ideas for new material for the band and we recorded a few demos," recalls Jamie Crompton. "I really can't remember what the songs were apart from the fact that 'Hard Times' (a track which would later resurface on the 1991 *Strange Affair* album) was written during this time."

Andy Powell has slightly clearer recollections of these sessions. "I remember recording some demos with Jamie at Surrey Sound around that time. We had a couple of songs with titles like 'Nkomo' and 'Valley of Tears' – it may have been these. I remember Phil Palmer also played on a track or two at Surrey Sound".

So 1986 saw no fewer than three different incarnations of Wishbone Ash with the band's future looking more and more precarious. It was about time for a drastic change and that change would happen within the next six months.

Chapter Nine

Phoenix Fly... Raise Your Head To The Sky

Following the relatively low-key mid-eighties, a period of seemingly endless personnel changes, not even the most optimistic Wishbone Ash fan could have predicted the events of 1987. In February, shortly after the band had returned from a European tour, former manager Miles Copeland (now head of IRS Records) approached Wishbone with a view to the four original members of Wishbone Ash – Andy Powell, Steve Upton, Martin Turner and Ted Turner – regrouping for a strictly instrumental project, as part of IRS's *No Speak* series of albums. Copeland laid it on the line: "Forget about having to come up with a single, don't worry about your image, and don't be concerned with lyrics. Just play your instruments, unencumbered by restraints."

Miles met Andy Powell and Steve Upton in London to discuss the possibility of the four original band members working together for this one-off.

"Miles remembered that a lot of our music was instrumentally based, so we were an ideal candidate," recalls Powell. "He wanted to see if the whole original band was interested in getting back together. We figured that there was enough water under the bridge and that it would be fun. Part of the appeal was that it was a "left-field" sort of project. There was no pressure, no stress."

Copeland also put the concept to Martin Turner on a visit to his studio, located in the basement of IRS's Ladbroke Grove headquarters. "I remember Miles coming into my studio saying, 'Mart, I've got a proposition to put to you!' I said, 'OK, Miles, let me guess – Wishbone Ash Mark II'. He said, 'Wrong – Wishbone Ash Mark I'." Martin was receptive to the idea, but only on the condition that it was the entire original group.

"With really good bands, they're good bands because you've got four individuals that are all strong in one area or another," says Martin. "I think that was the case with Wishbone Ash. For me, at that time, I felt there was only any point in doing it if it was the original band."

"That was my feeling too." agrees Powell, "although in reality it wasn't to pan out that way. What it did do was put Martin and myself back into a songwriting partnership mode again – something that hadn't been the case since the *Argus* days."

The other stipulation Martin had was that, now he was immersed in a record production career, he wanted to be involved in the production of the album. Copeland was agreeable to this, suggesting Kim Turner as co-producer.

With Ted Turner, the situation was more difficult. Living in Los Angeles and in the process of moving to Chicago, Ted admits he had distinct reservations about the project and working with his former colleagues again.

"To be honest," says Ted, "I wasn't sure if I wanted to come back after fourteen years, representing my past. I had a solo career planned and I wanted to represent Ted Turner 'now', a very different person to when he left. So that was the main consideration."[26]

Once again Andy Powell was to be the catalyst. He flew to Los Angeles and after much deliberation, managed to talk Ted into participating in the project, agreeing to work with the others later in the year. Meanwhile, the existing Wishbone Ash line-up, with Andy Pyle and Jamie Crompton on board embarked on a US tour running from March through to May.

On 11 May 1987, writing and rehearsal sessions for the instrumental reunion album got underway at Martin Turner's studio, with Andy, Steve and Martin working together for the first time since 1980. There was certainly no shortage of material being put forward. Studio jamming proved fruitful, whilst ideas from Andy and Martin's respective banks of unreleased material were reworked.

"If somebody comes along and asks you to do an instrumental, it's a great opportunity to use all your excess ideas that are not always suitable for a song," says Andy Powell. Tracks from Martin Turner's Wolf Gang period – originally written with lyrics – were among the pieces reworked for the album. Says Martin: "I was very surprised to see songs that I had written interpreted with no vocals – this only worked because the music contained such strong melodies, I believe." Tapes were running throughout the initial sessions and such was the strength of the recordings that many of these tracks would find their way onto the final project.

"The ideas started to flow fast and furious with Martin and I both editing or producing each other on real collaborations of some truly melodic and rhythmically interesting ideas," continues Powell. "He would come up with guitar ideas and I would come up with bass ideas. There were great arrangements, rhythmic shifts, interesting colours – all the old tricks. It was inspired."

Recording sessions were interrupted briefly when, on 24 May, Wishbone flew out to South Africa with Nazareth to make a live appearance at the controversial Sun City complex. At that time the apartheid policy of separation of blacks and whites was still in operation and the United Nations had urged entertainers and sportsmen and women of all persuasions to boycott visiting South Africa. Several rock bands and artists had already played at Sun City and as a result had been blacklisted by the United Nations and subsequently banned from playing live in certain other countries. Wishbone Ash found themselves blacklisted for a year until they formally apologised and explained their reasons for going in the first place. Steve Upton defended Wishbone's decision to play in Sun City:

"We decided to go to South Africa based on being told that we would be playing to a 50/50 multi-racial audience. The promoters were black and the ticket prices were low. The reality was not as expected. We were due to play another show in Cape Town, straight after Sun City, but after a band meeting we decided not to continue our tour and returned to England. On our return we wrote to the United Nations expressing our regret at playing South Africa and that we had no intentions of returning under the regime that existed then. A reply from the UN thanked us for our views and our support of the anti-apartheid cause."[5]

In spite of the band's qualms as a whole, Andy Pyle looks back on the South African visit with some fondness: "We were playing in the Las Vegas of South Africa. I found a back way round to the place where we were playing. Pete Agnew of Nazareth and I found this magic place – a cafe filled with real food and real people! The first day I would be the only white man in the place, but after two or three days I was accepted as a member. This place was really throbbing. Gradually other members of Wishbone or Nazareth would join me. It ended up that after we did our last show both bands all ended up going to this place which was little more than a tin shack. We all sang and played that night with the locals. That thing that we did with the locals I recorded it on my Walkman and listening to it brings tears to my eyes."

In July, work resumed on the instrumental album, but they encountered a setback. Kim Turner, who had originally been lined up to co-produce the album with Martin, had been asked to manage a tour by former Police guitarist Andy Summers. Miles Copeland suggested William Orbit as a substitute. Although somewhat unsure as to Orbit's compatibility (he is a respected figure on the dance music scene who would later achieve enormous success collaborating with artists such as Madonna), Martin agreed to work with him after several phone conversations. Recording continued at Guerrilla and Beethoven Studios, London, with William Orbit co-producing and Ted Turner finally entering the picture. (Due to visa problems, Ted had been unable to make the initial writing and rehearsal sessions for the album.)

"If he left the States," recalls Martin Turner, "he might not have been allowed back in, which would have been disastrous for him, so he arrived very late and we really didn't get much time to work with him. Although he was involved and played on the album, it didn't feel like a band. It was the three of us, with Ted playing on top."

"It was like, I got to meet the guys after fourteen years and had to go into the studio the next day," adds Ted. "They had actually compiled all of the music, and all there was for me to do was grace it in any way I could. I came into the situation very late and, to be honest, it was detrimental to the album, because there wasn't enough time left to finish it in the true sense."[26]

Above: The return of the Turners (l-r) Martin and Ted.
Photo: Nicky Masters

Andy Powell explains why the rest of the band had continued to work on the album in Ted's absence: "Unfortunately we didn't have the luxury to be seventies dilettantes about the proceedings. We had job to do, a tight budget and a hell of an opportunity. So when Ted's problems became an issue for him, we just had to push on. Actually I don't think the album suffered too much if the truth be known."

Aside from frustrations over the lack of time available to work with Ted, there were other problems during the sessions – most notably, the working relationship between Martin Turner and William Orbit, which soured somewhat when Orbit's manager got involved and insisted on replacing much of Steve Upton's work with programmed drum patterns. Looking back, Martin has this to say about that situation:

"William did an OK job on *Nouveau Calls*. It's a good album, but it would have been much better if I'd been able to produce it with my brother and if Steve Upton had played all the drums. We would have used much more distortion and made the guitars come more to the fore which you need on an instrumental album. It would have sounded more like a rock album. To some extent it ended up sounding sterile and clinical. It should have had a lot more emotional content in it. I think William is a very talented guy who has got a lot to offer, but he certainly didn't do any favours to Wishbone Ash."

Andy Powell has his own views about William Orbit's contribution and the way the album turned out: "Yeah sure, there were the usual ego trips concerning production from Martin's perspective, but William got the job done on time and in budget which is a huge part of what it's all about. Also, I think his brand of sampling percussion parts really added to the grooves but I too feel that the guitars could have used a little bit more oomph."

Steve Upton also looks back positively at the recording sessions: "The return of the original band working together was a very poignant time," says Upton. "There we were – Ted, Martin, Andy and myself all sitting together in a studio. We all looked pretty much the same as we did fifteen years earlier – just a few more wrinkles and a little less hair. We had travelled different paths and our experiences had forged much stronger characters than when we were boys. Not just musically, but we were now men and had our own formulated ideas. It was fascinating seeing how we had all developed both as people and musicians. The latter was like putting on a well worn glove – it fitted perfectly."[5]

With the recording of the instrumental album complete, the Powell/Upton/Crompton/Pyle line-up continued to honour all outstanding live commitments. During August the band made various one-off festival appearances in Germany and Spain, and in December, Wishbone Ash became one of the first Western rock bands to perform in the Soviet Union and Lithuania.

"We toured the Soviet Union before there was a big 'hoo-ha' about it," states Andy Powell. "We were playing to 5,000 people a night and this was before the wall came down and Gorbachev and the whole thing."

The Soviet tour commenced with a series of twelve concerts in Lenningrad, performed over a ten-day period. "Many of the fans were aware of the band due to the fact that we'd been to East Germany and they had seen the press," remembers Steve Upton. "They came with photographs that friends had sent them from German or Yugoslavian magazines and wanted us to sign. The weather was twenty degrees below zero, yet the people still came to the concerts. We had to submit lyrics and records before we went, because they didn't want any sort of anarchistic lines in the songs that would help to influence their public. All the time we had five or six interpreters with us, who were extremely intelligent young people. We had discussions on ideology and what it was like in the West. They didn't really have any concept of what it was really like. The security at the concerts was handled by soldiers who also acted as the road crew."[5]

Andy Powell recalls a heavy incident during the tour: "The interpreters turned out to be Junior KGB. My brother, who was crewing for us at the time, decided that after meeting a beautiful Russian girl, he was going to stay on and I was told in no uncertain terms that things could get very rough for him if he persisted – passports could go missing, etc..."

Jamie Crompton has nothing but good memories of the visit: "Russia was fantastic. We travelled on trains across Russia and would get invited into people's homes. Andy has always been very keen to travel to different places and see other cultures so we were able to visit museums and art galleries and zoos! The kids were great there and very keen to see acts from the West. The only downside to the trip was that as it was December, the weather was bitterly cold."

Following the Lenningrad stint, Wishbone Ash travelled to Vilnius, the capital of Lithuania, for five shows over three days. "There was a different feeling from these people to the people in Lenningrad," says Steve Upton. "They were more open and warmer in their personality."[5] These would be the final shows for this particular line-up of Wishbone Ash and Andy Pyle in particular.

Nouveau Calls was released through IRS in December. The title (by Steve Upton) was a subtle pun – no-vocals! As expected, influences not heard in Wishbone Ash's music for some time – notably Andy Powell's folk-tinged guitar melodies – were clearly evident in the music, and the overall sound was a far cry from the mainstream heavy rock of the previous two albums. However, far from being a nostalgic trawl through past history, *Nouveau Calls* was a wholehearted effort to give the classic Wishbone Ash sound a new dimension. As such, the album definitely had a contemporary feel, partly thanks to Martin Turner's willingness to embrace synthesisers and sequencers, which nestled comfortably alongside Andy and Ted's trademark twin lead guitars on tracks such as "Tangible Evidence" and "Real Guitars Have Wings". Album mentor Copeland (who had provided most of the song titles) was delighted with the end result claiming, "When I commissioned this album I knew it would be great. I am proud to have this album on my label and be associated with the first group I ever managed."

It was positively received by fans and press alike, with UK magazine *Raw* enthusing: "If you ever liked Wishbone Ash, you'll find plenty to enjoy here." Several of the tracks were later used on TV soundtracks. "One of the songs was used in a review of the first week of the 1990 World Cup," recalls Ted Turner. "I remember we were all sitting out in the garden and they played the song for about three minutes, so I guess about sixty million people must have heard that. That's how powerfully music can be used, and that's one of the reasons that attracted us to doing an instrumental album."

Although *Nouveau Calls* was aimed very firmly towards the album market, a single coupling the cuts "In the Skin" and "Tangible Evidence" was released. Also, despite the fact the reformation had originally been solely for the purpose of recording *Nouveau Calls*, the four original members agreed to undertake a UK concert tour to promote its release.

"It was obvious the magic was still there," says Martin Turner. "I'd been separated from the band for quite a few years and with Wishbone Ash there was a certain kind of chemistry that existed in the band, and that carried across to everyone that worked with us. I never imagined in a million years that we'd be out gigging – the original guys in the band. There was just a very good, warm feeling surrounding the whole thing."[4]

With a full-blown reunion now on the cards, this effectively meant that the services of Andy Pyle and Jamie Crompton were no longer required. However, as Crompton admits, the reformation of the Mark I line-up made sound business as well as musical sense. "It had got to the point where we'd really done as much as we could," reflects Jamie on the band's status circa 1987. "The work was beginning to dry up and the only way the band could really continue at that point was to get the original guys together. That was the only option available to them at the time. It was strange, because I'd been in the band all that time and we'd become pretty close."

Following his departure from Wishbone Ash, Jamie Crompton quit touring, taking up a managerial position at the Gibson Guitar Centre in London's West

End, before swapping sides and working for Fender guitars in Surrey. Andy Pyle, meanwhile, joined a reformed Blodwyn Pig before being invited by Gary Moore to record and tour with his Midnight Blues Band. Pyle appeared on the million-selling *Still Got the Blues* album.

With concerts already booked, the start of 1988 saw Martin, Andy and Steve ensconced in the rehearsal studios gathering together a new live set which would combine a selection from *Nouveau Calls* with classic material from the early days. A late arrival from Chicago meant that Ted was unable to make the bulk of the live rehearsals, resulting in him only playing the second half of the set on the first leg of the tour, with Jamie Crompton augmenting the band for the first part of the show. "It was really up in the air until the last minute as to whether Ted was going to be able to do the tour at all as he had visa problems stopping him getting out of the States," recalls Jamie. "There was me, him and Andy on guitar for different parts of the set. I tended to play the newer stuff, whilst Ted concentrated on the older material. At one stage in the show we would have three guitarists on stage! It was a bit fraught, but it was fun."

The reformed band made their first public appearance at Folkestone Leas Cliffe Hall on 27 February 1988, the start of a nationwide UK tour (support act for most of the UK shows was fellow No Speak artist and long-time friend Pete Haycock, formerly of old MCA stablemates the Climax Blues Band).

"The first concert was very strange, but it was also magical," recalls Ted. "There was so much adversity for me, personally. It was very high profile for me, because I was coming on halfway through the set, but it worked out very well and you could tell from the moment I walked on that it was just a completely different feeling. I would inspire the others and they would respond and the audience reacted."[26]

The set would include "Tangible Evidence", "Real Guitars Have Wings", "Something's Happening in Room 602", "In The Skin" and "Clousseau" all off *Nouveau Calls*. These were faithfully reproduced utilising pre-recorded backing tapes to cover the album's synth colourings and sat well alongside classic material from the band's earlier years. One of the highlights of the tour came just a few nights in, when a prestigious Hammersmith Odeon concert on 4 March was recorded and broadcast by BBC Radio One. Scenes from this gig were also later used in a promo video for "In The Skin". Another highpoint from Martin and Steve's perspective was their "homecoming" gig at the English Riviera Centre in Torquay on 9 March. Glenn Turner's band Mercedes opened the show, which Martin remembers well: "Obviously I knew that my family, old girlfriends, old mates, lots of people were there," says the bassist. "My brother Glenn was playing with his band, who I'd worked with in studios, trying to get them off the ground career-wise. The whole evening was really pleasurable."[4]

The Torquay concert was also the last to feature Jamie Crompton. A two-week break in the tour schedule allowed Ted time to rehearse fully with the band, and the second leg of the tour saw him playing the entire show. The reunion shows were positively received with *Kerrang* magazine claiming, "Wishbone Ash have satisfied all criteria with this tour." Old and new fans alike welcomed the return of Martin Turner's distinctive bass and vocal work, whilst the twin leads of Powell and Turner gelled as though they'd never been apart. Ted Turner was quoted as saying, "I do think Andy and I are one of the greatest teams in rock... period. It surprised Martin when we started playing and it was all still there."[26]

Following the UK dates, the reunion tour continued with a series of dates throughout Europe (including two German arena shows as special guests of Canadian superstars Rush). Pete Haycock once again provided support and on occasions either he or his band members would jam with Wishbone during the encore – usually a new Ted Turner song entitled "Rollin".

The summer of 1988 saw the reformed band back in the studio. The instrumental album had been a positive experience for all concerned, but there were still disappointments over the lack of time Ted had been able to devote to the recording. It was clear that both Ted and Martin had ample material composed that they were keen to record – fully fledged songs that had been unsuitable for the instrumental format of *Nouveau Calls*. As such, the band agreed to work on a second, song-orientated album for IRS.

Rather than attempting to co-write on a four-way basis, the band set about listening to each other's respective compositions in search of material suitable for the album. Aside from new compositions, prospective material included songs previously written by Martin and Ted during their time away from the band.

"After coming back into the band, I had a whole bank of songs," recalls Ted. "We didn't have a lot of time for rehearsals, so we sort of laid things out on the table and reviewed what we had to work with."[7]

Recording sessions for the album commenced in July and work took place primarily at Beethoven Studios, London, although there would be further sessions at the Beat Factory and Air Studios, London before the album reached its completion on 24 October. The sessions were produced by Martin Turner, alongside co-producer/engineer Adam Fuest.

In November Andy Powell and Ted Turner were involved in an extra-curricular project, the *Night of the Guitar* tour. Assembled by Miles Copeland as a promotional vehicle for the *No Speak* series of albums, the *Night of the Guitar* featured nine guitarists, each with their own distinctive style. In addition to Powell and Turner, the tour also showcased Randy California (Spirit), Pete Haycock (Climax Blues Band), Steve Howe (Yes), Steve Hunter (Alice Cooper/Peter Gabriel), Robbie Krieger (The Doors), Alvin Lee (Ten Years After) and Leslie West (Mountain). The tour took in seven dates in principal venues throughout the UK and the three-hour show saw the musicians performing individually and in various combinations. Andy and Ted naturally performed as a double act and their allocated slot featured *Nouveau Calls* numbers "Real Guitars Have Wings" and "In The Skin", plus crowd pleaser "The King Will Come". The culminating show of the *Night of the Guitar* tour was filmed and recorded for a double vinyl album, single CD and two-part video released in the Spring of 1989, the recordings being produced by Martin Turner.

Wishbone Ash's 20th anniversary year of 1989 began with Martin Turner upgrading the *Argus* 16-track master tapes to 24-track at Air Studios, London, before taking the tapes to his home recording studio to remix the album for a future CD reissue.

"*Argus* had always bugged me," admits Martin. "It was recorded in two weeks. The vocals were put down in a day or two and basically were not very well done – I was singing flat right the way through the album. At the time we never gave it a thought – it wasn't that important – but then later, that album ended up being revered as our best work ever. For years and years I'd always thought it would be nice one day to get the tapes out and knock them into shape. I didn't actually have to sing anything – all I needed to do was put it through a pitch changer and take the vocal up just enough to sharpen it a little bit. There were a few other bits and pieces – "The King Will Come" was recorded a bit slow and I wanted to speed that up a bit, and there were a couple of guitar licks that we weren't happy with that needed fixing."

It would, however, take two years of legal wrangles before Wishbone Ash's MCA back catalogue began to appear on CD and a further four years before the re-mixes surfaced. To date the fully renovated *Argus* album has yet to see the light of day though various tracks have been incorporated in collections including the US *Time Was* compilation and the *Distillation* box set.

In May 1989 the *Night of the Guitar* toured in Europe, with a bill similar to the previous year's UK tour minus Steve Howe and Alvin Lee who were unavailable due to other commitments. Phil Manzanera, Pino Danielle and Jan Akkerman were added to the show. As Wishbone Ash approached their twentieth anniversary, US rock publication *Traffic* listed Andy Powell and Ted Turner among the top ten most important guitarists in rock history, in an article written by John Sutherland, an honour which clearly delighted the band.

"It's a pleasant change to see someone acknowledge these guys, but I do hold that view myself," says Martin Turner. "I have to say that there are publications such as *Rolling Stone* that for some reason seem to have completely omitted the fact that the band existed, so it's nice to see an article like that in print acknowledging the influence of the band. I don't think I'm blowing my own trumpet if I say that Wishbone Ash really has contributed to rock music. You can turn on the radio any moment of the day and hear a record featuring harmony guitar and Wishbone Ash was without a doubt the band that pioneered that sound."[2]

The almost total lack of recognition of the band's influence by the music press also frustrated Ted Turner. "All I can say from looking at the papers is that I feel they're lacking in the sense of providing a service for people," says Ted. "I think they could be more comprehensive, maybe widen their angle instead of specialising. It seems they're writing about obscure bands that fit with the formula they think is right, but there is a lot more going on in the music world than that."[26]

Some eight months after its completion, *Here to Hear* was released in the USA on 15 June 1989 to coincide with the original Wishbone Ash making its first live appearances in the USA since 1974. A select series of shows on the East and West Coasts were preceded by dates in Rio de Janeiro and Sao Paulo in Brazil. Many of the shows were package bills featuring other IRS acts such as Spirit, Jan Akkerman, Robbie Krieger and Leslie West. This short series of North and South American concerts concluded with a double bill in New Orleans with the Allman Brothers. "It was a great gig," recalls Steve Upton, "because it was our twentieth anniversary, but coincidentally it was also the Allmans', and the production company that booked both bands way back – it was also their twentieth anniversary. It was by public demand that the people of New Orleans had asked for the concert to take place. It was a 10,000 seater sports arena."[4]

Back in June the *Here to Hear* track "Cosmic Jazz" had been released as a single in the UK, in both 7" and 12" format. The B-side of both versions featured "T-Bone Shuffle", an Andy Powell/Martin Turner-penned instrumental outtake from the *Nouveau Calls* sessions, while the 12" featured an additional new track "Bolan's Monument". Although the sleeve states that the song was to feature on the forthcoming *Here to Hear* album, this clearly did not happen. The sleeve also credited Martin Turner as sole writer, whereas in fact the song was very much a Martin Turner/Andy Powell collaboration which evolved in an unusual fashion.

"Bolan's Monument" was a bit of a hybrid," says Martin Turner. "It was an idea that came from Andy. We'd laid down a basic backing track, but never got around to finishing it. After the album had been recorded and everyone had gone their separate ways, I received a call from IRS asking if there was anything on tape suitable for a B-side. So I went back to this idea Andy had put down and basically sang some lyrics that I'd written, which seemed to fit, and added some keyboards. Lyrically, it's a very heavy song for me. I was going through heavy stuff, divorce, loads and loads of tears. One night I was going out of my mind, I just got out of bed, got in the car and went across Barnes Common. I was heading west from Putney Bridge, along the towpath by the River Thames. It was real misty, five or six o'clock in the morning, nobody about at all. Over in this pool – the stagnant pool it says in the song – there was a heron, and it just stood there. I thought it was stuffed, dead or whatever, but sure enough it rose straight up in the air. I know this to be a sign which has occurred several times in my life when I've been at a crossroads and things are about to change. On the way back home I drove past the tree where Marc Bolan had been killed. There were always flowers and messages left there, but on this occasion I saw a sign that really hit me hard and the message written on there was, "Why did you leave us?" I thought it was a particularly powerful statement because at that time I was so mentally down and was becoming suicidal. I had two little daughters and that's what they would say if I wasn't here any more. I felt like the whole exercise that morning had turned me around. I really love the guitar on the song. I thought Andy's guitar playing was so unusual – I was trying to push him in a similar direction to his playing on "Insomnia" from the *Just Testing* album. The sound is unusual, unique even, and is something very few players would be capable of coming up with."

Incidentally the music for "Bolan's Monument" would be further developed by Andy Powell during the *Illuminations* sessions and resurface in the song, "Another Time" which made it onto that album.

Here to Hear was finally released in the UK during August of 1989. Although well received by Wishbone Ash fans, the bias towards shorter songs and a contemporary sound did attract a certain amount of criticism from the music press, one publication labelling album opener and single release "Cosmic Jazz" as "tenth rate Police".

"I'm affected by what I hear like anyone else," said Andy Powell in defence, "and if our album copped anything from the Police it's because Stewart (Copeland) used to come home from school in his short trousers when we rehearsed in Miles' basement and play along with us. Basically, the focus was more on the songs rather than just the guitar playing. We knew we could do the harmony lead thing, but we didn't want to go over old ground. It was important to do something fresh."[27]

Martin Turner adds: "The album is a product of its time and the way it sounds reflects the way everyone in the band had evolved on both a musical and personal level. For example, I was going through a heavy time personally, with the breakdown of my marriage, and many of the songs were an outflow of the intense emotions I was experiencing at that time."

"Cosmic Jazz", penned and sung by Martin Turner, sets the blueprint for the remainder of the *Here to Hear* album – concise, upbeat and melodic, containing finely-honed instrumental work, yet never at any time over indulgent. A streamlined, modern day Wishbone Ash sound which had a rightful place on the late eighties music scene. "Cosmic Jazz" was a particularly involved track for its composer, Martin Turner. "The song is like a musical exorcism," reveals Martin, "where I am requesting a mischievous spirit to leave me alone. I was in an unbelievable mess mentally, and I actually visited a Jung analyst who ended up performing a magic ceremony at my request, because I'd dreamt that's what I needed to do in order to avoid running headlong into my destruction. Musically, the band played note-for-note what I had presented to them on my home demo. I put in a lot of energy into that song, and I'd never had such an intense creative experience. "Cosmic Jazz" is loaded with psychic energy. At the time I can remember visualising a video for the song. It was really off the wall."

"Keeper of the Light", a joint composition by Ted Turner and Steve Upton marked Ted's first lead vocal on a Wishbone Ash album since "Rock 'n' Roll Widow" on *Wishbone Four* back in 1973. Upton's lyrics, according to Martin Turner were "about motherhood and inspired by his wife and her role as a mother". Ted Turner's lap steel guitar skills – again first used on *Wishbone Four* – resurfaced on the next track "Mental Radio", also featuring backing vocals from session singer Angie Giles.

"Walk on Water" had originally been written by Martin Turner in the early eighties and was originally intended for his band the Wolf Gang. According to Martin: "The version on *Here to Hear* is very similar and, although it's hard for me to think of it as a Wishbone song, the band played it really well. Lyrically, it's about someone stuck in a poverty trap."

An interesting collaboration between Ted Turner and Squeeze's Chris Difford resulted in the atmospheric "Witness To Wonder". The basic structure of the song had been worked out during sessions for *Nouveau Calls*, but was not completed. "I had written the song," says Ted, "but we felt the lyrics could be improved. Miles Copeland offered Chris Difford a go and he took the best of what I had and it finished up a beautiful song." Andy Powell adds: "The whole feel is very dreamlike. Ted played an old Burns Double Six electric 12-string guitar and I supplied the lead guitar work."

Despite Wishbone Ash being regarded as one of the ultimate "guitar" bands, Martin Turner's "Lost Cause in Paradise" demonstrated that keyboards and synthesisers could be incorporated successfully. "It was inspired by my two little daughters," reveals Martin, "who when I left my wife, I knew would be the victims of that situation."

"Why Don't We" was written by Ted Turner during his time with the World Man Band in America in the early eighties. A plea for living together in peace and using technology to solve the world's problems, the lyrics are based on the revolutionary teachings of Buckmaster Fuller, whose motto was "More with Less". As Ted explains:

"He devoted his life to the human condition and knew that if you really want to make this planet a success, this could only be achieved through technology and artefacts, not economics and politics. This work was done in the early eighties, prior to the 'green' awareness that exists today." Martin Turner adds: "I thought 'Why Don't We' was a really good song. It emerged from the album as one of the strongest in terms of live performance."[22]

The Ted Turner-penned instrumental, "In the Case", "may have appeared on *Nouveau Calls* had Ted got to England in time," Martin Turner explains, in reference to the immigration problems which resulted in Ted missing the initial writing/rehearsal sessions for the instrumental album.

The two-part mini-epic "Hole in My Heart", described by Ted as "son of 'Phoenix'" certainly has a similar structure to the perennial favourite from the band's first album. Opening with a short intro section led by Martin Turner's distinctive bass work and a short but heartfelt lyric, the track subsequently breaks into an instrumental showcase featuring all four members of the band playing to the very peak of their abilities.

Although *Here to Hear* features material predominately composed by Martin and Ted, Martin is keen to stress that, "Everyone in the band contributed to the creative process in one way or another. For example, Andy Powell played some really nice guitar solos. There is one solo he plays in 'Why Don't We', immediately after the bass solo, which I'm particularly fond of. It's just so concise and tidy."

The strength of the songwriting on *Here to Hear* is underlined by the sheer quality of the material left off the album. Two further instrumentals were recorded. The first, "Heaven Is", a haunting Martin Turner penned piece performed by the trio of Martin, Andy and Steve later turned up on Martin Turner's solo collection *Walking the Reeperbahn*. "It's pure spontaneity from everyone," says Martin. "Andy sounds particularly relaxed and this is a fine example of his great guitar playing." A further instrumental, "Duffle Shuffle", later surfaced on the 1997 German 4CD collection *Distillation*.

One further piece from the *Here to Hear* sessions remains in Martin Turner's tape archive to this day. Given the working title of "Sienna", this instrumental backing track was never completed and Martin concludes that the piece "would need a lot of work to qualify for release. There are some really nice bits in it, but it really needs a vocal. I haven't been able to come up with anything to date and it really doesn't stand as an instrumental in its unfinished state."

Another full scale UK tour began on 8 September that year at the Eastbourne Winter Gardens. The tour, which took in most principal towns, included several shows featuring IRS labelmates Spirit as special guests. The Bristol Colston Hall show on 26 September was filmed by Central Television for its *Bedrock* series. The recording would later be released on video cassette by PMI as *Wishbone Ash Live*. The UK tour was followed immediately by an extensive European tour, running until 12 November.

Chapter Ten

Had Enough Of This Strange Affair

As the final decade of the twentieth century began, touring to promote *Here to Hear* resumed in January with a short string of UK dates. March saw Wishbone Ash making their first visit to former East Germany since the reunification for an appearance at the *East Meets West* concert. Like many other visitors they all chipped away souvenir pieces of the wall. On returning from Berlin the band performed a one-off date at London's Town and Country Club, which was filmed by Thames TV and broadcast later in the year as part of a series entitled *The Concert*.

In the summer, Wishbone Ash began work on their third album for the IRS label, interrupted briefly for concert appearances at the Isle of Man TT Race event and the Heineken Big Top festival in Swansea. For the new album, the band elected to record in an informal fashion – similar to the approach adopted for the *New England* sessions some fourteen years previously. This time though, instead of using a mobile recording unit, Martin Turner installed his 24-track studio from his London home at Andy Powell's UK base – Ivy Lane Farm in Great Brickhill, Buckinghamshire. Martin takes up the story:

"Andy had a house near Milton Keynes which he would rent out. At that time it was empty so we agreed to pay him some rent, take the house and record the album. I agreed to move my whole studio out of my house in London and take it up to Milton Keynes to install there so that we could record the album."

Powell adds: "Just as it was with the recording of the *New England* album, it was my suggestion that we try to be more self-sufficient and capitalise on our own assets and abilities for this album. I'd done pretty well financially up to that point and wanted to use that good fortune for the benefit of the band. Martin had a slew of recording gear. I had the perfect location. So it made sense that we pool our resources for the recording of the next album. I think also that I was trying to get us to return to that collective band spirit – you know, 'all for one and one for all!'"

The recording process, which would not be trouble-free, took the best part of eight months – the longest period spent recording since *Just Testing*. The first setback came during the early sessions for the album when it became apparent that Steve Upton was having problems getting it together in the studio.

"That whole period was not always a happy time," recalls Martin Turner. "Steve had personal problems with his marriage breaking down and because of this his playing was so lame. I was trying to help Steve play and Ted would come to me and say, 'Martin, you're wasting your time, mate'. We had a major problem and we had to do something about it rather than just keep on bashing our heads against the wall. In the end we said, 'We'll have to get someone else in or else use a machine'. At the same time we were all trying to help Steve with his problems. It was a very strained time and in the end Steve just walked out, basically. I felt so sorry for him. He was very lonely, very down."

With the band having a tight schedule to keep and a large investment made on the whole recording process, the net result was that founder member Steve Upton ended up parting company with Wishbone Ash after twenty-one years of loyal service. Andy Powell remembers the seeds of this split emerging whilst the band were on tour in Russia a few years earlier:

"I'd been somewhat aware of Steve's impending crisis during our trip to Russia when he'd gone into an uncharacteristic fit of manic depression. His marriage was breaking down. The band and his family commitments had all become intertwined. I remember Jamie (Crompton) in particular would try and console him. 'Don't bottle it up mate,' he'd say. One day the pressure just blew and he just walked out after 20 odd years with the band, never to be seen again. I tried to make contact a few days later, but there was no response – zilch. It was very shocking and confusing and we all felt a great sense of loss – myself in particular, since in recent years Steve and I had leant on each other quite a lot, forming a pretty strong alliance. We'd weathered a lot on a business level and we'd both struggled to keep our families together during tough times and the picture to my eyes was looking pretty good."

Following his sad departure from the band, Steve moved to the Bordeaux region in the South of France, where he now manages Miles Copeland's large chateaux, largely as a result of Andy Powell's intervention: "Miles asked if I knew anyone, since I'd lived in the country. I said, 'What about Steve?' He'd always loved the land and growing things. He was a prudent manager and was in desperate need of a new start. One thing led to another and eventually it all came together for him. Miles was later to thank me personally, but I never did hear from Steve on that score."

Unfortunately, Steve is no longer directly involved in music – an extremely sad loss to the industry. To this day Steve refuses to discuss any aspect of his time with Wishbone Ash. Steve's departure was a great loss to the band – not just in terms of the music, but also the tremendous amount of work that he put in on the band's behalf behind the scenes:

"Steve was not just 'the drummer' in Wishbone Ash," elaborates Martin. "He was crucially important in terms of organisation, liasing with agents, managers, gigs and dealing with money. He was great at organising road crews, transport, hotels – you name it. He was scrupulously honest which meant that everyone got the money that they were due. Steve did a huge number of things over and above playing the drums and, when he left, a lot of that responsibility was left up in the air."

Looking back to that disturbing period in the band's history still brings personal regret to Martin, who in retrospect thinks more should have been done to keep Steve in the band:

"I do think the way in which Steve was treated by all of us, myself included (I'd been with him since the mid-sixties, way before Wishbone Ash), was not what it could have been. I felt that we really, really should have helped him through an extremely difficult period in his life, even if it meant getting in another drummer to make the album. Steve should have stayed involved with Wishbone Ash. He was a very important part of the band. He decided because he was so upset that if he couldn't play drums then he was going to pack his bags and just take off, which is what he did. It was very, very strange for the rest of us. We were just not used to Steve not being around, especially with the background stuff, like the day to day running of the band, which really suffered. I thought he was very badly treated. I regret the fact that we were not able to stay together and get through that bad patch. It was a great shame that he left the band because that really did put the mockers on it."

Andy Powell is not so sure however: "I spent a lot of time listening to Steve's problems, as did my mother. For instance I gave him a place to stay when he left his family. I had always backed him up business-wise and I think he relied on my contacts when it came to recruiting new members for the band, since he was always a bit of a musical recluse. At the end of the day though, as close as a band becomes, it proved to me that you never really know someone."

The band now had the pressing problem of finding a drummer to take Steve's place. As well as the need to complete the album, an autumn tour of the UK was already booked. As Martin Turner recalls:

"We started recording with a drum machine, which was not ideal after the William Orbit experience, but we had no drummer in mind that we could call up at that time, except for Ray Weston who I did phone. He was off working in Germany so wasn't available. Eventually somebody came up with Robbie France".

Robbie France was an experienced session drummer who had previously played with Diamond Head, UFO, One Nation and Ellis, Beggs & Howard. "I was asked to go and have an audition," recalls Robbie, "so I went and had a play and the next day Andy Powell rang to ask me to join".

With Robbie France recruited, recording for the new album got seriously underway at Ivy Lane with Martin Turner producing and engineering. Several tracks were eventually laid down before Wishbone broke off to undertake an extensive UK tour.

Andy Powell in particular was pleased with the way the new drummer fitted into the band: "In the studio, Robbie was a dream. He picked up on every nuance and I particularly loved the way he pushed everything, which was kind of the way I played. I could never get Martin, or Steve for that matter, to play accents, but with Robbie it was natural. You can particularly hear how Robbie connected on the song, 'Dream Train'. It flies!"

Robbie France made his live debut with the band in Eastbourne on 30 August and the live set featured new songs such as "Dream Train" and "Hard Times" – the latter having been tried out previously, back in 1986/87. One highlight for Robbie was when the band played at Guildford:

"The most poignant moment was backstage at Guildford when Steve Upton's family came backstage to say, 'hello'. Steve's son was very nice and said how much he enjoyed my drumming."

However, although the band's new sticksman had been accepted by the fans and had been reported by the music press as having injected new life into the band's live show, Martin Turner in particular was not entirely comfortable with France's style, which was more technically orientated than that of Steve Upton.

"Robbie was very chirpy and confident and full of himself," recalls Martin Turner. "In fact he was an extremely good drummer in a somewhat jazzy kind of way, which, being the bass player, I found quite hard work. I speak as a bass player who was always used to hearing the drummer play square. Robbie never hit the bass drum dead on four. Robbie had kind of temporarily 'joined' the band, although I don't feel he was particularly suited to Wishbone Ash. We were getting onstage and Robbie was playing the songs far too fast. Ted started getting annoyed with it and so did I – and Andy too. It was messy and inevitably we parted company."

Robbie explains his version of the events: "I thought I was in the band permanently. However, Martin and I never really gelled as a rhythm section, in his opinion. I thought we sounded great. However after the tour, I heard that Ray Weston was doing some stuff with the band. No one had told me. I heard about it through a friend – a shame really as Ted and I were great mates. Ted and I would wander up the road from Ivy Lane and spend hours chatting over a couple of pints."

Ray Weston (ironically a former pupil of Robbie France) was eventually recruited as a more permanent replacement for Steve Upton. Already a noted figure on the London studio scene, Glasgow-born Ray had previously played with artists such as Bill Wyman, Cliff Richard, Ultravox and Big Audio Dynamite as well as playing on numerous EMI sessions. He had also crossed paths with former Wishbone Ash guitarist Jamie Crompton in an earlier band called the Blue Meanies and had worked with Martin Turner on a number of studio projects during the early to mid eighties, notably the Wolf Gang sessions. Ray would eventually play on six of the album's ten tracks, with Robbie France playing on three and the drum machine being used for the other track.

"Eventually, I did get Ray up there and he did a great job," admits Martin, "especially on 'Standing in the Rain'. When you superimpose a drummer on top of an existing track, you don't get that organic interaction between musicians, but Ray did really well."

Recording for the new album continued well into the early months of 1991 and at times, when Andy and Ted were at their US homes and therefore absent from the recording process, Martin Turner would continue work on the album alone. As Martin explains, it was somewhat fitting that the album would eventually be titled *Strange Affair*.

"Because things were going on too long, Andy and Ted would have to pop backwards and forwards," recalls Martin. "I got left to do a lot of it on my own and I don't think I did the greatest job. I was stuck between playing bass, writing, singing, keyboards, producing. I just needed the other guys to be around. It really was very messy indeed. It's funny how these things get named and years later you realise that it was not a coincidence – like *Locked In*. It really was a *Strange Affair* ".

Andy explains the difficulties he faced working on an album in England and living in America: "The whole dynamic changed during the recording with different drummers and so on. I was working my butt off writing songs and acting as chief cook and bottle washer and, due to the time things were taking, I was severely neglecting my family. I was also borrowing money from the bank on the band's behalf in order to pay for the extra time we were taking on the record. It was major stress for me."

As with *Here to Hear*, compositions penned by the individual members of the band dominated *Strange Affair*. The material chosen covered a diverse range of styles but, to a certain extent, indicated that Andy, Ted and Martin were pulling in three vastly different musical directions and as a result the album lacked the consistency of *Here to Hear*, though it did contain some worthy moments. Andy Powell, who had written little of the previous album, was particularly prolific this time around and, by his own admission, was edging the band towards an overall bluesier feel, especially on the songs he'd written such as "Renegade", "Dream Train" and "Hard Times" where he took lead vocal. Ted Turner, meanwhile, contributed a real mixed bag ranging from dreamlike to all-out rock while Martin continued his use of synth textures to add colour to the music.

Strange Affair was released by IRS on 21 April 1991 and, somewhat surprisingly in view of the traumatic circumstances in which it was recorded, received favourable reviews. Staff at *Metal Hammer* magazine voted the album number two album of the month and claimed, "1991 has Wishbone Ash with a keener edge than I've heard from them for a long time". Dave Ling of *Raw* magazine held similar views: "The quartet seem to have balanced the scales perfectly, blending the dual guitars with just the right amount of contemporary feel."

The cover, a cartoon strip-like picture, was designed by Ian Harris, who had designed the *Twin Barrels Burning* cover nine years earlier.

The album opens with title track "Strange Affair" – a song written by Andy Powell and former Wishbone Ash sideman Andy Pyle with whom Powell had maintained a friendship and songwriting partnership. A straight ahead boogie number, the track boasts some fine twin lead work as well as a tasty lap steel break from Ted Turner, and would become a mainstay of the band's live set. Andy Powell, often criticised for his vocal work on albums such as *Twin Barrels Burning*, sounds particularly at ease handling lead vocals here. Co-writer Andy Pyle recalls how the song came about:

"I'd written a song called 'Strange Affair' in the days before I joined Wishbone for the first time, but it wasn't quite Wishbone Ash and I said to Andy, 'If you want to use it, then use it,' but he said he'd have to change some bits. So he changed it and made it into what it is now and we went half each. It's not as if we sat down and wrote it together. The riff part was from Andy."

Andy Powell elaborates further: "'Strange Affair' is a classic example of how a demo which sounded like a Roger Whitaker outtake could be transformed into a very credible rocker. I love this song and put a lot of energy into writing it, upgrading the lyrics and producing the music as a whole."

The melodic "Wings of Desire" – originally intended as the album title – was another Andy Powell collaboration, this time with former Wishbone Ash publicist Rod Lynton. Inspired by the Wim Wenders film of the same title, the track was written on acoustic guitars at Ivy Lane Farm. One of the true highlights of the album, the track was originally recorded with Andy on vocals, although the album version features vocals shared by Ted and Martin.

Andy Powell describes "Renegade" as having a "swamp blues" feel and was an excellent showcase for Ted's lap steel playing. "The lyric is somewhat autobiographical and the song itself was composed using an open tuning on acoustic guitar," says Powell. "Dream Train", another Andy Powell composition that had been previewed on stage during the Autumn 1990 UK tour, has a distinct shuffle feel and was recorded without Ted. "I remember recording the vocal in one of the bedrooms at the farm," says Powell. "I was very pleased with the way this came out and particularly loved the compressed rhythm guitar sound which was overlaid, using a Gibson Chet Atkins guitar."

"Some Conversation" was written by Paul Young sideman Matt Irving. A powerful ballad which would have made a perfect choice for a single, the track features Martin Turner in particularly fine voice. Ironically, Martin had been suffering from a heavy cold at the time he laid the vocal down. Ted Turner's "Say You Will" contains some beautiful yet sad guitar parts, highly reminiscent of "Alone" from the *Pilgrimage* album, yet seems to lack direction.

While much of the material on *Strange Affair* was first rate, even the most tolerant of Wishbone Ash fans could not comprehend the inclusion of Ted Turner's "Rollin'". Often performed onstage as an encore number, as an album track it comes across as nothing short of a filler. and it is rumoured that Miles Copeland was not overly impressed upon being played the finished track. In a 1993 readers poll in the band's official fan club magazine, *Hot Ash*, "Rollin'" was voted the second worst Wishbone Ash song ever, in the same league as some of the tracks off *Locked In*.

As an interesting footnote, "Rollin'", "Strange Affair" and "Dream Train" were originally recorded with a four-piece brass section who came to the sessions fresh from a tour with Gary Moore. This experiment, a throwback to Andy Powell's formative days with the Sugarband, did not meet with the approval of IRS who insisted on the brass parts being removed from the final mix. One of the brass mixes – "Dream Train" – did surface at a later date on the *Distillation* box-set. The other two remain locked away in the vaults.

"You" had been written by Martin Turner during his Wolf Gang period. Of all the compositions from Martin's bank of unreleased songs, this seemed the most unlikely choice for a Wishbone Ash project. Indeed, songs such as "Strangers" or "Broken Down House" would probably have lent themselves better to the band format than this more offbeat composition. "You" is, however, a fine song in its own right and emphasises that Martin was always keen to experiment with different styles and sounds. "You" was Martin's sole songwriting contribution to *Strange Affair*. Martin explains the lyrics behind the song:

"'You' was a very important song for me. I'd recorded it with my own band in the eighties. It was very important lyrically because it was a song I'd written about my then girlfriend, who'd gone off with Andy Summers. Later on I became involved with her once more and she ended up becoming my wife and I still live with her! It's a somewhat bitchy song in some places, but it's a song I'm very proud of, as I know there's a lot of very powerful emotional energy in it. I would describe it as one of the best songs I ever wrote."

Andy Powell's "Hard Times" had been in circulation since the Pyle/Palmer incarnation of Wishbone Ash but like "Rollin'" had not been committed to tape until *Strange Affair*. Although the track became a live favourite and would close many future concerts in much the same way as "Bad Weather Blues" had in the past, the version on *Strange Affair* fails to capture the song's live energy.

Described by Andy Powell as the album's "magnum opus", Ted Turner's "Standing in the Rain" closes *Strange Affair* in fine style. Arguably one of the true highlights of the reunion period, "Standing in the Rain" would, in 1993, be voted the most popular Wishbone Ash track of all time in the aforementioned fan club poll. The song, which emerged from an earlier song Ted had written during his time with the Choice called "Possession Obsession", was inspired by Ted's infamous immigration problems.

"Standing in the Rain" gives an indication of the problems behind the scenes that can be encountered in a rock 'n' roll band," says Andy Powell. "The song deals with a trip home to the US by Ted which was thwarted by immigration officials who didn't feel that his papers were in order. This resulted in a quick turnaround flight back to the UK to put things right and then a third transatlantic flight to finally get a night's sleep in his own bed."

One track which did not make the final running order of *Strange Affair* was the Andy Powell composition "Chimes of Freedom". Inspired by the recent fall of the Berlin Wall, the track was sung by Martin Turner. Although by no means the greatest piece of music ever recorded by Wishbone Ash, it is difficult to comprehend its exclusion when viewed alongside "Rollin'" or indeed several of the other tracks featured on the album. Martin puts the record straight:

"Chimes of Freedom" was written by Andy but he wasn't happy with the lyrics or the vocal. In fact, he wasn't really happy with the music too – so the track was never finished. It needed a lot more work doing on it and so didn't make the album." Says Powell, "Quite simply, we ran out of time in order to bring the song to completion."

Strange Affair would mark the end of the road for Wishbone and Miles Copeland for a second time in the band's career. It would also be the final album that

Blowin' Free

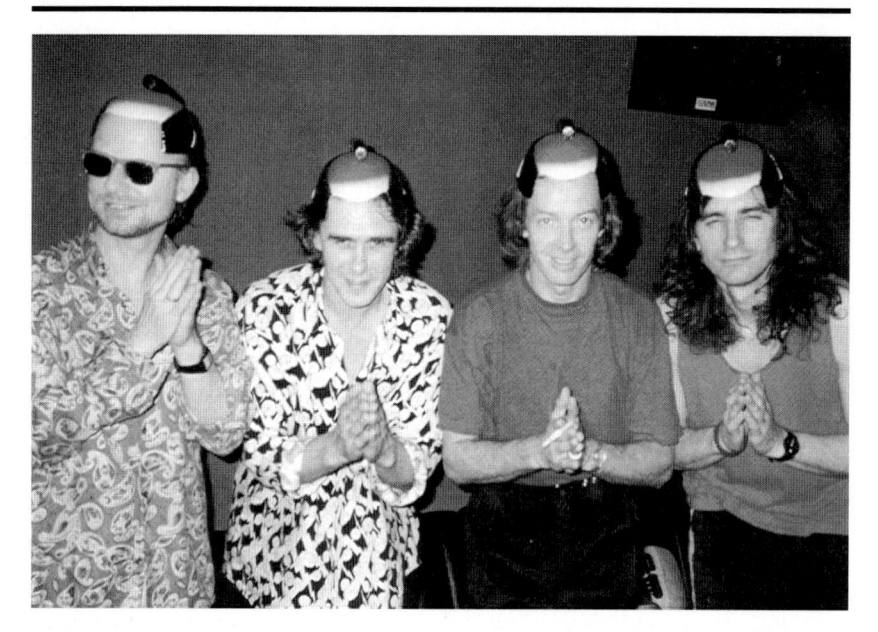

Above: Three out of four of the original line-up, Andy Powell, Martin Turner, Ted Turner and new drummer Ray Weston. *Photo: Wishbone Ash Fan Club Archives.*

IRS Records (Copeland's record label) would release. Andy Powell explains what happened:

"Miles had plans to sell the label to EMI and we were just like many of the other acts caught up in his master plan. It wasn't to do with not particularly wanting to keep us on. The whole *Night of the Guitar* concept raised the profile of the label sufficiently so that he was able to get a really good deal for it. It's always about making money, you see. Sentiment doesn't come into it. Our three album deal had run its course and had probably lost money so it was time for him to move on."

The release of *Strange Affair* was given little publicity by IRS but the band did make concert appearances in Spain, Switzerland, England, Japan and Germany throughout April and June 1991. Former bassist Andy Pyle attended the London Marquee and Milton Keynes shows and the UK leg of the tour concluded with a highly memorable concert at London's Walthamstow Assembly Hall on 16 May which saw Laurie Wisefield reunited with Wishbone Ash for the first time in over five years. History was made as Laurie played guitar alongside both Ted and Andy on "Jailbait" and his own composition "Living Proof".

"Walthamstow was really a last minute thing," remembers Laurie. "It was really out of the blue. We did 'Living Proof', but the band at the time were into this thing where they had a tape going, with a click track. It was all kind of mapped out with backing vocals or something, so everything had to be spot on. I went on playing the opening riff for ages, not realising the whole thing had to be kept in sync, but it was fun."

The day after the Walthamstow concert, Wishbone Ash departed for a tour of Japan, their first visit since 1978. In Japan they witnessed a number of changes that had occurred during their twelve-year absence from the country.

"With a band like Wishbone Ash, you are privileged to get an amazing overview of change in a first hand manner," says Andy Powell. "This is a position that very few people are fortunate to be in. I often think a few politicians could benefit from more world travel. Also, with a band, the culture directly touches you because you learn to accept foreign customs, cuisine, humour, manners, thought patterns, etc. When we first went to Japan, the country was opening up to Western music and culture in a big way. There is still this very forward looking, exciting feeling about the future there. It's not dissimilar to the way America must have been in the 1950s. The difference now is that it is tempered with a lot more experience and commercial success which the country has enjoyed. The wealth of the country is much more apparent now. In a city like Nagoya, for example, you really get a glimpse of the 21st Century with aerodynamic buildings, computerised route finder screens in cars, 24 hour facilities, etc. The mood of the people is very confident too. When we first went there audiences were very reserved and would only clap very quietly and deferentially after each song. Not so now – they are much more like Western audiences in their reactions. Another odd phenomenon we noticed was how the schoolchildren, who you see everywhere, are so much bigger in stature than their elders. We thought this must be a result of a more Western-style diet. I know the same was true of the post-war generations in England, who received a better diet than their parents who suffered through the shortages of the war years."

The Japanese tour was well documented by the local media. Part of the Kawasaki concert of 21 May was aired by local radio, and the Nagoya show of 23 May was filmed for TV broadcast. The latter would also surface on the CD *Live Timeline*, released by Receiver Records in 1997.

After three years of contractual wrangles, 1991 also saw the start of MCA's CD reissue programme of the back catalogue. This commenced with *Pilgrimage* and *Argus*, although sadly MCA did not use Martin Turner's 1989 remix of the latter.

September saw the CD release of *BBC Radio One Live In Concert*. It was a recording of a 1972 show at the BBC's Paris Theatre in London. Eagerly awaited by collectors, this release proved disappointing. The tracks were presented in the wrong order from the original concert, mono tapes were used despite stereo bootlegs of the concert already being in circulation and the release was poorly packaged – another wasted opportunity.

The following month saw further line-up changes with the band parting company with founder member Martin Turner for the second time. Following business differences with Martin, the band elected to continue with former sideman Andy Pyle filling the bass slot. Andy Powell, who by this stage was on the verge of taking over the management of the band, conveyed this group decision to Martin via a phone call on 1 October 1991 – Martin's forty-fourth birthday. Martin recalls what happened:

"I got a phone call from Andy. He rang me up on my birthday, would you believe. I picked up the phone and thought, 'How sweet. He's calling me up to wish me happy birthday!' Actually he was calling me up to tell me my services were no longer required. I think he felt that if he got someone in who wasn't going to give him as much shit as I did, it would be much better for him. That's when he got Andy Pyle in."

Andy Powell gives his version of events: "Things had simply run their course. So we called him up and told him that was what we'd decided to do. I think we all thought the reunion would just be one album. The fact that it kind of transmogrified into three albums was pushing it a little bit. Towards the end of *Strange Affair* it became apparent that it was the end of a little sequence of recording. I had decided to shoulder the debt this album had run up, since no one else was offering to. It had also been at my instigation that we try the commune approach to recording again, so I took the responsibility. It was back to survival mode and we needed to build a team again. I was totally committed to the project, but I just don't think the team spirit was there. However, I personally got an enormous amount of experience from it. For me it was trial by fire and in retrospect it gave me the strength to take Wishbone on to the millennium."

Martin Turner looks back at the problems that led to the disintegration of the reformed band:"During that period it was quite hard to make the thing work financially and we would say, 'Is it worth putting in all this effort?' I wouldn't call it resentment but I think we were all a little short-sighted. I don't think we appreciated that it was going to take time to rebuild the thing. Also, I think probably the timing wasn't right. I think maybe it would have been better to have left it for a few more years, to 1992/93 – maybe even later than that. To have put the band back together then would probably have attracted a lot more attention. It would have been a better time to do it, rather than when we were trying to do it. But I still feel that we did manage during that period to make some of the best music Wishbone Ash have ever produced."

Following his second split with Wishbone Ash, Martin Turner continued to pursue his love of studio and production work and also began reworking tracks from his archive of unreleased solo recordings with a view to a future album project. This would feature a mixture of new songs, previously unreleased tracks from the early eighties as well as several Wishbone Ash songs performed in the way they were originally written.

In spite of several line-up changes in the ranks of Wishbone Ash throughout both the eighties and nineties, Andy Powell has always remained philosophical:

"Hopefully, line-up changes can be integrated into the overall scheme of things and the players we have recruited generally have a good awareness or feel for Wishbone Ash's musical style. Some of the changes have been very easy to assimilate, whilst others take a little time getting used to that particular player's own personality."[28]

The new line-up wasted little time. Just three days after dropping founder member Martin Turner, new bassist Andy Pyle joined the band onstage in Germany for a series of festival dates. These shows were followed by a lengthy European tour throughout November and December 1991 as special guests of Ten Years After, with Man opening the show. Original intentions were for the tour's Paris concerts to be recorded for a new live album – but these plans were scrapped. The tour was not without its problems, which included the theft of Ted Turner's Paul Reed Smith guitar en-route to London. As Ted recalls: "Just an empty flight

Above: Ted Turner 1992.
Photo: Donald Duggan

case turned up at customs." Wishbone's performance at London's Town and Country Club (the first of two nights at the venue) was also marred by a behind the scenes dispute when the band overran their allocated hour-long time slot. Steve Moore, who at this time was running the band's UK fan club and handling merchandising sales on the road, recalls the incident:

"All too soon the hour passed and the band left the stage. Up went the house lights and it was all over – but was it? Ted walked back onto the stage, plugged in and started playing again. The rest of the band followed close behind and soon the encore was in full flow. About halfway through 'Jailbait', Ted turned around and came out with a most uncharacteristic remark. Obviously trouble was brewing, so I nipped backstage at the end of the number to see what was up. A lot of chest prodding and pointing was going on. Somebody had turned the band's monitors off expecting them perhaps to walk off halfway through a number. The dressing

Left: With Martin Turner's second departure Andy Pyle found himself back on bass. **Right:** Andy Powell smiles bravely. *Photos: Trevor Vanderplank.*

room was not a happy place. There were threats of recriminations and the feeling I got was the band would not turn up to play on the Sunday."

In fact, Wishbone did turn up for the second Town and Country show and as Steve Moore recollects: "An extra five minutes had been added to Wishbone's time by the stage manager, who couldn't stand any more grief."

The early months of 1992 saw the new Wishbone Ash line-up touring the midwest US states. On 24 and 25 January the band performed at Easy Street Club, Glenview, on the outskirts of Chicago for the recording of their new live album – the first official Wishbone Ash live album release since *Live Dates Volume II* back in 1980. For this occasion, the band was augmented by keyboards player Dan Gillogly, a local musician and friend of Ted Turner. *The Ash Live in Chicago*, produced by Ted Turner, Andy Powell and Fred Breitberg, was released on 6 April that year. The album was released in the UK by Permanent Records, a London based company formed by John Leonard and Dave Betteridge, formerly of the Agency group, who had been the band's concert booking agents for several years. The relationship with the label would be short lived and messy to say the least.

The live album received excellent reviews from the music press. *Record Collector* magazine claimed, "Instrumentally, Wishbone Ash have lost none of their versatility and the current line-up certainly doesn't disgrace the band's legacy." Fans, however, were divided in their thoughts on the new line-up. Most welcomed the long overdue live set but many were naturally disappointed that the album had not been recorded while the reformed original line-up had been intact. Certainly the album was not without its faults, with a particularly cloudy mix which, whilst highlighting that Powell and Turner's guitar work had lost none of its magic, did little justice to their vocal work which had been mixed extremely low. Most notable was the void left by Martin Turner's departure. Andy Pyle, by his own admission, made no attempt to reproduce the classic Wishbone Ash bass lines which had been such an integral part of the band's music: "I don't play like Martin," says Pyle. "Martin tends to play upfront, while I'm more in with the kick and rhythm."

During the spring, Wishbone Ash undertook a major UK tour, opening at Newcastle Playhouse on 10 April. For most, this tour was the first sighting of the new line-up and reactions were mixed. Many felt the departure of Martin Turner signified Ash on the decline, once again fearing an endless succession of replacements as per the mid-eighties. Former member Trevor Bolder, however, was clearly impressed by the show he attended in his home town of Hull: "I thought they were brilliant. I was very impressed – they sounded great. I didn't expect them to be that good, but from where I was standing it was just superb. I was going to get up and play with them but they were late arriving and we couldn't organise it."

For many, the fears about personnel changes were confirmed when Brad Lang (a session player who had guested on *Raw to the Bone*) stepped into the bass slot for a series of dates which Andy Pyle was unable to honour due to prior commitments with Gary Moore.

Midway through the UK tour, on 7 May, Andy Powell and Ted Turner made a personal appearance at Birmingham's Central Library, as part of the second city's "City of Music" celebrations. They held a question and answer session, as well as performing "In the Skin" and "Real Guitars Have Wings" live, against a prerecorded backing track. On 13 May, Wishbone Ash performed a live "unplugged" set for Richard Skinner's BBC show on Greater London Radio. The broadcast went out at prime listening time and Andy Powell and Ted Turner were interviewed in between semi-acoustic versions of "Strange Affair", "Throw Down the Sword" and "Wings of Desire". Brad Lang played fretless bass and the band was also augmented by former Fashion guitarist Alan Darby, an old friend of Ray Weston. Another unusual performance followed an appearance at the Sommarfestivaler in Malmo, Sweden. Due to the routing of their plane tickets, Wishbone had a day off. Andy Powell mentioned to the promoter (a lifelong Ash supporter) the possibility of staging an impromptu show. The band's hotel doubled as a venue for local bands and by 10 pm a PA was in place. Members of Nazareth, who had also appeared at the festival, joined Wishbone onstage for off-the-cuff covers of Little Feat tracks plus other standards.

In July, the band played a few dates in America including one in Little Rock, Arkansas where Andy and Ted were reunited with one of America's most famous groupies, Connie Hamzy, whose sexual exploits in the seventies had been immortalised in the song "We're An American Band" by Grand Funk Railroad. The band then returned to the UK for further live shows in August. Brad Lang again deputised on bass for Andy Pyle who was once again busy playing with Gary Moore. Alan Darby also joined the band onstage for several numbers at the Roadhouse, London on 10 and 11 August. These informal shows were notable for the inclusion of several unusual choices in the set list, such as Alan Darby's composition

"Drink the Wine", Stevie Ray Vaughan's "Cold Shot", Fleetwood Mac's "Stop Messin' Round" and the Steve Miller Band track "Mercury Blues". The mini-tour closed with an intimate show at Bobby Brown's in Nottingham, attended by former Ash member, Mervyn Spence. 1992 ended with a short tour of Sweden plus a further handful of UK shows during October and November.

Chapter Eleven

They Sure Do Hit Hard Times

After the UK/Swedish tour of October/November 1992 the members of Wishbone Ash returned to their individual bases – Andy Pyle and Ray Weston to their homes in England, while Ted Turner and Andy Powell returned to their Stateside residencies. (Powell had maintained bases on both sides of the Atlantic for several years, but in 1991 had quit the UK to take up permanent residency in Connecticut.)

In January 1993, a chance meeting between Powell and local Connecticut musician Roger Filgate, heralded the start of a highly productive songwriting partnership. Connecticut born Filgate began playing guitar at the age of ten, initially inspired by the music of the Beatles before developing a taste for the progressive rock music of bands such as Yes, Rush, ELP, Genesis and Wishbone Ash. In the early eighties, Filgate relocated to California, touring the club circuit with various bands, often appearing on the same bill as future stars such as Guns 'n' Roses. Roger also spent a year at Fender Guitars Custom Shop, building guitars and basses for celebrities, before returning to Connecticut in the early nineties, where he combined guitar teaching with work as a session player and engineer. While working at Danbury's East Coast Music Hall, a local music store, Roger was introduced to Andy Powell. Andy was looking for piano tuition for his youngest son, Lawrence, so Roger suggested his mother who was well known locally for her piano teaching skills. The two players immediately clicked as both musicians and friends. In addition to collaborating with Andy Powell, Filgate was soon enlisted as Wishbone Ash's "guitar technician" for a short burst of US dates in March covering Texas and the surrounding States. Roger explains the reality behind the title:

"After Andy and I had first met, we had been writing for a few weeks when he asked me if I'd be interested on going on a tour with them as a tech/roadie. At the time I thought it would be kind of cool to travel around and see how it all works. As it turned out I ended up being the roadie for the entire band. Basically, it was a nightmare – over worked, under paid, etc... It's a good thing that I liked the guys so much because the job itself sucked. You live and learn, but it really made me appreciate how hard a good crew works."

During the tour, the band premiered two new songs, "Love Abuse" (penned by Powell, Filgate and Weston) and "The Last Time" (a Ted Turner composition). It would be six years before "Love Abuse" would surface on a Wishbone Ash studio album.

With very little in the way of new releases from the band, MCA (USA) decided the time was right for a retrospective release of Ash material. In April of 1993 they released *Time Was – The Wishbone Ash Collection* – a 2CD set. Together with tracks from the band's MCA output recorded between 1970-81, the set featured a rare studio recording of "Where Were You Tomorrow" recorded during the *Pilgrimage* sessions as well as a version of "The Pilgrim" as featured on the promo *Live From Memphis* album. Furthermore, the *Argus* tracks featured were Martin Turner's 1989 remixes. The set was compiled with the full co-operation of Andy Powell and Ted Turner. Martin Turner, however, had no input into the compilation and was less than happy with how it had been packaged.

"I was pleased with the *Argus* re-mixes," the former bassist remarked, "although the CD artwork looked very 'cheapola' to me. The notes were inaccurate and the main photo was of the current band, who didn't play on the record. The whole thing was very sorry and sad – a missed opportunity."

In defence of the packaging, Andy Powell has this to say: "I thought that the artwork was cool and not in any way cheap! The photo on the cover was a great current shot of Ted and myself who did both play on the record. I'd initiated the deal with MCA, not Martin. I spent my time and money compiling it and it was a great opportunity for all members, past and present, and the overall concensus was that it worked really well for Wishbone on a global level."

Reaction to the *Time Was* set from fans in both America and Britain was fairly mixed. Some shared Martin Turner's frustrations, whilst others were disappointed by the almost total exclusion of Laurie Wisefield's work with the band. Only six of the album's twenty three tracks were from his period in the band. Certainly, the set failed to present a comprehensive overview of the band's MCA period, instead showing a distinct bias towards material by the original line-up. Sixteen of the tracks were taken from the band's first four albums, while the other seven MCA (US) albums were only afforded seven tracks. A little "top-heavy" to say the least. Co-compiler Andy Powell was quick to defend the album's intentions:

"MCA produced this to their specifications and would have done so with or without my input. It is intended for casual fans, not dyed in the wool addicts. Unfortunately, the Wisefield period did not sell many albums – this has nothing to do with Laurie's obvious talents and contribution."

The months of April to October saw Wishbone Ash taking a lengthy break from live work, giving the band members the opportunity to write and pursue other interests. Andy Powell, Ted Turner and Roger Filgate would sporadically assemble in Connecticut to compose new material for the next Wishbone Ash album, but some of Andy Powell's time was spent working with the Sure Thing – a seven piece New York/Connecticut based blues band complete with brass section.

The Sure Thing, formerly the Snap, was formed in 1991 by keyboard player/arranger Michael Mindel and vocalist Jon Moorehead, both veterans of the East Coast blues scene. Mindel had a day job as an insurance salesman while Moorehead was a commercial television/video producer. Mindel recalls his first meeting with Andy Powell:

"I mentioned that I had a band and he probably thought, 'Oh, great. Here's this guy in a suit trying to sell me insurance and he's got a band... right.' So I invited him to a gig in Poughkeepsie and he drove all the way out from Connecticut. After the show he came up and said, 'If ever you need a guitarist – give me a ring'. Our regular guitarist Mike Perko had moved to Texas, so I called Andy and reminded him of his offer, and it turned out he was serious."[29]

Powell, whilst stating that Wishbone Ash would remain his priority, clearly welcomed the opportunity to perform with other musicians: "I started out playing this kind of music in my late teens," says Powell. "This band keeps me from getting rusty when I'm off the road and takes me right back to my roots with the Sugarband, who also used horns. The fact that these guys are a local group didn't matter, because they're great players, driven by the love of music, not jaded like many of the pros I've worked with."[29] The Sure Thing's debut six-track demo cassette was issued as a limited edition Wishbone Ash Fan Club release.

In November 1993, Wishbone Ash regrouped for concert appearances in Canada and the USA as part of a package also featuring Uriah Heep, Blue Oyster Cult and Nazareth, under the banner *Total Recall*. Wishbone would be kicking off the show and as such would only be allowed a thirty-minute slot, playing just five songs. Also, rather than hire a tour bus, the band decided to drive the 16,000 miles themselves in a van with Andy Powell driving and Ted Turner doing the navigating. This tour would be the last time American and Canadian fans would see Wishbone Ash for several years. Apart from a couple of low-key gigs in 1997, there would be no tour of America until 1999.

A similar bill toured Germany during December under the title of *The Golden Age of Rock 'n' Roll*. On this tour Nazareth were replaced by Molly Hatchet and Girlschool, which meant that Wishbone were no longer the show openers. The closing date of this tour, in Vienna on 20 December 1993, would turn out to be the final Wishbone Ash performance to feature the line-up of Andy Powell, Ted Turner, Ray Weston and Andy Pyle, and the band's last show for fifteen months. Andy Pyle looks back on his days with "the Wishbones" as he calls them:

"When I was with them I felt I was 'one of the boys'. We had some wonderful times... I loved it. Sure I can't play like Martin but I do like the music and the chaps and we had a good time. Also the fans made me feel very welcome. They were always very nice."

However, there is one thing that still bugs Andy Pyle – namely the problems that surround the re-issuing of the *Live In Chicago* album on which he played. Since its first release in 1992, no less than fifteen different versions of the same album have surfaced. Although the precise circumstances remain unclear, the problem seems to stem from the fact that Permanent Records sold the album rights to an Italian record company who in turn re-sold them and so on, until several different record companies were releasing it under different titles – often with pictures of different Wishbone Ash line-ups that hadn't played on the record (see discography for details). Some band members feel that as a result of this they have not been paid their full royalties due.

"I went through a lot regarding *Live In Chicago*," says Andy Pyle, "not through any malice to anyone, but to see what had happened to the royalties. I know that Andy and the band didn't sign the best deal and they didn't have an easy time, but I was in a position to help Andy because I could get information as a publisher that he couldn't. My information was in the form of sales figures, and it looked as if somebody was due to pay out some money. As to who's responsibility that is, it's always passed along the chain, it's always somebody else's fault. It has to stop at the person who employed me, the person who agreed with me "Yes, you will have this percentage." It must rest there. The fact that he has had some trouble with the people above him is not my problem."

Andy Powell explains the situation: "I did my own investigation and got as much info as was available. The truth was that we'd all been the victims of a classic rip off. This happened to several other Permanent Records artists – people like John Martyn and Donovan were all victims of similar scams."

The following year (1994) should have been remembered as the year that Wishbone Ash celebrated their twenty fifth anniversary but instead it was a depressing year for the band and its fans. They say that things always happen in threes and in Wishbone Ash's case it was true to the saying.

The first piece of bad news was revealed in March, with Andy Powell announcing early in the new year that Ted Turner had handed in his notice. The official reason for Ted's (second) departure was "musical differences", although sources close to the band revealed that relations between Ted and Andy had become particularly strained during the previous tour, with much disagreement over the band's direction on a business as well as musical level. Early in 1994, Ted had moved south from his Chicago base to settle near Phoenix, Arizona with his wife Marianne, whom he had married in 1991.

"I think Ted felt he'd done as much as he could," says Andy Powell, who had co-written a number of songs for the intended new Wishbone Ash album with Ted. "I worked on material with him for over two years and it just didn't seem that he was really fired up about it. The things he was coming up with were in quite a different direction from what I thought we required for the band, and so I think there was a dissatisfaction. Ted is very much his own man – Ted does what Ted wants to do. I tend to be more of a team player. I think you've got to have that mentality for a band, but Ted was always on his own."

Since leaving Wishbone Ash, Ted Turner has continued to write and record but has maintained a low profile. Six years on from his departure, Ted has not yet released any new material or indeed revealed his future musical plans, though he did get together with Martin Turner in December 1998 to jam at Martin's London home.

thirty years of Wishbone Ash

Following Ted's departure, the new Wishbone album was starting to become more and more of a mountain to climb as each day passed, although the Powell-Filgate writing team was quietly going about its business. It was now over three years since the last studio album and there seemed little prospect to the fans of a new deal being negotiated in the foreseeable future. Also, Ted's departure meant that for the first time ever in the history of Wishbone Ash there was just one original member in band's line-up – Andy Powell. This would not help matters from a business standpoint, but Powell was in no way going to quit, determined instead to steer the good ship Wishbone Ash through the stormy seas that lay ahead.

Andy Powell explains what was going through his mind at the time: "I wasn't about to roll over and play dead. I'd been through so many situations where people would quit or get flaky. I could be that way too, but I just said, 'Fuck It! It's my life. What am I gonna do – give up on my life?'"

The second piece of bad news was that on April 8th, Wishbone's former agent and manager, John Sherry, passed away after a short battle against cancer. John had been the band's booking agent for many years, arranging their gigs from as far back as the early seventies. Taking over as manager of the band in 1977, he had been responsible for bringing the Ash back to the UK after a three-year exile in the US and over the ensuing years pushed Wishbone Ash into the enviable position of being one of the top live bands in Britain and Europe. In America he had successfully negotiated the reunion of Wishbone with their original American label, MCA. Although he jumped ship in 1983, he continued to be involved with the various ex-members of Wishbone Ash and, shortly before his death, had renewed his acquaintance with Andy and was offering advice once more. Martin Turner was also working with him at the time of his death:

"We were up at the studios that he had built on an island in the Thames working on a greatest hits album by the Flying Pickets. It was late, about 11 o'clock, and we decided to call it a day. It was just before Christmas and bitterly cold. As it was on an island we had about a fifteen-minute walk to get to the car park on the mainland. I said goodbye to John and was going to walk on ahead but felt as he was walking so slowly and didn't look very strong that I should stay with him. He told me that he had a lot of pain in his back and was talking about going to see a chiropractor. I said that he should seriously think about getting a second opinion, not knowing that at that time he had cancer. Eventually we made it to his car despite the fact that we were both shivering heavily in the cold. That was the last time that I saw him."

The third piece of bad news arrived just as the Wishbone Ash UK fan club was getting ready to make its own piece of Wishbone Ash history by organising the first ever Wishbone Ash fan club convention in Solihull. This one would shock fans everywhere and, by comparison, the uncertain musical future of Wishbone Ash seemed somewhat insignificant.

Ted Turner and his 11 year old son Christopher (fondly known as Kip to his family and friends) were walking along the pavement in the town of Scotsdale, Arizona when Kip was hit from behind by a speeding car and thrown several feet into the air. He was killed instantly. The driver of the car, a Rolls Royce, did not stop, but police later arrested 67 year old Edward Palenkas who was found to have been drinking heavily beforehand at a local restaurant. Palenkas was later tried and found guilty of the killing. He was sentenced to ten years imprisonment for reckless manslaughter and as a result of pressure from Ted and his former wife, Deborah Luck, the maximum penalty for hit and run drivers in Arizona was increased from two and a half to eight and a half years imprisonment.

On a happier note, the first ever Wishbone Ash fan convention took place on 29 May 1994 at the Saracen's Head, Solihull, near Birmingham, although even this did not run smoothly. No current members were able to attend but Martin Turner had agreed to come up from his west London home to make his first public appearance since his split with Wishbone two and a half years previously. However, just a few days before the convention, Martin's father was involved in a serious car crash and was in a critical condition in hospital. As a result Martin had no option but to miss the convention. (Martin's father sadly passed away on the morning of the convention.)

Although it looked as if no past or present member of Wishbone Ash would be present, Mervyn Spence saved the day by attending at short notice and performed three acoustic songs from his then current album, *Something Strong*, accompanied by his musical partner, Jason Fillingham, on piano. The convention also saw an early performance by Magma, an embryonic Wishbone Ash tribute band who, although only in their teens, performed a selection of Ash songs to the delight of the hundred or so fans in attendance. The convention also included rare video footage of the band as well as record and memorabilia stalls and a display of Wishbone Ash artefacts. There was also a quiz and a raffle in aid of the Kip Turner memorial fund. Most importantly, the convention gave the fans the chance to get together and there was much demand for the convention to become an annual event in the Wishbone Ash calendar.

On the other side of the Atlantic, Leon Tsilis who had left MCA and had lost contact with the band, was starting a website for Wishbone Ash. He explains how he came to set up one of Wishbone's most powerful publicity tools of the present era:

"After nearly a six year disassociation with nearly everyone in the record business, I figured it was time to make contact with some of my old friends and contacts to let them know that I was still alive and well and living in Washington DC. I had more or less kept up with what Wishbone were up to, but for the life of me could not get in contact with anyone in the band. It was through Dr John of the US fan club that I finally made contact with Andy Powell. Since my leaving the record business I had been tinkering with computers and the internet, but not the internet as we know it today. The web at that time was basically a text medium with no graphics, sound files or anything that it has evolved to today. I told Andy that Wishbone Ash was going to be one of the first bands on the Web and I went out and bought a book about HTML 1.0 and began to learn how to program to this new form of communication. Funny, I still have a copy of the original website that I wrote for the very first time and what was state-of-the-art back then now looks like someone's seven year daughter did it. I enjoyed doing the Wishbone Ash site so much that I decided to open my own internet company called Skymarshall Productions."

Further north in Connecticut, Andy Powell was injecting much of his energy into Blue Law, as the Sure Thing had by now been renamed. Blue Law recorded their debut album and also headlined a major jazz/blues festival in Ghent, Belgium. In addition, Andy performed with Connecticut musicians Jon Young and Mike Ware, recording an acoustic session for local radio. As fans patiently awaited new Wishbone Ash material, MCA licensed another superfluous compilation set, *Blowin' Free,* released through Nectar Records. This contained material recorded between 1970 and 1976 and offered nothing new.

The summer of 1994 saw a new incarnation of Wishbone Ash gradually taking shape. Andy Powell had wasted little time in finding a replacement for Ted Turner inviting Roger Filgate to join the Ash ranks. However, by this stage, drummer Ray Weston had begun lining up other projects, joining London-based band World of Leather. He would subsequently secure the drumseat in the house band for TV shows such as *Viva Cabaret* and *The Jack Dee Show*. In addition, Andy Powell made a conscious decision that the band's next studio album should attempt to recapture the magic of the early Wishbone Ash, within a modern setting. With Martin Turner's strident bass style being such a key element in the band's classic sound, Powell was keen to involve a player whose personal playing style was not dissimilar and was also capable of handling lead vocalist duties. As such, Andy Pyle's services were dispensed with – he would continue working with Gary Moore before subsequently joining the Moody/Marsden Band – and Tucson born musician Tony Kishman was drafted in.

Tony Kishman began his musical career in the early seventies, playing guitar with Cheap Trix, a covers band whose repertoire featured Top 40 material as well as a number of Wishbone Ash numbers. Tony went on to play bass, guitar and keyboards in a number of theatre shows touring the USA and Canada followed by a period in the early eighties working in England with producer Christopher Neil (later of Mike & the Mechanics fame). Tony released two singles in his own right, including "Staying With It". It was while working in England that Kishman was first introduced to Andy Powell and the pair remained in contact. Although Kishman had recently completed work on a solo album, he rose to the occasion when invited by Powell to audition for the new Wishbone Ash line-up.

"Andy asked me to come to the East Coast to audition and try some new material," remembers Kishman. "After we worked for a few days the band felt really tight and our vocals really came together. Seeing that I'd performed Wishbone Ash material in other groups, it became second nature for me to play with Wishbone."

Demo sessions for the new album got underway, with Powell, Filgate and Kishman (augmented by Connecticut based drummer Rob Hazard) laying down rough versions of new numbers "Mountainside", "Top of the World", "On Your Own", "No Joke", "Tales of the Wise" and "Love Abuse". Powell also had lengthy talks with respected US producer Elliott Scheiner, best known for his work with Bruce Hornsby and the Eagles. Scheiner expressed a keen interest in producing the new Wishbone Ash album and also put forward the suggestion of using top session man Simon Phillips as drummer. Scheiner's association with former Steely Dan member Gary Katz also promised great things for the future, as the pair planned to form a new record label, with Wishbone viewed as a potential signing.

It would be 1995 though before the fans got a chance to see and hear this new line-up of Wishbone Ash.

Andy Powell takes up the story: "It was by no means an easy feat getting all the components together for a new band and a new album. For example Roger and I wasted a few weeks on aborted recording sessions at Active Studios in the part of Manhatten known as Chelsea. This was to be the culmination of all the hard work we'd put into writing and rehearsing in various cold outbuildings and lofts in Connecticut, but unfortunately it just didn't work out soundwise. It ended up costing me a lot more money that I didn't have at the time! It was a real set-back."

1994 also saw the release of *From The Archives* – a US fan club release which collected together a series of Wishbone Ash recordings featuring the Mk.1 and Mk.2 line-ups, previously only available on bootleg albums and cassettes, in an attempt to "beat the bootleggers" at their own game. The release was promoted as being issued with the consent of the band – presumably the one which appeared on the album. Although Dr. John (president of the US fan club) had sincere motives for issuing the album, the release naturally prompted mixed reactions from fans – some were pleased to get hold of rare material, whilst others felt dissatisfied by the sound quality, which varied from excellent to relatively poor. The album and its two successors, were also less than favourably received by ex-band members. As Martin Turner states, "Dr. John is sincere, I am sure, but when the sleeve claims the product is issued with the "approval of the band", I think he must mean Andy. It strikes me that the copyright situation is very dubious and the recorded quality very poor."

1994 was to be the only year in Wishbone Ash's thirty year history when they didn't play live. In fact it would be a transitional year; a chance for Andy Powell (now the only original member) to take stock and work out a clear strategy for the future. In a special message to the readers of *Hot Ash* he stated what he had in mind for the future of Wishbone Ash:

"I want the music to carry forward and promote the best elements of the band's style. Wishbone Ash seems to be in a position to do that right now, with the present line-up, which is well schooled in this. I sometimes think the fans are more aware of what constitutes the Wishbone sound than some of the various members. To that end Tony and Roger are definitely fans, along with being two of the finest musicians I've ever had the pleasure to work with."

Chapter Twelve

I'll Return Again To Fight Another Day

When 1994 turned into 1995, UK fans were heartened to hear of dates set for March and April under the banner of the *Spring Skirmish* tour. Although the new Wishbone Ash were naturally wary of touring with no new product to promote, the idea of the tour was to break in the new line-up with some low-key dates. The venues would be a mix of clubs and small theatres. There was just one question unanswered. Who would be sitting on the drum stool? The answer came in the form of London resident Mike Sturgis, a Milwaukee born session musician who had previously performed with the likes of A-Ha, Phil Manzanera, Nina Hagen, Asia and Scott Gorham's 21 Guns. Sturgis' name had been suggested to Andy Powell by Mervyn Spence.

"I called Spam Spence and asked him if he knew any good drummers," recalls Andy. "I was thinking of maybe Cozy Powell. Spam had worked with Cozy, but he had also worked with Mike Sturgis. I called Mike, never met him, but spoke to him on the phone several times. After conversations with him and listening to his stuff with Scott Gorham's band and with Asia, I knew he could play, but when we met I just immediately clicked with the guy."

"Getting involved with Wishbone Ash happened quite unusually for me," adds Sturgis, "as it was the first time I'd been hired by a band of such stature, sight unseen. Mervyn Spence had recommended me for the drum chair and that was the extent of my audition."

With the line-up complete and dates booked, all that remained to be seen was what the reaction to the new incarnation of Wishbone Ash would be. Some were shocked to see that the quintessential English band had now become three-quarters American, whilst others saw the new-line up as merely a backing band for Andy Powell, the sole surviving original member. The rest were quietly reserving judgement. With the first date in Rotherham on 30 March at the Classic Rock Society's headquarters in England, many of these prejudices and fears soon evaporated. Roger Filgate showed that he was an excellent replacement, an experienced guitarist good enough to follow in the footsteps of Ted Turner and Laurie Wisefield, albeit a little nervously at first. Tony Kishman on the other hand was a natural – an out-and-out extrovert who could even sing and play such testing pieces as "Vas Dis", a scat song from the band's second album, *Pilgrimage*, which had not been performed since 1973. Mike Sturgis was also complimented on his playing and would be described by Andy Powell as the band's "best tub thumper to date". Fans were also pleased to see the now jaded set of the early nineties supplanted by rarely heard oldies such as "Sometime World" and "Runaway".

A selection of numbers from the promised new album also made their way into the live set. The likes of "Mountainside" and "Tales of the Wise" were epics in the classic Wishbone Ash style, whilst the more commercial "Top Of The World" was more in the AOR bracket and was certainly "radio-friendly". It was a song that split the English fans who attended the shows: some thought that Wishbone had finally sold out to the Americans, while others thought it was a daring but justifiable move especially if Wishbone were to attract airplay, particularly in the States.

After the UK dates the band flew over to Switzerland to record a special show in Geneva for a French satellite TV company, France Super Vision, the idea being that the show would later be released on video for sale to the general public. Although the show was later broadcast on French Satellite TV and the audio of the show would surface as the *Live in Geneva* CD, the proposed video never materialised. Overall, Andy Powell regarded the Spring tour an overwhelming success.

"I was mightily relieved that all the elements fell into place," admitted Sergeant Powell (as Mike Sturgis had dubbed the bandleader during tour rehearsals). "The new band worked their butts off to prepare for these few shows and, after all this preparation, things could have fallen short had we not had the support of the fans, which of course we did in abundance."

Wishbone Ash travelled to Europe for a short series of dates during May 1995, returning to play their first UK festival appearance for some years at the *Rock at the 'Quinns* event in Port Talbot, Wales. They then moved on to Germany for three shows also spending several days in the studio re-mixing audio tapes of the Geneva show for a future live album release.

Writing continued throughout the summer, although recording was put on ice as Wishbone waited patiently for Elliott Scheiner to find a suitable break in his hectic schedule to produce the new album. Meanwhile, a twenty-fifth anniversary tour of the UK and Europe had been booked for the tail end of the year. As the months rolled by, it became clear that, once again, there would be no new album to coincide with the tour.

Recording schedules aside, things appeared to be going well for the new line-up until just prior to the band flying to the UK, when new bassist/vocalist Tony Kishman informed Andy Powell that he would be unable to undertake the tour. Ill health was the "official" reason given, though Tony has since admitted that the real

Above: Tony Kishman. *Photo: Gary Carter*

reason was that he had "other gigs booked across the USA with his other band". (Kishman had been contracted to the sixties tribute show *Twist and Shout*, prior to his involvement with Wishbone Ash.) Faced with the grim prospect of cancelling the entire tour, Powell mulled over various options, such as using Blue Law bassist Al Payson. Mike Sturgis also put forward Asia's John Payne as a possible replacement for Tony Kishman.

Andy Powell explains the background to Tony Kishman's non-appearance for the Autumn tour: "Touring was always an issue with Tony since he had so many fingers in so many pies. His Beatles show, to which he owned the rights, was a big earner for him. He had a complicated life style. Also he was just starting a family with his wife. We've all been there – it ain't no easy road. For my part, it was a nightmare having to juggle all these balls in the air."

Coincidentally, just days before Kishman pulled out of the tour, Andy Powell had begun communicating with Martin Turner for the first time since the acrimonious split four years earlier with a view to collaborating on ideas for a planned 4-CD Wishbone Ash box-set. Andy Powell, knew that the fans would appreciate seeing Martin again. With Tony Kishman's role being such a vital part of the new line-up, Powell accepted that, in reality, there was possibly only one person able to fill the bass/vocal slot at such short notice. So he therefore invited Martin to join the band for the *25 Years* tour.

"Basically," recalls Martin, "Andy called me up and said that Tony had pulled out and that I was the only person who could step in at such short notice – so I said, 'No, I'm busy!' We spoke again and Andy said that he was faced with blowing out the entire tour. There are so many people who get involved in a tour and to just cancel is bad news, so I said to Andy, 'Send me a list of dates and I'll see if there's any possible way I can work it'."

Above: Martin Turner and Roger Filgate, Leicester 1995. *Photo: Alan Pye*

Despite being midway through mixing his debut solo album *Walking the Reeperbahn* and with various other projects lined up, Martin eventually agreed to tour. A demo tape of new material was promptly shipped to Martin from the States, the contents of which met with his instant approval.

"One of the reasons I was happy to be back working with Andy was the new material," says Turner. "I can't tell you how many tapes of Wishbone Ash demos I've heard over the years, but I've never been quite as impressed by the songs as I have with this one. I thought they sounded really nice."

Martin Turner was reunited with Wishbone Ash on 25 October for an intensive week of rehearsals. Selecting a suitable set list for the tour would not be easy. Martin was naturally keen to perform many of his contributions to the band's legacy, particularly IRS era material such as "Cosmic Jazz" and "Lost Cause in Paradise", but these choices eventually fell by the wayside and the set for the tour was similar to that performed in the spring with a few additions such as the reintroduction of "Real Guitars Have Wings" as set opener and an acoustic interlude featuring "Leaf and Stream", new number "Another Time" together with "Living Proof".

"I went with songs that would grab the audience in a live context," says Powell. "People wanted to hear Martin sing 'Living Proof'. They wanted to rock 'n' roll."

On the afternoon of the opening date of the *25 Years* tour (3 November), Wishbone Ash recorded the band's first UK TV broadcast for several years – a slot for Satellite TV station VH1's *Take it to the Bridge* show. Tommy Vance interviewed Martin and Andy about the band's lengthy career and the band performed an acoustic medley of "Leaf and Stream" and "Another Time".

Most surprising of all was the tone in which Martin and Andy spoke during the Tommy Vance interview about the current Wishbone Ash line-up and their forthcoming plans, not mentioning Martin's "guest" status thereby giving the impression he was very much part of the band once more. Did this signify that Tony Kishman was now out of the picture?

"I really wasn't too sure what the future held at that point," says Powell. "The only thing I knew for sure was that after the tour I was absolutely determined to produce a really good Wishbone Ash album, with whoever was best able to deliver the goods – on time and in budget. That was quite simply the criteria."

The *25 Years* tour got underway at the Bottom Line in Shepherd's Bush, London. Considering the lack of time the band had to rehearse with Martin, it was a pretty tight set. There were one or two rough edges, but these were soon ironed out as the tour progressed. Certainly by mid-tour, fans were witnessing Wishbone Ash at their very best and Martin Turner was clearly delighted to be back in the fold – on a temporary basis or otherwise.

During the period 26 November to 2 December the tour broke off briefly and initial recording sessions for the new album got underway at Element Studios, Kingston upon Thames with engineer John Etchels, veteran of Queen and Elton John albums. (The previous plans to work with Elliott Scheiner had come to nothing, since he was now virtually under contract to the Eagles and Fleetwood Mac who were both enjoying an extraordinary run of success with their respective reunions.) The studio, situated by the River Thames, had been built by former Wishbone Ash manager John Sherry and following his death had been taken over by his son, Jody. The basic backing tracks for five numbers were recorded at Element and Martin's involvement in the sessions again sparked rumours that he was back to stay.

The *25 Years* tour resumed on 3 December at Leicester University, the evening's concert being part of the second annual Wishbone Ash fan convention. *Ash-Con '95* was an altogether grander affair than its 1994 predecessor. Following an afternoon of archive video screenings, audio rarities, stalls and a performance by German tribute band Hot Ash, all four members of Wishbone Ash made personal appearances and spent considerable time talking to fans, signing autographs, answering questions, etc. The main question on everyone's lips was whether or not Martin was staying. Martin diplomatically replied, "Hopefully," not committing himself, but publicly stating his keenness to be involved in any future projects, something he would confirm several weeks later in a candid interview for the band's official fan club magazine. All in all the convention was a memorable occasion for both the band and fans – many citing the evening's performance as the finest of the entire tour.

The *25 Years* tour drew to a close with two live concerts plus a TV show in Warsaw, Poland. "The last time we'd been to Poland was 1984," recalls Andy Powell, "but people certainly remembered the show and made us feel very welcome. Poland was not without its problems for us, with a ten-hour drive through a snow storm to name one, but everyone in the band had a great time. I think the vodka may have had something to do with it."

In December the *Live at the BBC* CD was released through Band of Joy. A compilation of several BBC sessions covering the years 1971, 1972 and 1977, this must surely rank as one of the most poorly conceived collections bearing the Wishbone Ash name. Eagerly awaited by fans, the album was a grave disappointment with a short running time and sub-bootleg sound quality on some tracks. The album was aimed very much at the collector yet boasted a predictable "greatest hits" style track list, which ignored the band's most worthy BBC recordings and, in reality, was geared more towards the casual listener.

In March of 1996 another live Wishbone album saw the light of day. This was the *Live in Geneva* album, on Hengest Records, the label of Martin Looby, the band's booking agent since 1992. The album (which incidentally was the first Wishbone Ash release to be recorded using 48-track digital equipment) had been taped during the previous year's spring tour and featured the Powell/Filgate/Kishman/Sturgis line-up. Similar in running order to the previous *Live in Chicago* collection, *Geneva* saw the band performing with a much keener edge. However, when comparing the live album to the TV broadcast of the same show, it was blatantly obvious that much studio overdubbing had taken place.

May saw Andy Powell taking a break from Wishbone Ash and touring the UK with Blue Law to coincide with the release of the band's debut album *Gonna Getcha* through Hengest Records (UK) and Griffin (US). The UK tour was probably an over-ambitious move as the band were totally unknown in the UK and their brand of brassy R&B would clearly be of very limited interest. Not surprisingly the shows were poorly attended. At some gigs there were as few as twenty people present (the majority of those being Wishbone Ash fan club members). Those who did attend enjoyed a fine set by a band of extremely talented musicians who played their hearts out regardless. With hindsight, the tour could be described as a well-intentioned, but misguided exercise due to the inexpert booking of the band's agent. Blue Law would have probably fared better had they toured the dedicated blues club circuit rather than relying totally on Andy Powell's rock following for support.

In June, Wishbone Ash flew to Eastern Europe to make a one-off festival appearance in Yugoslavia. Once again, Martin Turner held down bass and vocal duties. As for the Wishbone Ash album in progress, the project had once again come to a halt. Armed with a selection of unfinished backing tracks from the Element sessions, Andy Powell and Roger Filgate were keen to resume recording as soon as possible. However, although several record labels had expressed an interest in releasing the album, none of these were prepared to provide funding for the recording.

"Roger and I realised that we were banging our heads against a brick wall by sending our demo tapes around to labels and getting no response," says Andy Powell. "We decided to go it alone and finance the $50,000 required to make the record by ourselves. I was already working with Leon Tsilis in setting up a website for the band. He and I decided to put word out through the internet that we were looking for investors for the project. To our amazement, various friends started to respond to our business plan, based on a 15% return. Before long we had a consortium of people all rooting for us."

In the summer of 1996 work on the new album resumed at Studio Unicorn in Powell's home town of Redding, with himself and Roger Filgate producing the sessions alongside resident Unicorn engineer and owner Paul Avgerinos. Meanwhile, with a lengthy UK and European tour booked to commence on 31 October, the issue of band's line-up once again flared up. Andy Powell had announced that he planned for both Martin Turner and Tony Kishman to be involved in the album and tour in some way. The reality however, proved to be different from Powell's predictions as, although both Turner and Kishman had signed up for different sections of the tour, Martin Turner, who was due to perform the vast majority of the upcoming concert dates, was not invited to rejoin the band in the studio. Work continued with Tony Kishman on vocals and Roger Filgate providing all bass parts. Andy Powell explains the reason for Martin Turner's exclusion from the recording project:

"We'd started recording at John Sherry's studio during the 1995 tour and had invited Martin to participate with vocal/bass duties, together with coming up with some extra songs. This didn't really work out, since he'd exhausted most of his song material for *Walking the Reeperbahn* and felt a little constricted having to play bass lines which we'd already written. The reason Roger played bass was due to the fact that he'd largely compiled all the bass lines in the process of compiling the demo tapes and because we didn't want to waste any more time or other people's money waiting for either Martin or Tony to come up with the goods in that area. To have the luxury of deciding between different singers or bassists just wasn't even an issue."

Martin Turner explains his version of events: "I offered Andy and Roger the opportunity to record at my studio for a mere fraction of what they eventually spent on studio time in the States," says Martin. "The album may not have ended up sounding quite as posh, but it would have had an energy that, I feel, the album lacked. In my mind the amount of money they eventually spent on recording that album was crazy – you just don't spend that kind of money on an album unless you're prepared to spend the same amount of money again on promoting it. I thought the songs that Andy and Roger had written sounded great and would like to have taken the best of what they had and put my stamp on it, where I felt it could add something to the music. After the sessions at John Sherry's studio, I'd offered to take the multi-track tapes back to my studio and work on the bass parts, which I could have recorded for free, but Andy and Roger insisted on taking the tapes back to the States. Roger is actually a very good bass player and did a decent job on recording the bass parts but it does have a tendency to sound like what it is – a guitarist playing bass."

Andy Powell has this to say in response to Martin's criticisms: "To have taken Martin's option would have meant handing over two years of blood, sweat and tears to Martin who had no real involvement in, or emotional and financial commitment to, the project. The outcome of that course of action would have by no means been certain. It made no sense at all, other than for sentimental reasons. We decided to trust our instincts which ultimately served us well."

The split of touring duties between Martin Turner and Tony Kishman far from keeping all parties satisfied, only promoted further controversy. Some felt that Kishman was the key to future success. Others questioned his commitment to Wishbone Ash, feeling his priorities lay elsewhere. Certainly Kishman had no shortage of other engagements.

Illuminations, as the long awaited new album was titled, finally hit the UK racks on 27 October 1996 released by the small independent label HTD Records. Those who had personally invested thousands of dollars or pounds to help finance the project had their names printed in a special insert included with the initial pressing of the CD. Release in other territories followed soon after.

Andy Powell explains: "The idea of self-financing came to me after hearing of a similar situation with an American solo singer who had outlined her experiences while being interviewed on public radio in the States. I am eternally grateful for those people for getting into the spirit of the thing and for making this album a reality. It could have been risky for them, but they gave a big vote of confidence with their investments."

Although many were naturally disappointed by the non-involvement of Martin Turner, particularly in view of the commitment he'd made to both the previous and forthcoming tours, *Illuminations* was met with a highly favourable press reaction. It certainly marked a departure from the three contemporary-sounding IRS albums, with a conscious return to the band's earlier style and sound. Musically the album could be split into two distinct halves. One half was a return to the classic Ash of old, while the other had a distinct commercial flavour, with songs that sounded suitable for American radio.

Some sceptics felt that much of the album sounded somewhat contrived and appeared to be little more than an identikit pastiche of earlier achievements. In retrospect, the album was maybe not quite the "*Argus* for the nineties" which Andy Powell had promised in press interviews, yet on the other hand, it was far from an artistic failure.

Album opener "Mountainside" sets the tone for much of the album, the emphasis being on tight vocal harmonies, catchy hooklines and twin lead guitar lines aplenty.

"I think 'Mountainside' really shows what this band is about – power and melody," says Andy Powell. "The music came together during a jam session in an old carriage house in Norwalk, Connecticut. Roger and I simultaneously hit on the monster opening riff, which we couldn't stop playing all night. A couple of days later, I got to thinking about Steve Upton and wondering what he was up to and the lyric came to me in one go while I was doing some farm work. It's about an event that happened on the road in Wales a long time ago. Steve had tried unsuccessfully to reunite with his estranged father and was understandably pretty brought down by it. Coincidentally, my father had recently passed away and so that event was very much in my mind. I live on the side of a small mountain and would spend a lot of time meditating on losing my dad; coming to terms with my grief."

"On Your Own", with a similar shuffle feel to "Blowin' Free", was originally written during Ted Turner's final days with the band and features some searing slide guitar.

"Roger and I introduced the groove to Ted, during a visit he made to us in Connecticut," recalls Andy Powell. "He was inspired to try some slide parts and Ted and I put the lyric together. Originally the chorus was, 'You got me hanging by my fingernails'. The lyrical concept is all about being responsible for one's own actions, hence the chorus changed to 'On Your Own', which later seemed pretty apt considering Ted bailed out of the recording project."

"Top of the World" has a more commercial feel, retaining the essential hallmarks of the classic Wishbone Ash sound with some excellent twin guitar breaks and some fine three-part vocal harmonies. The chorus gave it its "radio friendly" sound.

"This is largely a Roger Filgate song," says Andy Powell. "I collaborated on lyrics and guitar parts. The sentiment comes from a situation a lot of people can relate to, where one's partner takes off in a new career or life leaving an embittered mate behind."

"No Joke" has a distinct funk-rock feel and this, combined with its Andy Powell vocals, invites comparison to the *Number the Brave* album. There is even a mention of 'Blowin' Free' in the lyric. "Tales of the Wise" is undoubtedly the traditional Wishbone epic, which Andy Powell admitted was inspired by the earlier "Sometime World". Certainly the song is similar in structure, with its jazzy middle section and strident lead bass line. It also reflects the influence of Yes guitarist Steve Howe heard in Roger's brilliant solo.

"Roger presented me with a demo of this one, pretty much in the form it went down on album," remembers Powell. "I put the melody and words together. It's a song about parental responsibility."

"Another Time" was based on the same Andy Powell theme around which Martin Turner had written "Bolan's Monument". "I'd always had something different in mind," admits Powell, "so I decided to revamp it along the lines of my original concept, making it more guitar orientated, giving the song more of a rock feel. Roger does some stellar nylon guitar work in the verse and I put down the strange over-compressed solo after the middle eight vocal section."

Perhaps the album's heaviest endeavour is "Comfort Zone", with its riff sound similar in style to *Twin Barrels Burning*. "Lyrically it follows on from the last verse of 'On Your Own'," says Powell. "The title came whilst trying to figure out the heating system in an American hotel room. They have the setting 'Comfort Zone', where the temperature is most relaxing. Musicians are often notoriously bad at holding down relationships because they get itchy feet when life and relationships get too cosy. It's about making sure that you keep that sense of dynamics, about not staying in that comfort zone where apathy sets in. It's about keeping your edge."

"(Once in a) Thousand Years" proved that the band were not only borrowing from their own back catalogue, but also absorbing influences from elsewhere. This particular track boasts a distinct Beatles influence to the bridge section and some definite Yes-isms throughout.

"The title came from a phrase I heard while listening to a radio programme," recalls Andy Powell. "The song celebrates the turn of the Millennium and has a very optimistic 'up' vibe."

Arguably one of the album's true highlights, "The Ring" is largely an acoustic song with a folky melody and historic "*Argus*-esque" lyrics.

"'The Ring' harks back to an earlier set of influences in Wishbone's career," says Powell. "The song was inspired, as others have, by folklore. I was reading a book on legends from the history of Scottish clans and put the words to a piece of music I had in mind. Roger collaborated on the choruses and part of the middle section, and Tony did a really nice job of interpreting the lyric."

"Mystery Man" is less successful. A Roger Filgate sole composition, the song has a blues-rock feel with a generous helping of slide guitar, but is musically one of the weakest tracks on the album.

"The song explores the outsider in society," says Powell. "There are a lot of guys in the USA who were promised a lot by their government and later felt let down and even betrayed. Some ex-Vietnam vets and assorted other fringe groups that we've read about can be found living in the backwoods, harbouring deep feelings of resentment. They are the 'mystery men'."

"Wait Out the Storm" is a slice of mainstream American rock, hardly recognisable as being Wishbone Ash. Indeed the only point of real merit is the reggae-like middle section which, ironically, was added by Andy Pyle who was still involved when the song was written.

"'Wait Out the Storm' is basically a song about keeping the faith – kind of what this album is all about," says Powell. "The mandolin makes a brief appearance and this must be one of the few Ash songs without a guitar solo. I think it harks back to 'Time Was' and other power-chord dominated songs of the past."

The instrumental number "Crack of Dawn" (formerly known as "Ship of Dreams" when released in its original form on an exclusive fan club cassette back in 1995) closes *Illuminations* in classic style, having added twin electric guitars layered over the chorus section and echoes of "Alone" in its feel.

Long time Wishbone fan Colin Harper, writing in *Mojo*, had this to say about *Illuminations*. "This is an hour's worth of brand new Ash that positively pirouettes along the tightrope of balancing analogue power... This is the one where the present meets the past and remembers the hook lines and the amp settings."

Those who had been disappointed by Martin Turner's absence from the *Illuminations* recording sessions were comforted somewhat by the almost simultaneous release of *Walking The Reeperbahn*, the bassist's long-overdue debut solo album. Naturally comparisons to *Illuminations* were made, which was somewhat unfair on both Martin and Wishbone since the two projects were of a vastly different nature. Whereas *Illuminations* was a new album in the truest form, *Walking The Reeperbahn* delved deep into Martin's personal archive of unreleased recordings and featured material spanning a fifteen year period – even though most of the music was "new" to listeners. The album covered demo recordings made during the early eighties; material from the shelved Wolf Gang tapes, original versions of songs later reworked for Wishbone during the reunion era, and brand new compositions recorded with brother Glenn during 1996. The album proved to be a mixed bag, highlighting the many facets of Martin's talent. Many of the songs were far removed from the Wishbone Ash style, whilst others had the band's hallmark stamped firmly on them. Many of the lyrics were, as expected, of a highly personal nature.

"For me personally, writing lyrics, it can only be about direct experiences, things that happened in my life," admits Martin. "When I write those things, I'm totally naked, on the line. It's not something that is contrived, although there are people

Above: Martin Turner in his home studio, March 1996. *Photo: Ewa Goodman*

who are extremely successful that seem to be able to put together songs very easily which are somewhat contrived. I'm not claiming either way is better, but for me, there is a certain amount of purity involved, which I regard as a gift in my case, disregarding how commercially successful something is."[5]

The *Illuminations* UK/European tour kicked off at a packed Leeds Irish Centre on 31 October with Martin Turner once again joining the band on the road. The lengthy trek, which took in dates in Germany and Poland before winding up with a final UK date at the Brook, Southampton on 16 December, provided the opportunity to perform several songs which had been overlooked on recent tours, such as "Warrior", "Errors Of My Way" and "Front Page News". Naturally a fair proportion of *Illuminations* made its way into the set. But it was only when Kishman himself arrived for four performances mid-tour that the band were able to do the new songs justice.

One of the highlights of the UK leg was the third annual Wishbone Ash fan club convention, held at Mansfield Leisure Centre on 17 November – thanks to the efforts of Andy Yates and his dedicated team at *Sound Barrier* who co-organised the event. The format was largely the same as the previous year's event, the convention being followed by a full-length evening concert performance by the band. UK tribute band Magma (who had debuted at the 1994 convention and by this time had blossomed into a highly polished act) opened the proceedings, followed by the usual afternoon feast of video screenings. Wishbone Ash once again made personal appearances, this time with a new twist – Andy Powell and Roger Filgate performing a short acoustic set featuring "Crack of Dawn" from *Illuminations*, "East Coast Boogie" from the acoustic fan club cassette and "A Rose is a Rose" from *Nouveau Calls*. There then followed a communal question and answer session. Most original question? "Martin, is that the same piece of gum you've been chewing all tour?"

1997 began with yet more Wishbone Ash CD releases. *Live Timeline*, released in the UK by Receiver Records, featured extracts from a 1991 concert recorded in Nagoya for Japanese TV. Hardly the most creditable recording from the reunion period, this one is really for completists only. In addition to the concert tracks, several tracks from early seventies BBC sessions were added. All in all, an extremely suspicious looking package containing no indication on the sleeve as to where and when the set was recorded. Only a set of Andy Powell sleeve notes gave the release any "official" seal of approval. Several months later, part of the Nagoya show surfaced on another CD entitled *Archive Series*, this one released by Rialto Records. Again, the disc was padded out with BBC cuts, most of them from the Mark I line-up, although differing in selection to the Receiver release. To add to the confusion a photo of the Mark II line-up taken from the *New England* photo shoot sessions in 1976 appeared on the cover.

Touring to promote *Illuminations* resumed in May with a further batch of European shows. By now, Martin Turner appeared to be out of the frame for good and it was Tony Kishman who was retained to enable the band to "perform a more varied selection from *Illuminations*" to quote Andy Powell. Ironically, the set eventually chosen for these dates largely reverted to the Spring 1995 playlist.

August saw the release of yet another US CD compilation of classic Wishbone Ash material, *The Best of Wishbone Ash*. The time-honoured marketing ploy of including previously unreleased tracks to tempt ardent fans was employed, the album featuring a live take of "Lorelei" recorded in Liverpool in 1976 plus a new acoustic rendition of "Blowin' Free" recorded by Andy Powell, Roger Filgate, Tony Kishman and Andy's son AJ Powell on drums. Many fans, however, thought the purchase price was worth it for that track alone. (MCA UK would later issue this set to the home market in February 1998.)

In direct contrast to somewhat superfluous releases such as *The Best of Wishbone Ash, Live Timeline* and *Archive Series*, the release of *Distillation*, through Germany's Repertoire Records, in September 1997 was met with an extremely enthusiastic response. This was a lavishly packaged 4 CD boxed-set with all the tracks re-mastered by Martin Turner. Ideas for a definitive Wishbone Ash boxed set had been floating around for several years. The band had initially attempted to persuade their former record label MCA to pursue the idea, but to no avail. Andy Powell takes up the story:

"An old friend of ours, Stuart Watson, was at the helm at MCA London for a major part of our career," says the guitarist. "In his new role as an independent deal maker, he and I threw back and forth the idea of MCA doing a boxed set. Unfortunately, it proved difficult to get any one person within the company to commit to the idea and make it their 'baby'. To our minds, Wishbone Ash was an ideal candidate for a boxed set, with a career spanning 25 years, and yet in talking to MCA, they were not prepared to take the gamble. Finally, Stuart located Repertoire Records, a German label specialising in back catalogue releases. I met the president, Thomas Neelson, several times and was greatly pleased to find that I was talking to a man with a deep knowledge of music rooted in the seventies. It was apparent that Thomas was a person committed to following the same ideals as ourselves, namely allowing the artists to have a major input in their release."

Thomas Neelson and Andy Powell began to assemble a rough tracklist, which was subsequently opened up to various Wishbone Ash archivists for their suggestions. The idea was to present a definitive career retrospective, presenting music from all periods of the band's history and taking in its many musical facets, yet at the same time providing a selection of previously unreleased recordings. It was with the latter in mind that Martin Turner was initially asked for his involvement, since Turner had in his possession the largest collection of Wishbone Ash multi-tracks. In September 1996, Martin began wading through numerous boxes of live and studio tapes to select material for inclusion.

"It's always very difficult for artists to carry out this job of going over old ground," recalls Andy Powell. "So at this point Gary Carter stepped in and offered his assistance and ears. Each week Gary would fax me an update of what had been recovered and gradually the choices were honed down."

Quality control was kept in mind at all times and the fact that a particular recording was rare or of collectors interest did not automatically justify its inclusion on the album, which had to represent the definitive Wishbone Ash. For example, the outtakes of the original *Live Dates* album sessions were reviewed, but considered by Martin to be unsatisfactory. The live recordings eventually chosen for the album came largely from outtakes of shows originally taped for the *Live Dates Volume II* album. These songs, which had not been previously released in a live format, included "Outward Bound", "Rest in Peace" and "Insomnia", as well as rare Mark II renditions of classics such as "Sometime World", "Errors of my Way" and even "Lookin' For A Reason" – a Martin Turner song which had never even made the recording studio, but had been performed live shortly before the bassist's first split with the band in 1980.

On the studio front, Wishbone Ash had never been a band to record an excessive amount of surplus material for each album, but there existed on tape a handful of songs which, for various reasons, had not seen the light of day. However, early eighties recordings such as "Hard on You", "Cat and Dog Fight", and "Going for Gold" were clearly not up to scratch and it was not difficult to see why they had previously been consigned to the vaults. Other songs were rejected on different grounds. "Chimes of Freedom" from the *Strange Affair* sessions was considered unfinished, as was the instrumental "Sienna" from the *Here To Hear* outtakes. "Heaven Is", another *Here To Hear* outtake, was favoured by Martin but was considered to sound "more along the lines of solo Martin Turner" by Andy.

However, other sources proved more fruitful, particularly the *No Smoke Without Fire* sessions, from which the Martin Turner mini-epic "Time and Space" was taken. The *Here to Hear* recordings also spawned a superb instrumental entitled "Duffle Shuffle". Perhaps the biggest surprise of all was "She's Still Alive", a Mervyn Spence composition dating from 1984 which proved to be quite different in style from anything recorded during this period, having more of a traditional Wishbone Ash feel.

In addition to a selection of previously unreleased live and studio recordings, several of the tracks on *Distillation* appeared in re-mixed form. For example, "Dream Train" appeared with its original brass parts intact, "Standing in the Rain" had a Martin Turner vocal (instead of Ted) which had been laid down at the original sessions as an experiment whilst "Alone" was presented in its original form, as a full song rather than the instrumental extract which features on *Pilgrimage*.

The format of *Distillation* largely satisfied both casual and ardent fans. For those unfamiliar with the band, the first two and a half CDs contained at least one track from every Wishbone Ash studio album (with the exception of *Raw to the Bone*). The third CD also contained a sizeable helping of rare B-sides plus re-mixed and previously unavailable studio recordings, whilst the fourth CD contained previously unreleased live tracks from the Mark II period of the band which would please the hard-core fans. A short history of the band written by former *Melody Maker* scribe Chris Welch was also included, backed by several rare photographs of different Wishbone Ash line-ups. Finally, Andy and Martin gave their comments on each track.

The original cover was to have been designed by Storm Thorgesson, but his prototype based on the album's original title, "Twin Rivers", bore more than a passing resemblance to a vagina and was scrapped! Instead, a more tasteful picture of some ancient standing stones designed by Jon Crossland was used.

Distillation is undoubtedly the best career retrospective so far and even received favourable reactions from the music press. In a review for *Vox* magazine, Dominic Wills described the album as "an absolute must for their still huge army of fans, as well as all real students of music" whilst *Record Collector* stated that "*Distillation* has been worth the wait" and "the later discs will convince you that there are many interesting facets to one of rock's great survivors".

Coinciding with the release of *Distillation*, Wishbone Ash embarked on a short UK tour commencing on 6 November in Milton Keynes. Two days later, on 8 November, the fourth annual Wishbone Ash fan convention took place at Mansfield Leisure Centre. The format was similar to Ash-Con '96, although the evening concert saw Martin Turner making a guest appearance for the bulk of the second part of the show, marking his last onstage appearance with Wishbone Ash to date. At the time of writing Martin is planning a new touring band to perform both Wishbone Ash and solo material, tentatively titled "Wishbone-Ish". In addition, Martin has been working with London blues-rockers the Blue Bishops, producing their forthcoming CD as well as playing live dates "just for fun and to keep me from getting sterile, which can happen when you spend too much time in the studio".

Former backing vocalist Claire Hamill, who had performed a set with her partner, Andrew Warren, on keyboards during the afternoon, also guested during "Living Proof". In addition, Chris Auld of Moonstone (formerly Magma) augmented the band for several songs. This was dream come true for Chris, the son of Billy Auld, who had for many years been involved with Wishbone Ash's UK fan club and had assisted in the organisation of previous conventions. Chris – a big Wishbone Ash fan – was able to play the material with ease.

Once again, the convention proved to be a highly memorable event, the highlight of the night being the outstanding version of 'Blowin Free' with past and present members of the band on stage together.

If the convention was the highpoint of the November tour for both the band and its fans, then the Bradford show on 13 November was certainly a low for

Above: Claire Hamill. *Photo: Mark Chatterton*

Roger Filgate who was hospitalised for the night, forcing him to miss the show. Faced with the prospect of cancelling the Bradford show at very short notice, Andy Powell contacted Chris Auld, who had proved more than capable in Mansfield, with a view to him stepping into Roger's shoes for the night. This meant a slightly rearranged set list, but Chris rose to the occasion and delivered the goods.

There were doubts as to whether or not Roger would be fit enough to finish the tour but as things turned out he soldiered on bravely, albeit with the band playing a slightly abbreviated set for the remaining dates. Meanwhile, as the current Wishbone Ash line-up toured the UK, original member Martin Turner headed for Poland for a series of radio and public appearances promoting *Distillation* and *Walking The Reeperbahn*.

Chapter Thirteen

Wings Of Desire Will Keep Us Flying

By January 1998 Wishbone Ash's line-up carrousel seemed to be spinning faster than ever. To the band's following it had been obvious for some time that Tony Kishman was only partly committed to Wishbone Ash and it came as little surprise when, mid way through the UK 1997 tour, the bassist announced that the tour in progress would be his last. His intention was to concentrate on promoting his recently released solo album *Catch 22* and to spend more time with his family in the States. What did come as a shock, however, was Roger Filgate's decision to follow suit. As Andy Powell's right hand man since 1994 and a key musical impetus behind *Illuminations,* Filgate had appeared dedicated to the cause. Numerous stories concerning Filgate's departure began to circulate, ranging from ongoing health problems to business differences. Roger puts the record straight on why he left Wishbone Ash:

"Eventually the negatives outweighed the positives, which ultimately led up to my leaving. For me there was a lot of frustration because it never really felt like a 'band' – mainly because it was sort of thrown together in a hurry for the purposes of touring. It's not to say that we didn't get along or that we didn't have our moments musically, but I feel it lacked the chemistry needed to make it a magical combination. And as a result of being anchored to the past, the majority of our live show was dedicated to covering older material and I was primarily interested in playing the new stuff – which isn't realistic with a band that's been around this long. I did enjoy seeing places and meeting new people. I guess like with anything else, the first couple of times you do something, it's all new and exciting but after a while it wears off a bit. The schedule and pace that you have to keep up with can

Above: Roger Filgate and Tony Kishman (left and right) would leave Andy Powell and Mike Sturgis (centre) to an uncertain future in 1998. *Photo: Gary Carter.*

run you down quickly. It's also very easy to get sick of each other! When you're locked up with the same guys day after day it tends to get old. Basically, it was a great learning experience and although it ended up not being what I wanted, I appreciated the opportunity to be part of it and if what I did made some people happy, then it was worth doing."

Powell adds: "It was great working with Roger. He's an excellent musician and a good man. He was able to keep his ideals and focus, despite the rigours of the road, which was largely a new experience for him. Also, as a fan of the band's music, he had a really good feel and understanding for Wishbone Ash. We had a few good years, which would be considered a career for some these days, but at the end of the day, change is inevitable. I've become quite accustomed to that, after 30 years."

Filgate and Kishman would be sorely missed. The pair had been responsible for injecting new life into Wishbone Ash and the November 1997 tour had seen this particular incarnation of Wishbone Ash playing better than ever.

UK and European shows had been arranged and announced from January through to March 1998 and Andy Powell was now faced with the now usual dilemma of having a tour booked, but no band to play it. Ironically, Andy Powell appeared to have anticipated the departure of Tony Kishman and Roger Filgate and had been sounding out members of the Mark II line-up about a possible reformation early in 1998. "Faxes were sent to Martin in London and Laurie in Munich. Even Steve Upton was contacted," says Powell. Martin Turner and Laurie Wisefield were up for a reunion, but the plan did not get beyond the drawing board stage. Martin was willing, although had stated that any future involvement he had with Wishbone Ash would need to be as a fully-fledged member – not the session basis on which he had appeared in 1995/96. Likewise, Laurie was willing to commit in theory, but was not particularly enthralled by the type of tour on offer or the fees that were available. The trek was going to be, by and large, a small club/pub tour and Wisefield felt strongly that a reunion of arguably the band's most prolific line-up should have a higher profile.

Laurie explains his views: "Andy phoned me and swore me to secrecy about it! He said, 'With the box set due out how do you feel about rejoining Wishbone Ash to promote it?' My initial view was that if we were going to do it, it would be good to have all the boys in the band at the time together – me, Martin and Steve. I gave Steve a call and he seemed well, etc and we left it that when he was next in London he would give us a call. The problem was that the whole thing raised so many questions which couldn't really be sorted out in such a small space of time."

"Laurie came up with what he considered was a reasonable financial overview for a tour and it was, quite frankly, something that was not attainable," states Powell, who by now had garnered a lot of experience of running bands and making ends meet on the road.

As events turned out the Mark II band reunion was not to be and Andy Powell began the search for a new band. Guitarist Alan Darby was one musician that he seriously considered. Alan had sat in with the Ash a few years earlier on an unplugged show on London's GLR radio. Andy did actually invite him to join the band, but this fell through as Eric Clapton had asked Alan to join his band for his 1998 US tour. As Andy Powell later admitted, "I wasn't about to pull rank on 'God'!"

Most outsiders were oblivious to what was happening behind the scenes, so it came as a shock to fan club members when they received a letter from Andy Powell early in January confirming the changes within the band. The news was that despite the resignations Wishbone Ash would not be calling it a day. A young guitarist called Mark Birch would take over Roger's place, whilst the more mature Bob Skeat would take over bass duties. Mike Sturgis would continue on drums, though for most of the UK dates that spring his place was taken by another former Wishbone Ash drummer, Ray Weston. In effect the wheel had turned full circle and Wishbone Ash would once again be a completely British band. The new recruits came about largely due to the influence of Mike Bennett, co-ordinator of *Trance Visionary*, an album project released later that year, which combined Wishbone Ash's guitar orientated rock with a dance/trance sound.

Bob Skeat came from a musical family, his father being a well-respected jazz musician, and has a long musical heritage, as he recalls: "I have been in the thousand and one bands you've never heard of, but the main ones have included Colin Blunstone's band and then I toured the world with Princess Stephanie of Monaco. I've also worked with Gilbert O'Sullivan and Toyah Wilcox as well as doing lots of sessions and TV adverts."

Bob Skeat's association with Wishbone Ash and Andy Powell came about while he was working on the *Live Timeline* album at the Northamptonshire studios in 1997. "I did a little bit of 'repair work' on the *Live Timeline* album," recalls Bob, "adding some organ parts and re-doing some bass lines. But it was Mike Bennett who got me involved with the *Trance Visionary* album where I played bass lines on several tracks. Then later on when Andy needed a bass player, I got a call."

thirty years of Wishbone Ash

Above: Bob Skeat . *Photo: Mark Chatterton*

    Mark Birch, on the other hand, was the baby of the line up, being born in the year that Wishbone Ash was first formed. A lookalike to the hippy character Neil from BBC TV's *The Young Ones* sit-com, Mark is a very easy going and has fitted very well into the guitar twin spot in Wishbone Ash. He also plays from time to time with Bob Skeat in a fun covers band called Mike Fab Gere. It was via the internet that he "auditioned" for Wishbone Ash, sending biographies and e-mails to Andy Powell. When the new line-up convened in London in January 1998, Mark and Bob had just three weeks to learn all the Wishbone material.

    The 1998 Winter tour – 43 dates in all – began in Cork, Ireland on 28 January and progressed through England, Belgium, Holland, Austria and Germany. Someone must having been watching over Andy Powell as on the way to JFK airport in New York to catch the flight to London, Andy and his wife Pauline were involved in a collision with a Mack truck (juggernaut) at 60 mph. Their car was a write-off, but luckily no one was hurt and the pair were able to continue with their journey. Another near-disaster occurred as the band arrived for the opening show in Cork. All of their stage equipment had been held up at the port in Wales. Dedicated fan Alan Creedon came to the rescue, as Andy Powell remembers:

"Alan turned up with an offer of the use of his personal equipment collection, together with his brother's, uncle's cousin's, etc. After a frantic drive around the backstreets of Cork, we had what we needed and the show went on. I think for Bob and Mark, the rest of the tour was a breeze after that 'baptism of fire' so to speak."

Fortune again smiled on 7 February at the Standard in Walthamstow, London where a reunion of sorts took place. Laurie Wisefield made a guest appearance with the band, joining them for an encore which consisted of "Living Proof", and the medley of "Lady Whiskey", "Jailbait", "Phoenix" and "The Pilgrim". A few days later, Wishbone played possibly the smallest venue they have ever played. Holding not much more than a hundred people, the 12 Bar Club in London's Denmark Street was to host the launch party for *Trance Visionary* but due to production problems, the album wasn't yet ready and the band played two shows instead.

The new line-up sparked further debate amongst Wishbone Ash fans. Some welcomed the rawer edge that guitarist Mark Birch in particular had brought to the band. He was noticed not only for his guitar skills, but also because he was able to tackle some of the higher register vocal parts on long lost favourites like "Phoenix".

Bob Skeat (almost a deadringer for former Ash bassman Andy Pyle) ably fitted in on bass, playing more in the style of Martin Turner than many previous Wishbone bassists as well as adding falsetto vocals and harmony parts when needed. As the tour progressed through Europe, Ray Weston replaced Mike Sturgis on some dates and by the end of the year it was Weston who held down the drum stool on a permanent basis. Mike Sturgis had decided that due to having a young family he didn't want to be away on the road for long periods of time. This also coincided with the offer of a steady job at the Academy of Contemporary Music in Guildford.

Possibly the most controversial episode in the band's career, however, was still to come. In April 1998 the *Trance Visionary* album was released. This was basically a collaboration between Andy Powell and producer/remix specialist Mike Bennett, who had previously worked with The Fall, The Specials and the Sweet. It was through Bennett's production work at Trojan and Receiver Records that he had crossed paths with Andy Powell, when he was given the job of remixing the *Live Timeline* album. There had been a lot of pre-publicity around the album from the record company, Invisible Hands Music, but when it was finally released the reaction was very mixed. Diehard Wishbone Ash fans in the main hated it, though it must be said that there was a significant minority who accepted it for what it was – a sideline project treading new ground in the 'drum 'n' bass' arena to be exact. Although the album went under the name of Wishbone Ash, it was mainly electronic music with tape loops of previous Wishbone songs such as "F.U.B.B.", "The Pilgrim" and "Front Page News" with the addition of soundbites of the voices of Martin Turner and Miles Copeland added to the final mix. Producer Mike Bennett explained what it was all about:

"The idea for *Trance Visionary* was to be faithful to the Wishbone Ash guitar brief, whilst manipulating the technology available to enhance the possibilities of exploring a wider spectrum, at the same time experimenting with an exciting assortment of hypnotic sounds and pulses."

Although the *Trance Visionary* album was largely disowned by dyed in the wool fans – some claiming the album should never have boasted the group's name – the album sold extremely well amongst the dance fraternity, by far outstripping the sales of *Illuminations*. It was extensively featured in London dance clubs, though the majority of dance music fans had no idea who Wishbone Ash were.

A brace of releases *did* please the majority of fans of old – the long-awaited *No Smoke Without Fire* and *Just Testing* on CD by MCA/Universal. This came to light, partly through a petition organised by the Wishbone Ash Fan Club and partly through individual badgering of various executives at MCA Records in London over a number of years. It was mainly due to the efforts of Alan Hodgson at MCA/Universal in London that the project was able to come to fruition. He sanctioned the use of bonus tracks from the period, as well as comprehensive sleeve notes and the printing of the albums' lyrics.

Martin Turner had the job of re-mastering the tracks but, although it was finished in the summer of 1997, it was put back at Andy Powell's request so as not to clash with the release of the *Distillation* box set. Such was the response that sales of both albums exceeded the expectations. As a result Alan Hodgson was happy to proceed with the release of the final two Wishbone Ash albums never to have been released on CD – namely *Number the Brave* and *Live Dates Volume II*. Unfortunately, with the merger of Universal Records with several other record companies, the project got shelved when Hodgson was promoted. To this day, the release of these two Wishbone Ash CDs is still eagerly awaited by fans despite a 500 strong fan petition being handed in to Universal Music in 1999.

Meanwhile, the new Wishbone Ash line-up performed at several German festivals including the Weil der Stadt Summer Night Festival on 17 July and the Burg Herzburg the following day. The latter show was attended by 70,000 music fans. The next night the band played a much smaller impromptu club gig in Frankfurt but, as Ray Weston had another gig booked in the UK, a drummer was needed fast. At the last moment, Andy Powell's youngest son, sixteen year old "AJ", stepped in to take his place and, like Chris Auld the year before, saved the day for the band. The band also played their first corporate event in August for the executives of Trimedia at Zurich in Switzerland through the efforts of Trimedia boss, Bodo Kirf.

"These kind of events are often actually a lot of fun," says Andy Powell. "Many of our fans of old have been quietly getting on with their lives and some find themselves heading up important companies these days. This particular show as put together by such fans and with a corporate expense budget, we found ourselves playing on a mini-stage which had been erected on the roof top terrace of the company headquarters, with the whole of Lake Zurich as a backdrop. Our audience consisted of the marketing and corporate heads of companies like Coca Cola, VW and Burger King. What a strange world rock and roll can be!"

Before the Swiss show, the UK "tour" to promote the *Trance Visionary* album started and then stumbled at Camden Town in London. On paper the *Trance Visionary* tour sounded an exciting concept, if not exactly one which met with the average Wishbone Ash fan's approval. The show would be in two parts, one featuring an augmented Wishbone Ash line-up featuring Mike Bennett on keyboards and guest vocalist Tacye, performing music based around the *Trance Visionary* album. The second part would see the band stripping down to a four piece to perform a traditional Wishbone Ash set. *Trance Visionary* producer Mike Bennett would sound engineer for the tour, which would take the band away from the rock clubs and back to the 1500-2000 capacity venues they had headlined in their heyday. To entice the new dance-influenced audience various name DJs would be "supporting" the band.

For all it faults, *Trance Visionary* was without doubt the most radical and ambitious project to bear the Wishbone Ash name in years. VH-1's *Talk Music* show highlighted the album and interviewed Mike Bennett. A promo video for "Wonderful Stash", shot by French producer Christian Guyonnet, was also shown.

The *Trance Visionary* tour kicked off at London's Camden Palace on 6 August. The show featured a stunning lighting show provided by the venue's newly installed laser set-up, and the *Trance* set attracted positive reviews. The show, however, was poorly attended. There were few dance fans in attendance, whilst the majority of Ash die-hards stayed away. The band, meanwhile, would not appear on stage until after midnight. The *Sunday Telegraph* reviewed the show claiming "there were about 20 people inside the Camden Palace's vast cavern". The London show would be the sole *Trance Visionary* performance with all other scheduled dates being cancelled, mainly through lack of advance ticket sales. Andy Powell blamed tour's collapse on the promoters, Kicking Up a Storm, citing "financial problems within the company and mistakes in strategy. As a result the band lost a lot of money and wasted time, as well as the good name of Wishbone Ash being damaged". Mike Bennett too had his ideas about the failure of the tour:

"It was total devastation. We had the best DJs that money could buy, but it was ill-conceived because the promoter put the DJs on at eight/nine o'clock. People who come to see those kind of DJs turn up at about one in the morning. The band on the other hand were meant to come on at about one in the morning. I think it was too fragmented to bill Wishbone Ash in the drum 'n' bass trance idiom. But you live and learn."

The *Trance Visionary* saga was not over yet, though. Following the cancellation of the tour, Andy Powell and Mike Bennett decided to record the music as it would have been experienced live. Bennett, Powell, the entire Wishbone Ash band, plus Tacye entered Far Heath Studios, Northamptonshire during August 1998 to record *Psychic Terrorism* – the "live" sequel to *Trance Visionary* – an altogether rockier variation on the *Trance Visionary* themes, with heavier emphasis on guitars. As Mike Bennett explained: "The funny thing was that had the tour not collapsed, we wouldn't have recorded *Psychic Terrorism*." The recordings would eventually come out on a new label to be distributed by Rob Ayling at respected UK independent label Voiceprint Records.

In the Autumn of 1998, Wishbone undertook its now customary annual Winter UK/European tour, opening in Market Harborough on 31 October. The performances on this jaunt were received rather more enthusiastically by fans than the new line-up's debut earlier in the year, largely due to greater use of Mark Birch's vocal skills and the reintroduction of several back-catalogue favourites such as "Phoenix" (in its entirety), "F.U.B.B.", "Clousseau", "Ballad of the Beacon", "Underground" and "Persephone".

On 7 November 1998 the fifth annual Wishbone Ash fan convention took place once again at Mansfield Leisure Centre. As in previous years, the event featured a full-length concert appearance, although this time the event placed a greater emphasis on live music. Wishbone Ash, augmented by Tacye and Mike Bennett, performed a *Psychic Terrorism* set during the afternoon session, whilst the opening slot was ably filled by Otis, who performed a mixture of Wishbone covers and original material. Claire Hamill once again played a short set and also performed "Living Proof" with the band during the evening concert, whilst Ben Granfelt filled the evening support slot.

On the other side of the Atlantic, America had only seen a couple of Wishbone Ash concerts in more than five years, but in 1999 they finally got a tour off the ground. The year began on a hopeful note when the Ash were invited to perform at the 35th Anniversary celebrations of the Whisky-A-Go-Go in Los Angeles on 20 January. This was the very first West Coast venue that Wishbone had played all those years ago in 1971, so it was a somewhat poignant return for Andy Powell. The gig was scheduled to be broadcast live over the internet, but due to technical problems, this failed to go out live that night. (Fans were, however, able to download it at a later date.) Also on the bill at the Whisky were Canned Heat, Edgar Winter and Badfinger and in the audience was Mick Fleetwood, no doubt checking to see what Wishbone was like after all those years. The next morning the band had the pleasure of taking breakfast with Bonnie Raitt, who was in LA writing songs with a former part-time Ash member, Alan Darby. Then it was back to Connecticut to start work on the next Wishbone album, tentatively titled, *Bare Bones* – a project that had been on Andy Powell's drawing board for a good three or four years.

Like many rock groups in the nineties, Andy Powell had been toying for some time with the idea of recording a completely acoustic album. Indeed he had already recorded and released a couple of acoustic duets with Roger Filgate. The brief was to give the latest line-up a chance to re-work some old Ash standards in an acoustic vein as well as record some new songs.

British audiences were treated to a sneak preview of the *Bare Bones* album in February 1999 when once again the Ash took to the road. Although there was no album to accompany the tour, it gave the band a chance to try out some of the songs slated for *Bare Bones* before a live audience. These included "Master of Disguise" from *Just Testing*, "Everybody Needs a Friend" from *Wishbone Four* (with Mark Birch taking lead vocals) and, most controversially of all, a completely reworked acoustic version of "Living Proof", which once again split the fans down the middle.

March saw the first ever German Wishbone Ash fan convention take place in Oberhausen. The Americans too organised their own convention a couple of months later in May, when Leon Tsilis, with the able assistance of Mary Beth Rowley and Fred Warnock, hosted the first ever US Ash convention in Chicago at the Beaumont Club. The night before the band played to a sell-out crowd at Chicago's House Of Blues. Parts of this concert were again available for downloading off the internet. The convention went well with the Catholic Girls opening events and Ben Granfelt being flown over from Finland to take the support slot. The whole event was videoed and released a few months later.

The band headlined a bikers festival in Florence, Italy in the spring. Then it was over to the Isle of Man to play in Douglas at the culmination of the annual TT Races on the island. Yet again they played several German festivals over the summer as well as putting the finishing touches to the "unplugged" album that they had started recording earlier in the year in Connecticut with Powell's old friend, Alec Head, handling the engineering duties. Final overdubs and mixing were done at Spotlight Studios in Willesden, London during August. Claire Hamill popped over to add backing vocals to the track "Love Abuse".

In September, Wishbone Ash played a 15-date tour of France – their first for many years – largely due to the efforts of Christian Guyonnet. The tour included a date at the Euro Disney theme park near Paris, as well as one at "Le Plan" in Ris Orangis, just outside Paris, which was recorded live in Dolby surround sound for a projected 2000 release.

In between the French dates and the annual UK Autumn tour, the long promised acoustic album *Bare Bones* was released on HTD Records. It contained a mixture of old numbers reworked in the unplugged format plus three new tracks and a cover version of the old Solomon Burke hit, "(Won't You Give Him) One More Chance".

The album opens with a new version of "Wings Of Desire" from the *Strange Affair* album, complete with mandolin from Andy Powell. The next track "Errors of My Way" from the very first Wishbone Ash album was lifted by the addition of accordion played by Mick Parker and fiddle by Lewis Gibson.

"Master of Disguise" off *Just Testing* was another song that had featured acoustic guitars in its original form. This version has violin courtesy of Morwenna Lasko as well as Hammond organ (as did the original) from Paul Moran. Andy Powell, this time around, took over the lead vocal and explains: "I had always had the idea to sing this song, since it was a very personal song for me." Four new songs followed consecutively. "You Won't Take Me Down" was written by Mike Bennett. Andy Powell explains: "Mike's original living room demo was actually a much heavier version but the song's haunting atmosphere immediately caught my ear, with potential for an acoustic treatment."

"Love Abuse", credited to Andy Powell and Ray Weston, follows. Fans had heard this song before on the *Archive* 3 CD, but the new version was much more laid back and had the added attraction of Claire Hamill on backing vocals.

Andy Powell: "I think subconsciously the meeting with Bonnie Raitt had influenced me on this one and so I decided to take the song in the kind of direction that she might have employed." The song had been played in the band's live set on a handful of occasions dating back to the 1993 US tour when Ted Turner was still with the band and had also been demoed for possible inclusion on *Illuminations*.

The old Solomon Burke song, "(Wont You Give Him) One More Chance" had been a chart hit in the UK during the sixties and is perhaps the most soulful track on the album. Powell reminisces: "This song is very dear to my heart since it was a favourite of my wife Pauline's from the old days. As fledgling Mods in the sixties we used to go and see this band called Gary Farr and the T-Bones who would perform it and who later took it into the UK charts. I'd demoed it twenty years earlier, waiting for just the right time to record it. You could say it was a present for her."

"Baby Don't Mind" is another Andy Powell composition and had originally been recorded by Wishbone Ash back in 1979, but was never released. This version features Mick Parker on accordion. It is essentially Wishbone playing country music and is perhaps the least successful track on the album.

The radical new arrangement of "Living Proof" almost sounds Spanish. Andy's son Aynsley "AJ" Powell played percussion. Andy states: "Regarding 'Living Proof' – it's a true mark of a great song when it can be embraced by a fresh new arrangement. It was a very rewarding exercise in this case."

"Hard Times" has more of a blues treatment compared to the version on the *Strange Affair* album. It features a mellow-shuffle beat with both guitarists, Birch and Powell, duetting on the vocal. "Strange Affair" was a natural choice for inclusion on the album and got the blues harp treatment from Giles Headly. It also featured a tasty Dobro solo from Chris Davis. With Ray Weston's brush work, it caught the band in a relaxed feel.

The final track, "Everybody Needs A Friend" was perhaps the most lauded track on the album and got the full treatment with electric guitars, Hammond organ and Mark Birch shining on vocals. The album climaxed with an Andy Powell Flying V guitar solo, harking back to the band's glory days, thus drawing the album to a fitting conclusion.

In November, it was time for a second British tour of the year, plus the annual UK convention at Mansfield Leisure Centre. As in 1998, Otis and the Ben Granfelt Band played and Andy Powell was present in the afternoon to answer questions and sign album sleeves. To show that the band's 30th anniversary had not been forgotten, Andy Powell announced that a special 30th Anniversary concert would take place at the Shepherds Bush Empire the following Easter.

For some of the later gigs on the UK jaunt, the band committed the unforgivable sin of actually dropping "Blowin' Free" from the set! Despite the numerous line-up changes, the track had been performed at every Wishbone Ash gig since 1972. Two older numbers which hadn't been played for many years did get an airing. They were "Lifeline" from the *Just Testing* album and "Come In From The Rain" from 1977's *Front Page News* – both from the Mark II line-up of the band. The tour continued with a series of dates in Germany and Holland during December.

The 30th Anniversary Concert
Opposite: Andy Powell, Mark Birch, Laurie Wisefield. *Photo: Carol Farnworth*
Above: The cake and a priceless entry ticket. *Photo: Carol Farnworth*
Below: Wishbone Ash outside the Shepherd's Bush Empire.
Photo: Alan Workman

As the 21st century began, Wishbone Ash continued the organisation of a 30th anniversary concert at the Shepherd's Bush Empire in London, with plans to video the entire show for release as a fitting memorial. Meanwhile, over in the States, news came through that sadly Ann Bixby had passed away. Ann had assisted Leon Tsilis with the website having first become a fan of the band through the song "Living Proof" and had been a major figure behind the scenes of both the website and the US convention.

Over in Europe Wishbone undertook a fourteen date tour of France, Belgium and Holland whilst behind the scenes Andy Powell enlisted the services of Michael Bisping as the band's new German agent. In the UK Wishbone Ash parted company with their agent, Martin Looby, after working together for most of the 1990s. His successor was to be Andy Nye, a friend of Bob Skeat. His first task was to arrange some dates around the Shepherds Bush 30th anniversary gig. The most memorable was one at the Cavern in Liverpool, not long after Paul McCartney had played a triumphant homecoming gig there. Wishbone's show was arranged so that it occured thirty years to the day since Wishbone Ash had first played there in 1970. A commemorative plaque had been put up outside the Cavern at the time to commemorate the band's original performance there. As a tribute to the Beatles, the band played "Let It Be" as an encore. Andy Powell found the whole evening an emotional experience, especially when a surprise gift was waiting for him at the venue:

"I had my family in tow and Leon Tsilis and some other Americans made it over, together with some German fans and a roaring crowd of Liverpudlians who proceeded to blow the roof off the joint. I needn't to have bothered singing any of the songs, since the audience took care of that. What a night! The manager said that we surpassed the reaction given to Sir Paul McCartney, who had played there earlier in the year, which is saying something. The biggest surprise of all, was presented to us in the dressing room by Julia Pugh in the form of an incredible cake, more like a work of art, celebrating our 30th. The pictures of this wondrous piece of confectionery don't do it justice. The detail was outstanding. All of the band's major albums were reproduced by hand, depicted in icing (or for the Americans, frosting), together with Julia's famous Wishbone Ash scarf which she always waves at our gigs at the Robin in Dudley. A fruitcake, laced with brandy, it was a true labour of love. Thank you Julia!"

The biggest event by far of that spring tour was undoubtedly the 30th Anniversary concert at the Shepherd's Bush Empire in West London. This quaint little theatre seemed the ideal venue for the concert and the date, Easter Saturday 2000 was set aside so that Ash fans from not just the UK, but also from other countries could make the gig.

Co-promoter Ramona Da Gama, who had previously booked the band into another West London venue, Blues W14, was enlisted by Andy Powell to help set up the show. Ben Granfelt was asked to support and German company, Eject TV, were booked to video and record the whole event. The musicians who had played with the band on *Bare Bones* were asked to play many of the songs from that album. These included, Paul Moran (Hammond organ), Mick Parker (accordion), Giles Hedley (blues harp), Lewis Gibson (violin) and Glen LeFleur (percussion).

Around 1,000 fans made the pilgrimage to this historical event from all parts of the globe, including the German fan club president Detleff Assenmacher, and Leon Tsilis, John Hahn and Fred Renz coming from America. One fan even flew in from Bangkok! Also so many relatives and friends of the band attended that a special section in the circle was set aside for them. Celebrity fan, Tommy Vance introduced the band with the words, "I play this band's music because I fucking love it!" From then on the audience was treated to almost three hours of classic Wishbone Ash music. For Andy Powell, after thirty years of ups and downs it was a very special night:

"At times it was a blur for me, since there was so much going on. I had spent an enjoyable three days in Germany prior to the event, producing the archived photo and video material which was used on the two giant screens featured at the Empire. There were times on stage when I would turn round to glimpse the footage and almost start to disassociate from the whole thing! It was if I was floating above the stage looking down on the last 30 years. This also happened when the guest musicians joined us for their interpretations of some of the Ash classics like 'Errors' and 'Ballad of the Beacon'. It was truly emotional and allowed me to look at those songs in a fresh light. Then to see the audience was amazing - so many familiar faces from all over the UK, and indeed many other parts of the world, under one roof. It did cause me to lose concentration a couple of times! I had family members over from Australia and even met school friends I hadn't seen in more than 30 years!"

From the words "with special guests" on the advertising for the 30th anniversary gig, some fans seemed to anticipate one big reunion party, with all the past members of Wishbone being present. This was perhaps a little over-optimistic to say the least. Claire Hamill did appear, as did *Trance Visionary* vocalist, Tacye. However, just one ex-member of Wishbone Ash made it to the gig and that was Laurie Wisefield, who agreed at the last minute to appear.

Claire Hamill thought that, "Seeing Laurie again was a highlight. The fans were marvellous and it was a great moment to be up there singing "Living Proof" with Laurie playing lead, just as we did it all those years ago."

Laurie's appearance on stage that night certainly raised the atmosphere to fever pitch as he played alongside Andy Powell on old favourites "Come in from the Rain" and "Blowin' Free", reliving the glory days of the seventies. Some fans however were puzzled by the non-appearance of the other ex-members of the band. It turns out that Martin Turner was on holiday with his family in Florida. As for the other ex-members of the Ash line-ups from the seventies, eighties and nineties, there was no sign of them either, although throughout the evening various pictures of the different line-ups appeared on two giant back projection screens. As Andy Powell explains:

"A complete reunion of ex-members was never on the table although, no doubt, some fans would have wished it so. That's understandable. So much water had flowed under the bridge that it would have taken a bigger man than I to have arranged a complete reunion, and also someone with extremely deep pockets, no doubt! As it was, we put on a hell of a show lasting almost three hours, which was a fitting tribute to the music of what I'm proud to be associated with - a great band!"

Which brings us to the present. It is hard to believe Wishbone Ash has survived thirty years as a band, albeit with numerous changes in line-up. How many other bands that started out in 1969 can you think of who have consistently continued to write, record and perform right up to the present day? While they may never have enjoyed the level of world-wide success that some of their "premier division" contemporaries such as Genesis, Queen or Deep Purple achieved, they have nonetheless remained one of the most enduring and influential British bands of their era, emerging from the rock 'n' roll circus with their dignity and integrity intact. Throughout the three decades of their career to date, the band has inspired respect from its dedicated legion of followers, forever keeping them guessing, challenged and entertained. Unlike many of their contemporaries who were, perhaps, guilty of finding a successful formula and milking it for all it was worth, Wishbone Ash have constantly evolved – adding and shedding members and influences along the way. While it could be argued that the band might have achieved a greater degree of commercial success had they compromised their ideals somewhat, would they have lasted as long or still be held in such high regard? The back catalogue continues to attract the attention of new followers. As founder member Martin Turner stated in 1999: "It is quite amazing that a band who peaked in 1973 still has so many records available, twenty six years on." Speaking about the legacy of music, Andy Powell adds: "I think it will offer future generations a glimpse into what will be seen to have been a very productive era in popular music. I want to see the band's name kept alive in this context."

With ever-changing personnel, the name Wishbone Ash – rather than being a particular group of people – continues to represent a vehicle for high quality melodic rock music. The twin-lead harmony guitars, the minor chords, the strident bass sound, the vocal harmonies, the intricate, yet melodic arrangements and tight drumming – it is these factors, rather than a particular set of musicians' names, which truly define the music of Wishbone Ash. The music is, of course, the central reason for the band's success, but dedication and persistence have been the foundations for the band's longevity in the music industry and none have been more dedicated to keeping the Wishbone Ash flag flying than sole surviving original member Andy Powell.

"I came to terms a long time ago with the fact that the Ash was to be a way of life for myself and my family and that I would be hard pressed to find a better substitute," says Powell. "I view it as a unique 'university' to which I am privileged to belong; one which offers me membership to the world of music and a window on the world which few other situations could provide."

Wishbone Ash have weathered many peaks and troughs throughout their career – on an artistic, business and commercial level. On a purely commercial level, it is without question that the band peaked during their first wave of success in the early seventies with *Argus*. Many of their greatest musical achievements, however, would continue throughout the band's career, with a reputation as being one if not *the* best live band around. Band members, meanwhile, have come and gone and, whilst the changes have not always been to the liking of all the bands' fans, each addition to the Ash fold has contributed something new to the melting pot of musical ideas that is Wishbone Ash. As such, the band has never stagnated. It is also reassuring to know that of the many personalities that have passed through the Wishbone Ash ranks over the years, the vast majority of these musicians are still active within the music industry and have cited their time in the band as the most enjoyable of their careers.

Thirty years gone. Hard to believe. But there's still a lot more to come and who knows how many more years Wishbone Ash can go on for, be it in its current form, with the injection of fresh blood, or perhaps even a regrouping of one of its more familiar incarnations?

As always, the Phoenix will continue to rise from the Ashes!

Sources

1. Unknown Source
2. KBSU Radio, Boise, Idaho, interview by Dr John and Dick Skoro, July 1989
3. "No Smoke Without Fire" tour programme, 1978
4. Devon Sound interview, 1989
5. Wishbone Ash – A Pocket History by Steve Upton, 1989
6. Sounds, 1971
7. Vintage Guitar, interview by Willie Mosely, 1992
8. Beat Instrumental, 1973
9. Sounds, interview by Pete Makowski, October 1974
10. Zig Zag Issue 51.52, interview by Trevor Gardener, 1975
11. "Time Was Collection" sleevenotes, MCA Records, 1992
12. Beat Instrumental, interview by Gary Cooper, November 1978
13. Sounds, interview by Ray Telford, April 1971
14. International Musician and Recording World, June 1981
15. NME, interview by Julie Webb, October 1971
16. Rock On, BBC Radio, interview by Tommy Vance, January 1980
17. Sounds, December 1972
18. Sounds, March 1973
19. Beat Instrumental, 1977
20. Sounds, interview by Barbara Charone, October 1976
21. Melody Maker, interview by David Bootroyd, 1977
22. Rocksig, interview by Martin Rogers and Jan Krynski, 1993
23. Record Collector, November 1994
24. Kerrang, interview by Steve Gett, 1982
25. Guitar Heroes, interview by Ed Park, 1982
26. Guitarist, 1988
27. Raw, 1989
28. Feedback, interview by Martin Rogers and Jan Krynski, October 1992
29. Rhythm n News, 1994

Addresses

Wishbone Ash fan clubs:
UK – Hot Ash, PO Box 58, Matlock, Derbyshire, DE4 5ZX, Englnad
USA – US ASH 2428 McKinnney, Boise, Idaho, 83704, USA
Martin Turner Newsletter: PO Box 1041, Oxford, OX4 6XD
Wishbone Ash related websites:
UK Wishbone Ash website: www.wishboneash.co.uk
Official Wishbone Ash website: www.wishboneash.com
Dr.John's US Ash site: www.usash.com
German Wishbone Ash website: www.wishboneash.de
Japanese Wishbone Ash website: www. bekkoame.or.jp
The other Wishbone Ash website: www.weidelt-web.de/ash
Rainer Frilund's Wishbone Ash discography: www.saunalahti.fi
Mark Birch website: www.markbirch.com
Claire Hamill website: www. clairehamill.co.uk
John Wetton website: www.johnwetton.co.uk

Wishbone Ash Concert Listing 1969-2000

The following list of concert dates is by no means complete, but we have attempted to list all known Wishbone Ash concert appearances to date, including radio and television shows. We have also attempted to detail which performances are known to have been recorded or filmed, either officially or otherwise. The key for this is:
R – radio broadcast/tape recording (official)
B – bootleg tape recording made by a member of the audience (unofficial)
T – Television broadcast/film recording (official)
V – bootleg video/film recording made by a member of the audience (unofficial)
If you know of any additional dates not recorded here please contact the authors via the publisher with your additions/alterations. Thank you.

1969
Nov 10	Civic Hall Dunstable	Eng
Nov 18	Tiffany's Exeter	Eng
Dec	Klooks Kleek Hampstead London	Eng

1970
Feb 12	Polytechnic Kingston-Upon-Thames	Eng
Feb 19	The Temple London	Eng
Feb 20	Bedford College London	Eng
Mar 13	Connaught Hall London	Eng
Mar 14	University College London	Eng
Mar 19	St Martin's School Of Art London	Eng
Mar 21	The Swan Yardley Birmingham	Eng
Mar 23	The Speakeasy London	Eng
Apr 2	Le Bilbouquet Paris	Fra
Apr 3	Le Bilbouquet Paris	Fra
Apr 4	The Golf Drout Paris	Fra
Apr 5	The Golf Drout Paris	Fra
Apr 6	Le Rock 'n Roll Circus Paris	Fra
Apr 5	Le Rock 'n Roll Circus Paris	Fra
Apr 12	Youth Club Bletchley	Eng
Apr 13	College of Architecture Leeds	Eng
Apr 16	Imperial Colleg London	Eng
Apr 17	Trent Park College Barnet	Eng
Apr 18	The Cavern Liverpool	Eng
May 2	University College London	Eng
May 8	Marquee Club London	Eng
May 9	Imperial College London	Eng
May 14	Country Club Hampstead	Eng
May 15	College Of Education Coventry	Eng
May 16	Toft's Folkestone	Eng
May 18	Civic Hall Dunstable	Eng
May 19	Speakeasy London	Eng
May 23	Bath City Pop Festival	Eng
Jun	College Guildford	Eng
Jun	Roundhouse London	Eng
Jun	Henry's Blue's House Newcastle	Eng
Jun	Marquee Club London	Eng
Jun	Dorchester Hotel London	Eng
Jul	The Old Granary Bristol	Eng
Jul	Farx Club Bardford	Eng
Jul 25	Civic Hall Dunstable	Eng
Jul 31	Town Hall Torquay	Eng
Aug 1	Town Hall Torquay	Eng
Aug 6	BBC Paris Studios London	Eng R
Aug 14	Fishmonger's Arms Wood Green	Eng
Aug 21	Lyceum London	Eng
Sep 16	Marquee Club London	Eng
Sep 25	City Hall St Albans	Eng
Sep 26	Starlight Rooms Boston	Eng
Sep 27	De Montford Hall Leicester	Eng
Oct 1	Town Hall Leeds	Eng
Oct 4	City Hall Newcastle	Eng
Oct 7	The Dome Brighton	Eng
Oct 9	Durham	Eng
Oct 10	Polytechnic Kingston-Upon-Thames	Eng
Dec 4	Technical College Waltham Forest	Eng
Dec 5	BBC TV Studios "Disco 2"	Eng T
Dec	1932 Windsor	Eng
Dec	Cooks Ferry Inn Edmonton	Eng
Dec	Railway Tavern London E15	Eng

1971
Jan 1	BBC Maida Vale Studios London	Eng R
Jan 9	Van Dyke Plymouth	Eng
Jan 17	Eel Pie Island Twickenham	Eng
Jan 18	Civic Hall Dunstable	Eng
Jan 27	Albert Hall Nottingham	Eng
Jan 28	City Hall Newcastle	Eng
Jan 29	City Hall Sheffield	Eng
Jan 30	City Hall Hull	Eng
Jan 31	St George's Hall Bradford	Eng
Feb 5	Il Rondo Ballroom Leicester	Eng
Feb 19	Adelphi West Bromwich	Eng
Feb 20	Shenstone College Worcester	Eng
Feb 21	Roundhouse London	Eng
Feb 25	Austin Texas	USA
Feb 26	Dallas Texas	USA
Feb 27	Houston Texas	USA
Mar 5	Whisky A Go Go Los Angeles	USA B
Mar 6	Whisky A Go Go Los Angeles	USA
Mar 7	Whisky A Go Go Los Angeles	USA
Mar 9	San Diego	USA
Mar 11	Filmore West San Francisco	USA
Mar 12	Filmore West San Francisco	USA
Mar 13	Filmore West San Francisco	USA
Mar 14	Filmore West San Francisco	USA T
Apr	Detroit	USA
Apr	Chicago	USA
Apr 8	Filmore West San Francisco	USA
Apr 9	Filmore West San Francisco	USA
Apr 10	Filmore West San Francisco	USA
Apr 21	BBC Maida Vale Studios London	Eng R
Apr 25	Lyceum London	Eng
Apr 28	Big Brother Hertford	Eng
Apr 29	Westbridge College Nottingham	Eng
Apr 30	Penthouse Club Scarborough	Eng
May 1	University Hull	Eng
May 2	Bowes Lyon House Stevenage	Eng
May 4	Marquee Club London	Eng
May 5	The Castle Tooting London	Eng
May 6	University Swansea	Wal
May 7	Polytechnic Lanchester	Eng

thirty years of Wishbone Ash

May 8	Van Dyke Plymouth	Eng
May 14	Red Lion Leytonstone London	Eng
May 15	University College London	Eng
May 21	Westfield College London	Eng
Jun 5	The Phonograph Finchley London	Eng
Jun 7	Town Hall Plymouth	Eng
Jun 9	Flamingo Redruth	Eng
Jun 10	Colston Hall Bristol	Eng
Jun 11	Guildhall Southampton	Eng
Jun 12	Town Hall Oxford	Eng
Jun 14	De Montfort Hall Leicester	Eng R
Jun 15	St George's Hall Bradford	Eng
Jun 16	Free Trade Hall Manchester	Eng
Jun 17	University Warwick	Eng
Jun 18	Town Hall Birmingham	Eng
Jun 19	City Hall Newcastle	Eng
Jun 20	City Hall Hull	Eng
Jun 22	City Hall Sheffield	Eng
Jun 23	Town Hall Leeds	Eng
Jun 24	Albert Hall Nottingham	Eng
Jun 25	Caird Hall Dundee	Sco
Jun 26	University Stirling	Sco
Jun 27	Caley Cinema Edinburgh	Sco
Jul 5	BBC Maida Vale Studios London	Eng R
Jul 17	Pioneer Club St Albans	Eng
Jul 26	Reading Festival	Eng
Aug 12	Public Hall Cleveland	USA
Aug 13	Hara Arena Dayton	USA
Aug 14	Cobo Arena Detroit	USA
Aug 15	Sports Centre Minneapolis	USA
Aug 16	South Illinois Univ. Edwardsville	USA
Sep 3	Satsop River Festival Seattle	USA
Sep 5	Austin Texas	USA
Sep	Alexandria Virginia	USA B
Sep	BBC TV The Old Grey Whistle Test	Eng T
Sep 24	The Hove Bournemouth	Eng
Sep 25	College Slough	Eng
Sep 26	Greyhound Croydon	Eng
Sep 28	Osborne Hotel Clacton-On-Sea	Eng
Oct 1	Polytechnic Bristol	Eng
Oct 2	Roundhouse Dagenham	Eng
Oct 3	Lyceum London	Eng
Oct 5	Town Hall Cheltenham	Eng
Oct 6	Patti Ballroom Swansea	Wal
Oct 8	Mayfair Ballroom Newcastle	Eng
Oct 9	University Sheffield	Eng
Oct 10	Jazz Festival Redcar	Eng
Oct 12	BBC TV Studios London	Eng T
Oct 15	Chez Leightonstone	Eng
Oct 16	Polytechnic Isleworth	Eng
Oct 18	BBC Maida Vale Studios London	Eng R
Oct 24	Empire Theatre Sunderland	Eng
Oct 28	College Alsager	Eng
Oct 29	University Bath	Eng
Oct 30	College Of Technology Watford	Eng
Oct 31	Starlight Ballroom Boston	Eng
Nov 1		Bel T
Nov 2		Bel T
Nov 4		Ita T
Nov		Ger
Nov		Fra
Nov		Swi
Nov 12	Rainbow London	Eng
Nov 13	Rainbow London	Eng
Nov 18	Kinetic Circus Birmingham	Eng
Nov 19	University York	Eng
Nov 27	Spa Hall Bridlington	Eng
Dec 1	Lyceum London	Eng
Dec 31	Marquee Club London	Eng

1972

Jan 14	Subscription Rooms Stroud	Eng
Jan 26	Civic Hall Dunstable	Eng
Jan 27	De Montfort Hall Leicester	Eng
Jan 28	Town Hall Birmingham	Eng
Jan 29	Colston Hall Bristol	Eng
Jan 31	University Exeter	Eng
Feb 5	Free Trade Hall Manchester	Eng
Feb 6	Greyhound Croydon	Eng
Feb 7	Oxford Polytechnic	Eng
Feb 8	Town Hall Watford	Eng
Feb 9	Civic Hall Guildford	Eng
Feb 10	City Hall Sheffield	Eng
Feb 11	Town Hall Leeds	Eng
Feb 12	City Hall Newcastle	Eng
Feb 13	Caley Cinema Edinburgh	Sco
Feb 14	City Hall Glasgow	Sco
Feb 16	Guildhall Southampton	Eng
Feb 17	Essex University Colchester	Eng
Feb 18	The Dome Brighton	Eng
Feb 19	Guild Hall Portsmouth	Eng
Feb 20	Winter Gardens Bournemouth	Eng
Mar 23	Schwabingerau Munich	Ger B
Apr	Camden Festival London	Eng
Apr 4	Kinetic Kenilworth	Eng
Apr 13	Central Hall Chatham	Eng
Apr 16	King George's Hall Blackburn	Eng
Apr 17	Top Rank Swansea	Wal
Apr 18	BBC Maida Vale Studios London	Eng R
Apr 19	City Hall Salisbury	Eng
Apr 20	Winter Gardens Malvern	Eng
Apr 22	St Albans City Hall	Eng
Apr 25		Swi
Apr 26		Swi
Apr 27		Swi
Apr 28		Bel
Apr 29		Bel
Apr 30		Eng
May 10	BBC Maida Vale Studios London	Eng R
May 12	University	Eng
May 14	Bristol Locarno	Eng
May	Bickershaw Festival Wigan	Eng
May 25	BBC Paris Theatre London	Eng R
May	Great Western Festival Lincoln	Eng
May 31	Aeolian Hall London	Eng R
Jun 19	St Louis	USA
Jul 27	Civic Auditorium San Francisco	USA
Jul 28	Long Beach Arena California	USA
Jul 30	Santa Monica California	USA
Jul 31	Santa Monica California	USA
Aug 11	Mecca Arena Milwaukee	USA
Aug 13	Arts Centre Saratoga	USA
Aug 17	Arie Crown Theatre Chicago	USA
Aug 19	Convention Hall Asbury Park	USA
Aug 20	Convention Hall Asbury Park	USA
Aug 21	Wcnk Studios Memphis	USA R
Sep 10	Pavilion Torquay	Eng
Sep 11	West Country TV	Eng T
Sep 15	Locarno Sunderland	Eng
Sep 16	Buxton Festival	Eng
Sep 30	The Oval Cricket Ground London	Eng
Oct	Massey Hall Toronto	Can B
Oct 28	Des Moines	USA
Oct 30	Electric Park Waterloo	USA
Nov 2	Kentucky State University	USA
Nov 8	Palladium Hollywood	USA
Nov 17	Rainbow London	Eng
Nov 18	Rainbow London	Eng
Nov 24	Dome Brighton	Eng
Nov 25	Winter Gardens Bournemouth	Eng
Nov 26	Colston Hall Bristol	Eng
Nov 27	Guildhall Southampton	Eng
Nov 29	Town Hall Birmingham	Eng

Blowin' Free

Date	Venue	Country
Nov 30	Stadium Liverpool	Eng
Dec 1	City Hall Sheffield	Eng
Dec 2	City Hall Newcastle	Eng
Dec 4	Free Trade Hall Manchester	Eng
Dec 6	Public Hall Preston	Eng
Dec 7	Greens Playhouse Glasgow	Sco
Dec 8	Empire Edinburgh	Sco
Dec 9	Caird Hall Dundee	Sco
Dec 12	Guildhall Portsmouth	Eng
Dec 15	Town Hall Leeds	Eng
Dec 17	Fairfield Halls Croydon	Eng
Dec 19	Civic Hall Dunstable	Eng

1973

Date	Venue	Country
Jan 10	Rainbow London	Eng B
Mar 17	Marquee Club London	Eng R
Mar 18	Marquee Club London	Eng R
Mar 29	Toronto	Can
Mar 30	Civic Centre Ottawa	Can
Mar 31	Lutheran University Theatre Waterloo	Can
Apr 1	State University Plattsburg	USA
Apr 3	Agora Theatre Columbus	USA
Apr 4	Dayton	USA
Apr 5	Cincinnati	USA
Apr 6	Ford Auditorium Detroit	USA
Apr 7	Morris Civic Centre South Bend	USA
Apr 8	Melody Skateland Indianapolis	USA
Apr 10	La Crosse	USA
Apr 11	Minneapolis	USA
Apr 12	Rochester	USA
Apr 13	Cow Town Ballroom Kansas City	USA
Apr 14	Kinetic Playground Chicago	USA
Apr 15	Kinetic Playground Chicago	USA
Apr 16	Sheboygan	USA B
Apr 17	Performing Arts Centre Milwaukee	USA
Apr 18	Louisville	USA
Apr 19	Auditorium Little Rock	USA
Apr 20	Municipal Auditorium Shreveport	USA
Apr 21	Independence Hall Baton Rouge	USA
Apr 22	Warehouse New Orleans	USA
Apr 23	Louis Tech University Ruston	USA
Apr 25	War Memorial Nashville	USA
Apr 26	Municipal Auditorium Atlanta	USA
Apr 27	Ellis Auditorium Memphis	USA
Apr 28	Municipal Auditorium Mobile	USA
Apr 29	Municipal Auditorium Birmingham	USA
May 11	Philadelphia	USA
May 12	New York	USA
May 13	Buffalo	USA
May 14	Hammond	USA
May 16	St Louis	USA
May 18	Miami	USA
May 19	Tampa	USA
May 20	Daytona Beach	USA
May 21	Fort Collins	USA
May 23	Colorado Springs	USA
May 24	Albuquerque	USA
May 25	Seattle	USA
May 26	Portland	USA
May 27	Hollywood Palladium	USA
Jun 10	Theatre Royal Norwich	Eng
Jun 11	Pink Pop Festival Galeen	Hol R
Jun 13	Swansea	Wal
Jun 14	City Hall Sheffield	Eng
Jun 16	University Leeds	Eng
Jun 17	Fairfield Halls Croydon	Eng R
Jun 21	Guildhall Portsmouth	Eng R
Jun 22	University Southampton	Eng
Jun 23	University Reading	Eng R
Jun 24	City Hall Newcastle	Eng R
Jun 25	City Hall Hull	Eng
Jun 26	Stadium Liverpool	Eng
Aug 4	Alexandra Palace London	Eng B
Aug 8	Houston Texas	USA
Aug 9	Merryweather Post Pavilion	USA
Aug 10	Asbury Park	USA
Aug 11	Central Park New York City	USA
Aug 15	Charlotte	USA
Aug 19	San Antonio	USA
Aug 21	Dallas	USA
Aug 22	Oklahoma City	USA
Aug 23	Wichita	USA
Sep	Houston	USA
Sep	Chicago	USA
Sep	Detroit	USA
Sep	County Fairground Wheaton Du Page	USA
Sep	Philadelphia	USA
Sep	Buffalo	USA
Sep	Birmingham	USA
Sep	New Orleans	USA
Sep 9		Ger
Oct 11	Guildhall Portsmouth	Eng
Oct 13	Kursaal Southend	Eng
Oct 14	Colston Hall Bristol	Eng
Oct 15	Stadium Liverpool	Eng
Oct 16	City Hall Sheffield	Eng
Oct 17	Apollo Glasgow	Sco
Oct 23	Lincoln	USA
Oct 24	Kansas City	USA
Oct 25	Oklahoma City	USA
Oct 26	Dallas	USA
Oct 27	San Antonio	USA
Oct 28	El Paso	USA
Oct 30	Denver	USA
Oct 31	Colorado Springs	USA
Nov 1	Vancouver	Can
Nov 2	Winterland San Francisco	USA
Nov 3	Winterland San Francisco	USA
Nov 4	San Diego	USA
Nov 7	San Bernadino	USA
Nov 8	Los Angeles	USA
Nov 9	Spokane	USA
Nov 10	Salem	USA
Nov 11	Seattle	USA
Nov 13	Boston	USA
Nov 14	Columbus	USA
Nov 15	Cincinnati	USA
Nov 17	New York City	USA
Nov 19	Minneapolis	USA
Nov 21	St.Louis	USA
Nov 22	Sheboygan	USA B
Nov 23	Wheeling	USA
Nov 24	Detroit	USA
Nov 25	Memphis	USA
Nov 26	Cleveland	USA
Nov 27	Shreveport	USA
Nov 29	Thibodaux	USA
Nov 30	Mobile	USA
Dec 1	Miami	USA
Dec 2	Tampa	USA
Dec	Paris	Fra
Dec		Swi
Dec 22	Alexandra Palace London	Eng R

1974

Date	Venue	Country
Jan		USA
Feb		USA
Feb 23	BBC Paris Theatre London	Eng R
Oct 2	Guildhall Plymouth	Eng
Oct 3	Colston Hall Bristol	Eng
Oct 4	Town Hall Leeds	Eng
Oct 5	City Hall Sheffield	Eng
Oct 7	De Montfort Hall Leicester	Eng
Oct 8	New Theatre Oxford	Eng

Date	Venue	Country
Oct 10	Odeon Newcastle	Eng
Oct 11	Apollo Glasgow	Eng
Oct 12	Empire Liverpool	Eng
Oct 13	Fairfield Halls Croydon	Eng
Oct 14	Dome Brighton	Eng
Oct 15	Guildhall Portsmouth	Eng
Oct 17	Rainbow London	Eng
Oct 18	Free Trade Hall Manchester	Eng
Oct 19	Odeon Birmingham	Eng
Oct 22	Volkshaus Zurich	Swi
Oct 23	Volkshaus Zurich	Swi B
Oct 24	Olympia Paris	Fra
Oct 25	Marni Brussels	Bel
Oct 26	Turfschip Breda	Hol
Oct 27	Evenementenhal Groningen	Hol
Oct 29	Musichalle Hamburg	Ger
Oct 30	Dusseldorf Phillipshalle	Ger B
Oct 31	Stadthalle Offenbach	Ger B
Nov 1	Fredrick Eberts Hale Ludwigschafen	Ger
Nov 2	Killesberghalle Stuttgart	Ger
Nov 3	Deutchemuseum Munich	Ger
Nov 5	Tivoli Copenhagen	Den
Nov 20	Tower Theatre Upper Darby	USA B
Nov 26	Convention Centre Indianapolis	USA
Nov 28	Keil Auditorium St.Louis	USA
Nov 29	Baseball Stadium Miami	USA
Dec 2	Masonic Temple Detroit	USA
Dec 3	State University Bloomingston	USA
Dec 4	Civic Centre St Paul	USA
Dec 5	Dane County Coliseum Madison	USA
Dec 6	The Auditorium Milwaukee	USA
Dec 7	The Forum Chicago	USA
Dec 8	Western Illinois State Uni. Macomb	USA
Dec 10	Brown City Arena Green Bay	USA
Dec 11	Sports Arena Toledo	USA
Dec 13	Public Arena Cleveland	USA
Dec 15	Century Theatre Buffalo	USA
Dec 16	State College Grand Rapids	USA
Dec 18	Atlanta	USA
Dec 19	Mobile	USA
Dec 20	Jacksonville	USA
Dec 21	Lakeland	USA
Dec 22	West Palm Beach	USA
Dec 23	Indiana	USA
Dec 27	Vets Memorial Coliseum Des Moines	USA
Dec 28	Aragon Ballroom Chicago	USA
Dec 29	Roberts Municipal Stadium Evansville	USA
Dec 30	Palmer College Davenport	USA
Dec 31	Hara Sports Arena Dayton	USA

1975

Date	Venue	Country
Jan 2	Civic Centre Baltimore	USA
Jan 3	International Building Oklahoma City	USA
Jan 4	The Music Hall Houston	USA
Jan 5	Hoffehit Pavilion Dallas	USA
Jan 6	Memorial Hall Kansas City	USA
Jan 7	Ellis Auditorium Memphis	USA
Jan 9	Hirsh Memorial Coliseum Shreveport	USA
Jan 10	Independence Hall Baton Rouge	USA
Jan 11	University New Orleans	USA
Jan 15	Masonic Temple Detroit	USA
Jan 17	Longbeach Arena Los Angeles	USA
Jan 19	Golden Hall San Diego	USA
Jan 22	Regis College Denver	USA
Jan 23	Terrace Ballroom Salt Lake City	USA
Jan 25	Winterland San Francisco	USA
Jan 26	Selland Arena Fresno	USA
Jan 28	Gonzaga University Spokane	USA
Jan 29	County Fairgrounds Eugene	USA
Jan 30	Paramount Theatre Portland	USA
Jan 31	Arena Seattle	USA
Feb 1	Agridome Vancouver	Can
Feb 3	The Coral Calgary	Can
Feb 4	Kinsmen Fieldhouse Edmonton	Can
Feb 7	Andrews Amphitheatre Honolulu	USA
Feb 15	Sun Plaza Tokyo	Jap
Feb 16	Sun Plaza Tokyo	Jap
Feb 17	Sun Plaza Tokyo	Jap
Feb 19	Koseinenkin Hall Osaka	Jap B
Feb 20	Koseinenkin Hall Osaka	Jap
Feb 21	Shi Kokaido Nagoya	Jap
Feb 27	Festival Hall Brisbane	Aus
Mar 1	Festival Hall Melbourne	Aus
Mar 2	Hordern Pavilion Sydney	Aus
Mar 4	Festival Hall Melbourne	Aus
Mar 6	Centennial Hall Adelaide	Aus
Mar 13	Wellington	NZ
Mar 14	Christchurch	NZ
Mar 15	Western Springs Stadium Auckland	NZ
Apr 12	Midnight Sun Upper Darby	USA
May 13	Lakeview Arena Marquette	USA
May 27	Cobo Hall Detroit	USA
May 28	Cobo Hall Detroit	USA
May 30	Outdoor Arts Arena Edwardsville	USA
May 31	Convention Centre Kentucky	USA
Jun 1	Roberts Stadium Evansville	USA
Jun 2	Morris Civic Auditorium South Bend	USA
Jun 3	Lake View Arena Marquette	USA
Jun 5	Brown County Arena Green Bay	USA
Jun 6	Arena Duluth	USA
Aug 5	Falkener Theatre Copenhagen	Den
Aug 7	Chat Noir Oslo	Nor
Aug 9	Runsala Folk Park Turku	Fin
Aug 11	Tivoli Stockholm	Swe B
Aug 14	Groendoorhallen Leiden	Hol R
Aug 15	Festival Bilzen	Bel
Aug 16	Stadion Gelende Ludwigsberg	Ger
Aug 17	Roman Amphitheatre Orange	Fra R
Aug 18	Plaza De Toros Marbella	Spa
Aug 24	Reading Festival	Eng B
Aug 27	Hallen Stadion Zurich	Swi
Aug 28	Munich	Ger
Aug 29	Sporthalle Vienna	Aut

1976

Date	Venue	Country
Mar 4	Arena Lubbock	USA
Mar 5	Municipal Auditorium San Antonio	USA
Mar 6	Kirsch Memorial Coliseum Scheveport	USA
Mar 7	Summit Houston	USA
Mar 8	Odessa	USA
Mar 10	Oklahoma City	USA
Mar 19	Arena Milwaukee	USA
Mar 22	Philadelphia	USA
Mar 24	Madison Square Gardens New York	USA
Mar 25	W Virginia Uni. Coliseum Morgantown	USA
Mar 26	Theatre For Performing Arts Elizabeth	USA
Mar 28	Convention Centre Indianapolis	USA
Mar 29	Largo Coliseum Washington DC	USA
Apr 2	Winterland San Francisco	USA
Apr 3	Sports Arena San Diego	USA
Apr 5	Terrace Ballroom Salt Lake City	USA
Apr 6	State Fairgrounds Boise	USA
Apr 8	Selland Arena Fresno	USA
Apr 9	Longbeach Arena Los Angeles	USA
Apr 10	Swing Auditorium San Bernadino	USA
Apr 12	Redding	USA
Apr 14	Medford	USA
Apr 16	Paramount Portland	USA
Apr 17	Convention Centre Spokane	USA
Apr 18	Arena Seattle	USA
Apr 23	Hayes	USA
Apr 24	Uptown Theatre Kansas City	USA
Apr 25	Dallas	USA
Apr 27	University Of Oklahoma Tuscaloosa	USA

Blowin' Free

Apr 28	Lincoln	USA		Sep 27	Munster	Ger
Apr 30	Hastings	USA		Sep 29	Heidelberg	Ger B
May 1	St Louis	USA		Sep 30	Esslingen	Ger
May 5	Peoria	USA		Oct 1	Munich	Ger
May 6	Davenport	USA R		Oct 2	Zurich	Swi
May 7	Madison	USA		Oct 4	Toulouse	Fra
May 8	Mount Prospect	USA		Oct 6	Lyons	Fra
Jun 6	Festival Frankfurt	Ger		Oct 7	Hippodrome Paris	Fra B
Jun 7	Dusseldorf	Ger		Oct 8	Tijenraan Raalte	Hol
Jun 8	Hamburg	Ger		Oct 9	Beynishal Haarlem	Hol B
Oct 3	Sun Plaza Tokyo	Jap B		Oct 11	BBC TV Studios London	Eng T
Oct 5	Kosei Nenkin Hall Osaka	Jap		Oct 16	City Hall Newcastle	Eng R
Oct 6	Kosei Nenkin Hall Osaka	Jap		Oct 17	Apollo Glasgow	Sco R
Oct 7	Hiroshima	Jap		Oct 18	City Hall Sheffield	Eng R
Oct 8	Kurashiki	Jap		Oct 20	Odeon Birmingham	Eng
Oct 10	Kosei Nenkin Hall Osaka	Jap		Oct 21	Empire Liverpool	Eng
Oct 11	Kokura	Jap		Oct 22	Belle Vue Manchester	Eng
Oct 13	Shi Kokaido Nagoya	Jap		Oct 24	De Montfort Hall Leicester	Eng
Oct 14	Sun Plaza Tokyo	Jap B		Oct 25	Theatre Coventry	Eng
Oct 22	Victoria Hall Hanley	Eng		Oct 26	Capitol Theatre Cardiff	Wal
Oct 23	City Hall Sheffield	Eng		Oct 27	Gaumont Southampton	Eng
Oct 26	Festival Hall Torbay	Eng		Oct 29	Marquee Club London	Eng R
Oct 27	University Exeter	Eng		Oct 31	Wembley Empire Pool	Eng R
Oct 28	Capitol Theatre Cardiff	Wal		Nov 5	Baden Baden German TV	Ger T
Oct 29	Colston Hall Bristol	Eng		Nov 11	Aragon Ballroom Chicago	USA
Oct 30	University Nottingham	Eng		Nov 12	Rock Island	USA
Oct 31	Fairfield Halls Croydon	Eng		Nov 14	Mike Douglas Show	USA T
Nov 1	Pavilion Hemel Hempstead	Eng		Nov 15	Masonic Temple Detroit	USA
Nov 2	Guildhall Portsmouth	Eng		Nov 18	Fox Theatre St Louis	USA
Nov 4	Gaumont Ipswich	Eng		Nov 22	Civic Auditorium, Bakersfield	USA
Nov 5	Hammersmith Odeon London	Eng		Nov 23	Selland Arena Fresno	USA
Nov 6	Hammersmith Odeon London	Eng		Nov 25	Longbeach Arena Los Angeles	USA
Nov 7	Odeon Birmingham	Eng		Nov 26	Swing Auditorium San Bernadino	USA
Nov 8	De Montfort Hall Leicester	Eng		Nov 27	Sports Arena San Diego	USA
Nov 12	Dome Brighton	Eng		Nov 29	Arena Seattle	USA B
Nov 13	Free Trade Hall Manchester	Eng		Nov 30	Armoury Salem	USA
Nov 14	City Hall Newcastle	Eng		Dec 2	Winterland San Francisco	USA
Nov 15	Empire Liverpool	Eng R		Dec 3	Winterland San Francisco	USA
Nov 16	City Hall Newcastle	Eng		Dec 4	Aladdin Theatre Las Vegas	USA
Nov 18	Usher Hall Edinburgh	Sco		Dec 7	Coliseum, Corpus Christi	USA
Nov 19	Apollo Glasgow	Sco R		Dec 8	Tarrant County Coliseum Fort Worth	USA
Nov 20	University Leeds	Eng		Dec 9	Joe Freemans Civic San Antonio	USA
Nov 21	University Lancaster	Eng		Dec 10	Sam Houston Coliseum Houston	USA
Nov 25	Niedersachsenhalle Hannover	Ger		Dec 11	Assembly Centre Tulsa	USA
Nov 26	Eissporthalle Berlin	Ger		**1978**		
Nov 27	Holstenhalle Neumunster	Ger		Sep 9	Stuttgart	Ger
Nov 28	Halle Munsterland Munster	Ger		Oct 6	Gaumont Ipswich	Eng
Nov 30	Stadthalle Bremen	Ger		Oct 7	Odeon Birmingham	Eng
Dec 1	Sporthalle Cologne	Ger T B		Oct 8	University Lancaster	Eng
Dec 2	Saarlandhalle Saarbrucken	Ger B		Oct 9	Apollo Glasgow	Sco R
Dec 3	Walter Kobel Halle Russelsheim	Ger		Oct 10	Odeon Edinburgh	Sco
Dec 4	Fredrich Bert Halle Ludwigsberg	Ger B		Oct 11	City Hall Newcastle	Eng
Dec 5	Messe Centrum Halle Nuremberg	Ger		Oct 12	Belle Vue Manchester	Eng
Dec 6	Naue Sporthalle Linz	Aut		Oct 13	Victoria Hall Hanley	Eng
Dec 9	Eishalle Innsbruck	Aut		Oct 15	Gaumont Southampton	Eng
Dec 10	Pavilion Des Sports Geneva	Swi		Oct 16	Dome Brighton	Eng
Dec 11	Sporthalle St Jacob Basle	Swi		Oct 17	Guildhall Portsmouth	Eng
Dec 12	Boblingen Sporthalle Stuttgart	Ger B		Oct 20	University Cardiff	Wal
Dec 14	Stadthalle Freiburg	Ger		Oct 21	City Hall Sheffield	Eng
Dec 14	Oberschwabenhalle Ravensburg	Ger		Oct 24	Hammersmith Odeon London	Eng
Dec 15	Olympiahalle Munich	Ger		Oct 25	Hammersmith Odeon London	Eng R
Dec 17	Olympia Paris	Fra B		Oct 27	Colston Hall Bristol	Eng R
Dec 18	Ljsselhal Zwolle	Hol		Oct 28	University Leeds	Eng R
1977				Oct 30	Winter Gardens Bournemouth	Eng R
Sep 18	Kiel	Ger		Oct 31	De Montfort Hall Leicester	Eng
Sep 20	Hamburg	Ger		Nov 2	Theatre Coventry	Eng
Sep 21	Bremen	Ger		Nov 3	Empire Liverpool	Eng
Sep 22	Dusseldorf	Ger		Nov 10	Sun Plaza Hall Tokyo	Jap R
Sep 23	Russelsheim	Ger B		Nov 13	Festival Hall Osaka	Jap
Sep 24	Nuremberg	Ger		Nov 15	Japanese TV Tokyo	Jap T
Sep 26	Wolfsburg	Ger		Nov 15	Koseinenkin Hall Tokyo	Jap R

thirty years of Wishbone Ash

1979
Nov 22	Wembley Empire Pool London	Eng R T

1980
Jan 18	Victoria Hall Hanley	Eng
Jan 19	City Hall Sheffield	Eng R
Jan 20	City Hall Sheffield	Eng R
Jan 21	City Hall Newcastle	Eng R
Jan 23	Odeon Edinburgh	Sco
Jan 24	Caird Hall Dundee	Sco
Jan 25	Capitol Theatre Aberdeen	Sco
Jan 26	Apollo Glasgow	Sco
Jan 27	Empire Liverpool	Eng
Jan 29	De Montford Hall Leicester	Eng
Jan 30	Assembly Rooms Derby	Eng
Jan 31	St George's Hall Bradford	Eng
Feb 1	Hammersmith Odeon London	Eng
Feb 2	Hammersmith Odeon London	Eng R
Feb 3	Fairfield Hall Croydon	Eng
Feb 4	Gaumont Ipswich	Eng B
Feb 5	Gaumont Southampton	Eng
Feb 7	Dome Brighton	Eng
Feb 8	Apollo Manchester	Eng
Feb 9	Odeon Birmingham	Eng
Feb 10	New Theatre Oxford	Eng
Feb 11	Pavilion Hemel Hempstead	Eng
Feb 12	Civic Hall Guildford	Eng
Feb 13	Winter Gardens Bournemouth	Eng
Feb 15	Guildhall Portsmouth	Eng
Feb 16	Colston Hall Bristol	Eng R
Feb 17	Festival Theatre Paignton	Eng B
Feb 19	University Cardiff	Wal
Feb 21	Stadium Dublin	Ire
Feb 22	Whitla Hall Belfast	N Ire
Feb 29	Hall Roma Antwerp	Bel
Mar 1	Palais Des Sportscambrai	Bel
Mar 2	Maison Des Sports Reims	Fra
Mar 3	Hippodrome Paris	Fra B
Mar 4	La Rotonede Le Mans	Fra
Mar 5	Maison Des Sports Clermont Ferrand	Fra
Mar 6	Palais Des Sports De Gerland Lyon	Fra
Mar 8	Parc Des Expositions Nancy	Fra
Mar 10	Deutches Museum Munich	Ger
Mar 11	Stadthalle Offenbach	Ger
Mar 12	Philipshalle Dusseldorf	Ger
Mar 14	Stadthalle Kassel	Ger
Mar 15	Hemmerleinhalle Nuremburg	Ger
Mar 16	Neue Welt Berlin	Ger
Mar 17	Musichalle Hamburg	Ger
Mar 18	Niedersachsenhalle Hannover	Ger
Mar 19	Ausstellungshalle Stuttgart	Ger
Mar 21	Friedrich Elbert Halle Ludwigshaven	Ger
Mar 22	Eurogress Aachen	Ger
Mar 23	Westfallenhalle Dortmund	Ger
Mar 25	Volkshaus Zurich	Swi
Mar 26	Sportshalle Linz	Aut
Mar 27	Sofienshalle Vienna	Aut T B
Mar 28	Udine	Ita
Mar 29	Turin	Ita
Mar 30	Milan	Ita B
Mar 31	Udine	Ita
Apr 1	Ljubliana	Yug
Apr 2	Belgrade	Yug
Apr 3	Zagreb	Yug
May 5	University Sheffield	Eng
May 24	Sports Centre Bracknell	Eng
May 25	Top Rank Cardiff	Wal
May 27	Town Hall Middlesborough	Eng B
May 28	Mayfair Sunderland	Eng
May 29	St George's Hall Blackburn	Eng B
May 31	Market Hall Carlisle	Eng
Jun 1	City Hall Hull	Eng R
Jun 2	Odeon Ilford	Eng
Jun 3	Odeon Chelmsford	Eng
Jun 4	Civic Hall Wolverhampton	Eng R
Jun 6	Pavilion Bath	Eng
Jun 22	Cameron Bear Park Loch Lommond	Sco
Aug 20	Bullring Santander	Spa
Aug 23	Lorelei Festival	Ger
Aug 24	Golden Summer Festival	Ger
Sep 20	Colmar Festival	Fra

1981
May 16	University Manchester	Eng
May 18	Odeon Taunton	Eng
May 19	Colston Hall Bristol	Eng
May 21	University Lancaster	Eng
May 22	City Hall Hull	Eng
May 23	Odeon Birmingham	Eng
May 24	De Montford Hall Leicester	Eng
May 26	Empire Liverpool	Eng B
May 27	City Hall Newcastle	Eng
May 28	Odeon Edinburgh	Sco
May 29	Apollo Glasgow	Sco
May 30	City Hall Sheffield	Eng
Jun 1	Guildhall Portsmouth	Eng
Jun 2	Hammersmith Odeon London	Eng R
Jun 3	Rainbow Theatre London	Eng
Jun 4	Civic Hall Guildford	Eng
Jun 5	The Dome Brighton	Eng R
Jun 6	New Theatre Oxford	Eng
Jun 12	Palais Des Sports Paris	Fra R
Jun	German TV	Ger T
Jun	Macroom Festival	Ire
Jul 14	Louis Rock City Washington	USA
Jul 15	My Father's Place New York	USA
Jul 16	The Ritz New York	USA
Jul 17	Tower Theatre Audabon	USA
Jul 20	Agora Atlanta	USA
Jul 21	Point After Orlando	USA
Jul 22	Agora Miami	USA
Jul 23	Brassy's Cocoa Florida	USA
Jul 25	The Warehouse New Orleans	USA
Jul 26	Cardis Houston	USA
Jul 27	Randy's Rodeo San Antonio	USA
Jul 28	Cardis Dallas	USA
Jul 29	The Rox Lubbock	USA
Jul 30	Cains Ballroom Tulsa	USA
Jul 31	The Uptown Theatre Kansas City	USA
Aug 1	Casa Loma St Louis	USA
Aug 3	Rockstage Festival Chicago	USA
Aug 4	Studio 1 Champaign	USA
Aug 6	Point East Lynwood	USA
Aug 7	Twin Lakes Wisconsin	USA
Aug 11	The Paradise Boston	USA
Aug 12	Concord New Hampshire	USA
Aug 16	The Bayou Washington DC	USA B
Aug 30	Reading Festival	Eng B
Nov 10	Casino Den Bosch	Hol
Nov 11	'T Heem Hattem	Hol B
Nov 21	University Of East Anglia Norwich	Eng
Nov 22	Brunel University Uxbridge	Eng
Nov 24	Caird Hall Dundee	Sco
Nov 25	Strathclyde University Glasgow	Sco
Dec 1	Polytechnic Hatfield	Eng
Dec 7	Bombay	Ind
Dec 8	Bombay	Ind
Dec 12	University Madras	Ind

1982
May 17	Queensway Hall Dunstable	Eng
May 18	Rock City Nottingham	Eng
May 19	Assembly Rooms Derby	Eng
May 20	Pier Theatre Colwyn Bay	Wal
May 21	Floral Hall Southport	Eng

Blowin' Free

Date	Venue	Country
May 22	Pavilion West Runton	Eng
May 23	Apollo Oxford	Eng B
May 24	Queen's Theatre Barnstaple	Eng
May 26	Town Hall Middlesborough	Eng
May 27	Leisure Centre Ashington	Eng
Jul	Lisdoonvarm Festival	Ire
Jul 20	Iron Horse Thibodaux Louisiana	USA
Jul 21	Ricky's Kenner Louisiana	USA
Jul 22	Southpaws Boiffer City Louisiana	USA
Sep 21	Cliff's Pavilion Southend	Eng
Sep 22	Civic Hall Guildford	Eng
Sep 24	City Hall Hull	Eng
Sep 25	Guildhall Preston	Eng
Sep 26	Royal Court Theatre Liverpool	Eng
Sep 27	Empire Sunderland	Eng
Sep 28	Thameside Theatre Ashton-U-Lyne	Eng B
Sep 29	Lyceum Sheffield	Eng
Oct 1	City Hall St Albans	Eng
Oct 2	Polytechnic Plymouth	Eng
Oct 3	Winter Gardens Margate	Eng
Oct 4	Guildhall Southampton	Eng
Oct 6	Assembly Hall Worthing	Eng
Oct 8	Dominion Theatre London	Eng
Oct 9	Rock Theatre Chippenham	Eng
Oct 10	Fairfield Halls Croydon	Eng
Oct 11	Anglia TV Norwich	Eng T
Oct 11	Theatre Royal Norwich	Eng
Oct 18	Ljubilana	Yug
Oct 19	Zagreb	Yug
Oct 20	Belgrade	Yug
Oct 21	Sarajevo	Yug
Oct 22	Split	Yug
Oct 24	Pula	Yug
Oct 26	Strasburg	Fra
Oct 27	Grenoble	Fra
Oct 28	Clermont Ferrand	Fra
Oct 29	Nugent Pavilion Baltard	Fra B
Oct 30	Lille	Fra
Oct 31	Rouen	Fra
Nov 2	Orleans	Fra
Nov 3	Poitiers	Fra
Nov 4	Pau	Fra
Nov 5	Bordeaux	Fra
Nov 7	Marseilles	Fra
Nov 8	Epinal	Fra
Nov 9	Lyons	Fra
Nov 10	Barcelona	Spa
Nov 11	Barcelona	Spa B
Nov 12	Madrid	Spa
Nov 13	Gijon	Spa
Nov 14	San Sebastian	Spa
Nov 18	Stuttgart	Ger B
Nov 19	Ulm	Ger
Nov 20	Erlangen	Ger
Nov 22	Reutlingen	Ger
Nov 23	Zurich	Swi
Nov 24	Mannheim	Ger
Nov 25	Bochum	Ger
Nov 26	Enden	Ger
Nov 27	Hamburg	Ger
Nov 28	Bremen	Ger
Nov 29	Pforzheim	Ger R
Nov 30	Hannover	Ger
Dec 1	Berlin	Ger
Dec 17	Wembley Arena London	Eng
1983		
Feb 15	Bombay	Ind
Feb 16	Poona	Ind
Feb 18	Madras	Ind
Feb 19	Bangalore	Ind
Feb 22	Marquee Club London	Eng
Feb 23	Marquee Club London	Eng T
Feb 25	Dublin	Ire
Feb 26	Queen's University Belfast	N Ire B
Mar 6	Teatro Tenda Milan	Ita B
Apr 13	Ons Huis Venlo	Hol
Apr 14	Berg Stichting Noordwijk	Hol
Apr 15	Alphen A/D Riijn	Hol
Apr 17	Spuug Vaal	Hol
Jun 5	Bayou Washington	USA B
Jun 8	Brandywine Club Chadd's Ford	USA
Jun 9	Paradise Boston	USA B
Dec 9	Mudd Club Gothenburg	Swe B
1984		
Jun	Athens	Gre
Jul 7	Parkzicht Rotterdam	Hol B V
Jul 8	Paradiso Amsterdam	Hol
Aug 25	Wakefield Music Festival	Eng
Oct 2	Bordeaux	Fra B
Nov 30	Basle	Swi
Dec 1	Bad Bergentheim	Ger
Dec 2	Osnabruck	Ger
Dec 4	Detmold	Ger
Dec 5	Bochum	Ger
Dec 6	Cologne	Ger
Dec 7	Simmern	Ger
Dec 8	Neuenstadt	Ger
Dec 10	Ulm	Ger
Dec 11	Landau	Ger
Dec 12	Rosenheim	Ger
Dec 13	Neunchen	Ger
Dec 14	Nuremburg	Ger
Dec 15	Pirmasens	Ger
Dec 16	Regensberg	Ger
Dec 17	Stuttgart	Ger B
Dec 19	Paradiso Amsterdam	Hol
Dec 20	Bonn	Ger
Dec 21	Hamburg	Ger
1985		
Feb 9	Bergen	Nor R
Jun 1	University Of Surrey Guildford	Eng
Jun 2	Goldiggers Chippenham	Eng
Jun 3	BBC Maida Vale Studios London	Eng R
Jun 4	The Pink Toothbrush Rayleigh	Eng B
Jun 5	Odeon Birmingham	Eng
Jun 6	Carnegie Theatre Workington	Eng
Jun 7	Pavilion Ayr	Sco
Jun 8	Playhouse Edinburgh	Sco
Jun 9	Albert Hall Stirling	Sco
Jun 10	Caird Hall Dundee	Sco
Jun 11	Rock City Nottingham	Eng B
Jun 12	University Manchester	Eng B
Jun 13	Assembly Hall Worthing	Eng
Jun 14	Leas Cliff Hall Folkestone	Eng
Jun 15	City Hall St Albans	Eng
Jun 16	New Ocean Club Cardiff	Eng
Jun 19	Theatre Royal Lincoln	Eng
Jun 20	Apollo Oxford	Eng
Jun 21	Hammersmith Odeon London	Eng B
Jun 28	TV Club Dublin	Ire
Jun 29	Larne Festival	Nir
Jul 5	BBC Friday Rock Show	Eng R
Jul 25	Rockfestival Vlissingen	Hol
Jul 26	Parkzicht Rotterdam	Hol
Jul 27	Elkerlijk Luttenberg	Hol
Jul 28	Paradiso Amsterdam	Hol B
Sep 14	Lorelei Festival	Ger R T
Oct 19	Belfast	N Ire B
Dec 2	Mutualite Paris	Fra
Dec 4	Queen's Theatre Barnstaple	Eng
Dec 5	Art's Centre Poole	Eng
Dec 6	Bar Gates Centre Burton-On-Trent	Eng

thirty years of Wishbone Ash

Dec 7	Spectrum Willington	Eng B
Dec 9	Hammersmith Odeon London	Eng R
Dec 14	Bombay	Ind R
Dec 15	Goa	Ind R
Dec 19	Madras	Ind R
Dec 21	Calcutta	Ind R

1986

Jan 7	Tuttlingen	Ger
Jan 8	Stuttgart	Ger B
Jan 9	Zurich	Ger
Jan 10	Freiburg	Ger
Jan 11	Bamburg	Ger
Jan 14	Bochum	Ger
Jan 16	Flensburg	Ger
Jan 20	Konsertuset Gothenburg	Swe B
Jan 24	Musicpub Uppsala	Swe B
Jan 25	Hard Rock Stockholm	Swe
Mar 17	Trocadero Philadelphia	USA
Mar 19	The Copa Springfield	USA
Mar 20	The Ritz New York	USA
Mar 21	The Boat House Norfolk	USA B
Mar 22	Harpo's Detroit	USA
Mar 25	Easy Streets Des Moines	USA
Mar 26	Stages East St Louis	USA B
Mar 27	Uptown Theatre Kansas City	USA
Mar 28	The Metro Chicago	USA
Mar 29	Zivko's Hartford Wisconsin	USA
Apr 1	Rockers Phoenix	USA
Apr 3	The Roxy Tuscon	USA
Apr 4	Joshua's Parlor Westminster	USA
Apr 5	Joshua's Parlor Westminster	USA
Apr 7	The Bacchanol San Diego	USA
Apr 8	The Oasis Sacramento	USA
Apr 9	The Keystone San Francisco	USA
Apr 10	The Keystone San Francisco	USA
Apr 12	Starry Night Portland	USA
Apr 13	Parker's Seattle	USA B
Apr 14	Commodore Ballroom Vancouver	Can
Apr 15	Parker's Seattle	USA B
Apr 16	Parker's Seattle	USA
Apr 17	Gatsby's Spokane	USA
Apr 18	Gatsby's Spokane	USA
Apr 22	The Club Turlock	USA
Apr 23	The Hill Oakland	USA
Apr 26	Rainbow Theatre Denver	USA
Apr 28	Krackers Las Vegas	USA
May 4	New West Club San Antonio	USA
May 5	Cardis Houston	USA
May 7	Jimmy's New Orleans	USA
May 9	The Boardwalk Huntsville	USA
May 10	Kidnappers Charlotte	USA B
May 12	Lone Star Cafe New York	USA
Aug 2	Festival Folkestone	Eng B T
Nov 20	Central Park Burton-Upon-Trent	Eng
Dec 12	Messehalle Leipzig	Ger
Dec 13	Messehalle Leipzig	Ger
Dec 14	Theatre Weimar	Ger
Dec 17	Marquee Club London	Eng
Dec 18	Marquee Club London	Eng

1987

Jan 2	Azotod De Meern	Hol
Jan 3	Paradiso Amsterdam	Hol
Jan 4	Noorderligt Tilberg	Hol
Jan 6	Akzente Tuttlingen	Ger B
Jan 7	Rockfabrick Bruchsal	Ger
Jan 8	Maxim Stuttgart	Ger B
Jan 9	Intertref Heilbron	Ger
Jan 10	Jurahalle Neumarkt	Ger
Jan 11	Hotel De Ville Saargemund	Ger
Jan 12	Theaterfabrick Unterfohring	Ger
Jan 13	Steinbruchtheater Darmstadt	Ger
Jan 14	Druckhaus Hanau	Ger
Jan 15	Zeche Bochum	Ger
Jan 16	Stollwerk Cologne	Ger
Jan 17	Freitzeitzentrum Bremerhaven	Ger
Jan 18	Knopfs Music Halle Hamburg	Ger
Jan 19	Sudhaus Berlin	Ger
Jan 21	Jugend-Und Kulterzentrum Bern	Swi
Jan 22	Rohrbach Bei Huttwill Baeren	Swi
Jan 23	Gigelberghalle Biberach	Swi
Jan 24	Maintauberhalle Wertheim	Swi
Jan 25	Rathaussaal Schaan	Lct B
Jan 26	Utopia Innsbruck	Aut
Jan 27	Posthof Linz	Aut
Jan 28	Metropol Vienna	Aut
Mar		USA
Apr		USA
May		USA
May 24	Sun City Complex	RSA
May 25	Sun City Complex	RSA
May 26	Sun City Complex	RSA
May 27	Sun City Complex	RSA
May 28	Sun City Complex	RSA
Aug		Ger
Aug		Spa
Dec 7	Jubilejnuj Leningrad	Rus
Dec 8	Jubilejnuj Leningrad	Rus
Dec 9	Jubilejnuj Leningrad	Rus
Dec 10	Jubilejnuj Leningrad	Rus
Dec 11	Jubilejnuj Leningrad	Rus
Dec 12	Jubilejnuj Leningrad	Rus
Dec 13	Jubilejnuj Leningrad	Rus
Dec 14	Jubilejnuj Leningrad	Rus
Dec 15	Jubilejnuj Leningrad	Rus
Dec 18	Sportshall Vilnius	Lit
Dec 19	Sportshall Vilnius	Lit
Dec 20	Sportshall Vilnius	Lit

1988

Feb 27	Lees Cliff Hall Folkestone	Eng
Feb 28	Hummingbird Birmingham	Eng
Mar 1	Gatehouse Theatre Stafford	Eng
Mar 2	International 2 Manchester	Eng B
Mar 3	Tivoli Ballroom Buckley	Wal
Mar 4	Hammersmith Odeon London	Eng R T
Mar 5	The Forum Hatfield	Eng
Mar 6	Arts Centre Poole	Eng
Mar 7	Assembly Hall Worthing	Eng
Mar 8	Assembly Hall Tunbridge Wells	Eng B
Mar 9	Riviera Centre Torquay	Eng
Mar 20	The Roxy Sheffield	Eng B
Mar 25	Mayfair Newcastle	Eng B
Mar 27	Royal Hall Harrogate	Eng
Mar 28	Astoria Nottingham	Eng
Mar 29	Roxy Sheffield	Eng B V
Apr 6	Metropole Aachen	Ger
Apr 7	Europasaal Bayreuth	Ger
Apr 8	E Werk Erlangen	Ger
Apr 9	Schutzenhalle Buren Harth	Ger
Apr 10	Modernes Bremen	Ger
Apr 11	Zeche Bochum	Ger
Apr 12	Akzente Tuttlingen	Ger B
Apr 13	Capital Hannover	Ger B
Apr 14	Grosse Freiheit Hamburg	Ger
Apr 15	Altepiesel Kunzell	Ger
Apr 16	Waldcafe Dudweiler	Ger B
Apr 17	Concertcentrum Gieselwind	Ger
Apr 18	Garage Rastatt	Ger
Apr 19	Theatrefabrik Munich	Ger
Apr 22	Biberach	Ger
Apr 23	Herenthout	Lux
Apr 24	Hunky Dory Musicalle Detmold	Ger
Apr 26	Darmstadt	Ger

Blowin' Free

Date	Venue	Country
Apr 28	Schlaghaus Wels	Aut
Apr 30	Stadtest Vienna	Aut
May 2	Burgerweeshuis Deventer	Hol
May 3	Paradiso Amsterdam	Hol
May 4	Festhalle Frankfurt	Ger B
May 5	Schleyerhalle Stuttgart	Ger B
May 6	Prasilia Kiel	Ger B V

1989

Date	Venue	Country
Jul 14	Sao Paulo	Bra B V
Jul 16	Rio De Janeiro	Bra B V
Jul 22	Theatre Of The Living Arts Pasadena	USA B
Jul 26	Coach House San Juan	USA B
Jul 27	Redondo Beach California	USA B V
Jul	New Orleans	USA
Sep 8	Winter Gardens Eastbourne	Eng
Sep 9	City Hall St Albans	Eng
Sep 10	Odeon Lewisham	Eng
Sep 11	The Borderline London	Eng B V
Sep 12	Assembly Hall Tunbridge Wells	Eng
Sep 13	Beck Theatre Hayes	Eng B
Sep 14	Princess Hall Aldershot	Eng
Sep 15	Assembly Hall Worthing	Eng
Sep 16	Leas Cliff HallFolkestone	Eng
Sep 17	Woughton Centre Milton Keynes	Eng
Sep 18	Riviera Centre Torquay	Eng V
Sep 20	Empire Theatre Sunderland	Eng B
Sep 21	Municipal Hall Colne	Eng
Sep 22	Royal Spa Centre Leamington Spa	Eng
Sep 23	Hammersmith Odeon London	Eng B
Sep 24	Festival Hall Corby	Eng B
Sep 25	Corn Exchange Cambridge	Eng B
Sep 26	Colston Hall Bristol	Eng T B
Sep 27	Royal Court Theatre Liverpool	Eng
Sep 28	Apollo Manchester	Eng
Oct 4	Rockfabrik Ludwigsberg	Ger B
Oct 12	Capitol Hannover	Ger
Oct 25	Music & Action Bonlanden	Ger B
Oct 26	Factory Regensburg	Ger
Oct 28	Haus Der Jugend Ingolstadt	Ger
Oct 29	Meddox Remscheid	Ger
Oct 30	Arche Waldkirch	Ger
Oct 31	Kultursaal Saarbrucken	Ger
Nov 1	Milieu Hausach	Ger
Nov 3	Baumgarten Bistensee	Ger
Nov 4	Miami Nice Berlin	Ger
Nov 5	Top Act Zapendorf	Ger
Nov 6	Hyde Park Osnabruck	Ger
Nov 7	Garage Luneberg	Ger
Nov 8	Felsenkeller Hoxter	Ger
Nov 9	Zeche Karl Essen	Ger
Nov 10	Audi Max Giessen	Ger
Nov 11	Kulturfabrik Krefeld	Ger
Nov 12	Gala Bremen	Ger

1990

Date	Venue	Country
Jan 26	Winter Gardens Margate	Eng
Jan 27	Civic Centre Aylesbury	Eng
Jan 28	Civic Centre Mansfield	Eng B
Jan 30	Civic Hall Camberley	Eng
Feb 1	Dome Brighton	Eng
Feb 2	Cliff's Pavilion Southend	Eng B
Feb 3	Hertsmere Centre Borehamwood	Eng B
Feb 4	Civic Centre Fareham	Eng
Feb 7	Marquee Club London	Eng B
Feb 9	Hummingbird Birmingham	Eng
Feb 10	University Exeter	Eng
Mar 2	East Meets West East Berlin	Ger
Mar 5	Town & Country Club London	Eng T B
Jun 3	Villa Marina Douglas	Iom
Jul	Zurich	Swi
Jul 7	Big Top Festival Swansea	Wal
Aug 30	Congress Theatre Eastbourne	Eng
Aug 31	Leisure Centre Brentwood	Eng B
Sep 1	Leas Cliff Pavilion Folkestone	Eng
Sep 2	Towngate Theatre Basildon	Eng
Sep 4	Guildhall Portsmouth	Eng
Sep 6	Irish Centre Birmingham	Eng
Sep 7	Civic Centre Mansfield	Eng
Sep 9	Queen Elizabeth Hall Oldham	Eng
Sep 10	Corn Exchange Maidstone	Eng
Sep 12	Beck Theatre Hayes	Eng B
Sep 14	Assembly Hall Worthing	Eng
Sep 15	Forum Hatfield	Eng B
Sep 16	Woughton Centre Milton Keynes	Eng
Sep 19	Central Hall Chatham	Eng
Sep 20	White Rock Theatre Hastings	Eng
Sep 21	Theatre Lewisham	Eng B
Sep 22	Queen's Hall Barnstaple	Eng
Sep 24	Civic Hall Guildford	Eng B
Sep 27	Ritz Theatre Lincoln	Eng
Sep 28	Civic Hall Wolverhampton	Eng
Sep 29	Royal Spa Centre Leamington Spa	Eng B
Sep 30	Leadmill Sheffield	Eng
Oct 1	St George's Hall Bradford	Eng
Oct 2	Cleethorpes	Eng
Oct 4	Arcadia Theatre Llandudno	Wal

1991

Date	Venue	Country
Apr 12	Zurich	Swi
Apr 13	Rubigen	Swi
Apr 19	Madrid	Spa
Apr 20	Barcelona	Spa
May 3	Forum Hatfield	Eng B
May 4	Winter Gardens Weston Super Mare	Eng B
May 5	Woughton Centre Milton Keynes	Eng
May 6	Marquee Club London	Eng B
May 7	Marquee Club London	Eng B
May 8	Prince's Hall Aldershot	Eng B
May 9	Assembly Hall Worthing	Eng B
May 11	King George's Hall Blackburn	Eng B
May 12	Civic Theatre Mansfield	Eng B
May 13	Thameside Theatre Ashton-U-Lyme	Eng B
May 16	Assembly Hall Walthamstow	Eng B V
May 20	Club Citta Kawasaki	Jap
May 21	Club Citta Kawasaki	Jap B
May 23	Bottom Line Nagoya (2 Shows)	Jap R T
May 24	Am Hall Osaka (2 Shows)	Jap
May 31	Festzelt Babenhausen	Ger B
Jun 2	Haus Neue Einheit Chemnitz	Ger
Jun 3	Capital Hannover	Ger
Jun 4	Music Hall Cologne	Ger
Jun 5	Longhorn Heligenwiessen	Ger B
Jun 6	Theater Fabrick Munich	Ger B
Jun 7	Serenadenhof Nuremberg	Ger
Jun 8	Stadthalle Neuenstadt	Ger
Jun 9	Music Galerie Uelzen	Ger
Jun 10	Fabrik Hamburg	Ger
Oct 25	Springfield Illinois	USA
Oct 26	Biddy Mulligans Chicago	USA B
Nov 1	St Louis Missouri	USA
Nov 15	Rockhaus Vienna	Aut B V
Nov 16	Weidhofen	Aut B
Nov 17	Feldkirch	Ger
Nov 18	Longhorn Stuttgart	Ger B
Nov 19	St Josefhaus Weiden	Ger
Nov 20	Resi Nuremburg	Ger
Nov 21	Elzer Hof Mainz	Ger
Nov 22	Schwabenhalle Augsburg	Ger
Nov 23	Stadthalle Saarburg	Ger
Nov 24	Westfelenhalle Dortmund	Ger
Nov 25	Metropol Berlin	Ger
Nov 26	Grosse Freiheit Hamburg	Ger
Nov 27	Rockheaven Herford	Ger
Nov 28	Stadthalle Cologne	Ger

thirty years of Wishbone Ash

Nov 29	Elysee Montmartre Paris	Fra
Nov 30	Mulhouse	Fra
Dec 1	Rockfestival Schinjndel	Hol
Dec 2	Aladdin Bremen	Ger
Dec 3	Paradiso Amsterdam	Hol
Dec 4	Schwabenhalle Augsburg	Ger
Dec 5	Town & Country Club London	Eng B
Dec 6	Elysee Montmartre Paris	Fra B
Dec 7	Vooruit Gaet	Hol
Dec 8	Town & Country Club London	Eng B

1992

Jan 24	Easy Street Glenview Illinois	USA R
Jan 25	Easy Street Glenview Illinois	USA R
Apr 10	Playhouse Theatre Newcastle	Eng B
Apr 11	Civic Hall Wolverhampton	Eng B
Apr 12	Bierkeller Bristol	Eng
Apr 13	Marina Swansea	Wal
Apr 15	Irish Centre Leeds	Eng B
Apr 17	Spring St Theatre Hull	Eng
Apr 19	Leadmill Sheffield	Eng B
Apr 24	Cotton Bowl Redcar	Eng
Apr 25	Olympia Dublin	Ire B
Apr 26	Carnegie Theatre Workington	Eng
Apr 28	Civic Theatre Mansfeild	Eng B
Apr 29	Old Frog Inn Newcastle-U-Lyme	Eng B
Apr 30	Rio Rokz Bradford	Eng
May 1	Leisure Centre Brentwood	Eng B
May 2	Woughton Centre Milton Keynes	Eng B
May 3	University Of East Anglia Norwich	Eng B
May 4	The Dome Ipswich	Eng B
May 5	Civic Hall Camberley	Eng B
May 8	Queens Hall Barnstaple	Eng
May 9	English Riviera Centre Torquay	Eng
May 11	Marquee Club London	Eng B
May 13	Greater London Radio Studios	Eng R
May 14	Playhouse Theatre Newcastle	Eng B V
May 15	Legends Dingwall	Sco
May 16	Pelican Club Aberdeen	Sco
May 17	SECC Glasgow	Sco
May 18	The Venue Edinburgh	Sco
May 19	The Grand Clapham London	Eng
Jun 4	Villa Marina Douglas	Iom B V
Jun 6	Antara Pub Olastrom	Swe
Jun 20	Montgomery Hall Wath-Upon-Dearne	Eng B V
Jul 18	Biddy Mulligans Chicago	USA
Jul 19	Big Hanka St Louis Missouri	USA B V
Jul 27	Cowboys Shreveport Louisiana	USA
Jul 29	Juanitas Little Rock Arkansas	USA
Aug 8	Olympia Dublin	Ire
Aug 10	Roadhouse London	Eng B
Aug 11	Roadhouse London	Eng B
Aug 13	Harvey's Stockton-On-Tees	Eng
Aug 15	Central Library Theatre Birmingham	Eng
Aug 16	Civic Theatre Barsnley	Eng B
Aug 18	Wytchwood Manchester	Eng
Aug 20	Bobby Browns Nottingham	Eng
Oct 22	Robin Hood Dudley	Eng B
Oct 24	Oval Rockhouse Norwich	Eng
Oct 26	Arts Guild Theatre Greenock	Sco
Oct 29	Kronprinzen Malmo	Swe
Oct 30	Bergan's Gothenberg	Swe B
Oct 31	Antara Olofstrom	Swe
Nov 5	The Wheatsheaf Stoke-On-Trent	Eng
Nov 30	Gothenburg	Swe B

1993

Mar 12	Flaherty's Evergreen Illinois	USA
Mar 13	Club Metropolis Glenview	USA
Mar 15	Juanita's Little Rock Arkansas	USA B
Mar 16	Cowboys Shreveport Louisiana	USA B
Mar 17	Sneakers Austin Texas	USA
Mar 18	Sneakers San Antonio Texas	USA
Mar 19	Santa Fe Cantina Texas	USA
Mar 20	Rockefeller's Houston Texas	USA
Nov 5	Pne Showmart Vancouver	Can
Nov 6	Pne Showmart Vancouver	Can
Nov 7	Riverside Coliseum Kamloops	Can
Nov 9	Max Bell Centre Calgary	Can
Nov 10	Convention Centre Edmonton	Can
Nov 11	Titan Place Saskatoon	Can
Nov 12	Convention Centre Winnipeg	Can
Nov 13	Target Centre Minneapolis	USA
Nov 14	Memorial Hall Kansas City	USA
Nov 16	Convention Centre Steven's Point	USA
Nov 17	Pierre's Fort Wayne	USA B
Nov 18	Seagate Centre Toledo	USA B
Nov 19	Rpm Warehouse Toronto	Can
Nov 20	Lulu's Kitchener	Can B
Nov 21	Eastbrook Theatre Grand Rapids	USA
Nov 22	Battelle Hall Columbus	USA
Nov 24	Boomers Martinsburg	USA
Nov 26	Music Fair Westbury	USA
Nov 27	Valley Forge Music Fair Devon	USA
Nov 29	Palmer Auditorium Davenport	USA
Nov 30	Coronade Theatre Rockford	USA
Dec 1	Club Eastbrook Grand Rapids	USA
Dec 2	American Theatre St Louis	USA
Dec 3	Horizons Rosemont	USA
Dec 4	The Palace Auburn Hills	USA
Dec 8	Stadthalle Offenbach	Ger
Dec 9	Stadthalle Fuerth	Ger
Dec 10	Heldenberghalle Goeppingen	Ger
Dec 11	Eissporthalle Halle	Ger
Dec 12	Phillipshalle Dusseldorf	Ger
Dec 14	Wikinghalle Flensburg	Ger
Dec 15	Musichall Hannover	Ger
Dec 17	Hessenhalle Alsfeld	Ger
Dec 18	Eberthalle Ludwigschafen	Ger
Dec 19	Terminal 1 Munich	Ger
Dec 20	Kurhalle Vienna	Aut

1994

No live dates were performed in 1994

1995

Mar 30	Leisure Centre Rotherham	Eng B
Mar 31	Fibbers York	Eng B
Apr 1	Concert Hall Blackheath London	Eng B
Apr 2	The Robin Hood Dudley	Eng
Apr 3	The Tivoli Theatre Wimborne	Eng B
Apr 4	The Wedgewood Rooms Portsmouth	Eng B V
Apr 5	The Lanterns Ashburton	Eng
Apr 6	Arthur's Club Geneva	Swi R T B
May 13	Rock At The Quin's Port Talbot	Wal B V
May 19	Soundgarden Ingleheim	Ger B
May 20	Park Kino Pirmasens	Ger
May 21	Centre Culturel Sandweiler	Lux
Nov 2	VH1 Studios London	Eng T B
Nov 2	Bottom Line London	Eng
Nov 4	Mean Fiddler Dublin	Ire
Nov 9	Never Never Land Blackburn	Eng B
Nov 11	Civic Theatre Mansfield	Eng B
Nov 12	Robin Hood Dudley	Eng
Nov 14	Ladle Ballroom Middlesborough	Eng B
Nov 15	Beachcomber Cleethorpes	Eng
Nov 16	Irish Centre Leeds	Eng
Nov 17	Civic Theatre Barnsley	Eng
Nov 18	Wheatsheaf Stoke-On-Trent	Eng
Nov 20	Wedgewood Rooms Portsmouth	Eng
Nov 21	The Lanterns Ashburton	Eng
Nov 22	The Tivoli Wimborne	Eng
Nov 23	New Morning Club Paris	Fra B
Nov 24	First Rock Cafe Geneva	Swi
Nov 25	Neuchatel	Swi
Dec 3	University Leicester	Eng B

Blowin' Free

Date	Venue	Country
Dec 4	Filling Station Newport	Wal
Dec 6	The Brook Southampton	Eng B
Dec 7	Pavilion Worthing	Eng B
Dec 9	Cellar Club South Shields	Eng B
Dec 11	Fleece & Firkin Bristol	Eng
Dec 13	Warsaw	Pol
Dec 14	Warsaw	Pol T
Dec 15	Warsaw	Pol

1996

Date	Venue	Country
June 30	Festival Budapest	Hun
Oct 31	Irish Centre Leeds	Eng
Nov 1	Municipal Hall Colne	Eng
Nov 2	Civic Theatre Barnsley	Eng V
Nov 3	Wheatsheaf Stoke-On-Trent	Eng B
Nov 4	Fleece & Firkin Bristol	Eng
Nov 6	Tivoli Theatre Wimborne	Eng B
Nov 8	Waterford	Ire
Nov 9	Mean Fiddler Dublin	Ire
Nov 10	The Quays Galway	Ire
Nov 14	Cathouse Glasgow	Sco
Nov 15	Cellar Club South Shields	Eng
Nov 16	Carnegie Theatre Workington	Eng
Nov 17	Leisure Centre Mansfield	Eng B V
Nov 18	The Stables Milton Keynes	Eng B
Nov 19	Beachcomber Cleethorpes	Eng B
Nov 20	Victoria Theatre Halifax	Eng B
Nov 21	Ladle Ballroom Middlesborough	Eng
Nov 22	Cellar Club South Shields	Eng B
Nov 23	Wilbarston Hall Market Harborough	Eng B
Nov 24	Robin Hood Dudley	Eng B
Nov 26	The Power Station Barry	Wal
Nov 27	New Pavilion Rhyl	Wal
Nov 28	Fernham Hall Fareham	Eng
Nov 30	The Lanterns Ashburton	Eng
Dec 1	Astoria 2 London	Eng B
Dec 4	Esplanade Southend	Eng B
Dec 6	Grosse Freiheit Hamburg	Ger
Dec 7	Rintelin	Ger
Dec 8	Leipzig	Ger
Dec 9	Berlin	Ger
Dec 10	Augsburg	Ger
Dec 11	Nuremburg	Ger
Dec 12	Mildstedt	Ger
Dec 13	Warmelskirchen	Ger
Dec 15	Schloss Wiessenfels	Ger
Dec 17	The Brook Southampton	Eng B

1997

Date	Venue	Country
May 5	Atlantis Basle	Swi
May 6	Atlantis Basle	Swi B
May 7	Scala Zurich	Swi
May 8	Mehrzweckhalle Oltenbach	Swi
May 9	Kammgarn Schaffhausen	Swi
May 10	Rossli Wattenwil	Swi
June 5	Summerland Douglas	IOM
June 6	Summerland Douglas	IOM V
June 7	Stramrock Hardenberg	Hol
June 8	Atlantis Alkmaar	Hol V
June 9	The Spirit Of '66 Verviers	Bel
June 10	Stadsdanszaal Middleburg	Hol
June 11	Zaal Schaaf Leeuwarden	Hol
June 19	Tuxedo Junction Danbury	USA B
June 20	Jaxx Springfield Virginia	USA B
Nov 6	The Stables Milton Keynes	Eng V
Nov 7	Wilbarston Hall Market Harborough	Eng
Nov 8	Leisure Centre Mansfield	Eng B T
Nov 9	Robin Hood Dudley	Eng B
Nov 10	The Brook Southampton	Eng B
Nov 11	Esplanade Southend	Eng B
Nov 12	Floral Pavilion Theatre New Brighton	Eng B
Nov 13	Rio Rock Club Bradford	Eng B V
Nov 14	Cellar Club South Shields	Eng B
Nov 15	Cellar Club South Shields	Eng B V
Nov 16	Boardwalk Sheffield	Eng B

1998

Date	Venue	Country
Jan 28	Old Oak Cork	Ire
Jan 29	The Quays Bar Galway	Ire
Jan 30	Mean Fiddler Dublin	Ire
Jan 31	Empire Music Hall Belfast	N Ire
Feb 4	The Lanterns Ashburton	Eng
Feb 5	Tivoli Theatre Wimborne	Eng
Feb 6	Recreation Centre Bridgend	Wal
Feb 8	Standard Walthamstow	Eng V B
Feb 9	Bier Keller Bristol	Eng
Feb 10	12 Bar Club London (2 Shows)	Eng
Feb 11	Cellar Club South Shields	Eng V
Feb 12	Ladle Ballroom Middlesborough	Eng V
Feb 13	Robin Hood Dudley	Eng
Feb 14	Leisure Centre Rotherham	Eng B V
Feb 15	Oval Rock House Norwich	Eng
Feb 16	Wheatsheaf Stoke-On-Trent	Eng
Feb 17	The Concorde Brighton	Eng
Feb 19	The Horn Of Plenty St Albans	Eng V
Feb 20	Rotplombe Erfurt	Ger
Feb 21	Grosse Freiheit Hamburg	Ger
Feb 22	Flensburg	Ger
Feb 23	Bad Hannover	Ger
Feb 24	B9 Aachen	Ger
Feb 25	Hirsch Nuremburg	Ger B
Feb 26	Alte Malzerei Regensburg	Ger
Feb 27	Anker Club Leipzig	Ger
Feb 28	Hafenbahn Offenbach	Ger B
Mar 1	Rock Haus Salzburg	Aut
Mar 2	Jazz Galerie Bonn	Ger
Mar 3	Schlutzenhaus Stuttgart	Ger B
Mar 4	Colos Saal Aschaffenburg	Ger
Mar 5	Substage Karlsruhe	Ger B
Mar 6	Star Club Oberhausen	Ger
Mar 7	Spektrum Solingen	Ger
Mar 8	Kufa Krefeld	Ger
Mar 9	Rock House Cologne	Ger
Mar 10	Aladdin Club Bremen	Ger
Mar 11	Jovel Music Hall Munster	Ger
Mar 12	Alts Zollhaus Leer	Ger
Mar 13	Ostend	Bel
Mar 14	Spirit Of '66 Verviers	Bel
Mar 15	Arnhem	Hol
Jul 17	Summer Night Festival Weil Der Stadt	Ger
Jul 18	Burg Herzberg Festival Alsfeld	Ger
Jul 19	Spritzhaus Frankfurt	Ger
Aug 6	Camden Palace London	Eng V
Oct 31	Leisure Centre Market Harborough	Eng V
Nov 1	Robin Hood Dudley	Eng
Nov 2	Riddles Music Bar Stoke-On-Trent	Eng B V
Nov 3	The Beachcomber Cleethorpes	Eng B V
Nov 4	Fleece & Firkin Bristol	Eng B
Nov 5	The Swan Swindon	Eng
Nov 6	Rio Rock Club Bradford	Eng V
Nov 7	Leisure Centre Mansfield	Eng T BV
Nov 9	The Boardwalk Sheffield	Eng
Nov 10	The Brook Southampton	Eng B
Nov 11	Blues W14 London	Eng
Nov 12	The Lanterns Ashburton	Eng
Nov 13	The Standard Walthamstow	Eng
Nov 14	The Stables Milton Keynes	Eng V
Nov 16	Lucky Break Bury St Edmunds	Eng
Nov 19	Carnegie Theatre Workington	Eng
Nov 21	Ladle Ballroom Middlesborough	Eng V
Nov 22	The Wytchwood Ashton-Under-Lyne	Eng B
Nov 23	Gwyn Hall Neath	Wal B
Nov 24	Ludwigs Swansea	Wal
Nov 26	The Quays Bar Galway	Ire
Nov 27	Whelans Dublin	Ire

thirty years of Wishbone Ash

Nov 28	Village Hall Narberth	Wal
Nov 30	Blue Note Gottingen	Ger
Dec 1	Bruckentorsaal Rinteln	Ger
Dec 3	Alter Schlachthof Soest	Ger
Dec 4	Kulturhaus Markers Dorndorf	Ger
Dec 6	Substage Karlsruhe	Ger
Dec 7	Jazz Gallerie Bonn	Ger
Dec 8	Hirsch Nuremberg	Ger
Dec 9	Alte Malzerei Regensberg	Ger
Dec 11	S'fon Renningen	Ger
Dec 12	Star Club Oberhausen	Ger
Dec 13	Tivoli Club Freiburg	Ger
Dec 15	Collosaal Aschaffenburg	Ger
Dec 16	Borderline Diest	Ger
Dec 17	Schwimmbad Club Heidelberg	Ger B
Dec 18	Stadthalle Rheinberg	Ger
Dec 19	Grosse Freiheit Hamburg	Ger
1999		
Jan 20	Whisky A Go Go Los Angeles	USA R
Mar 11	Horn Reborn St Albans	Eng
Mar 12	Recreational Centre Bridgend	Wal B
Mar 14	Ronnie Scotts Birmingham	Eng
Mar 18	Leisure Centre Market Harborough	Eng
Mar 19	Park Hotel Tynemouth	Eng
Mar 20	Oakwood Centre Rotherham	Eng V
Mar 21	Robin Hood Dudley	Eng B
Mar 23	The Brook Southampton	Eng B
Mar 24	The Standard Walthamstow	Eng
Mar 25	Blues W14 London	Eng
Mar 26	Krone Worms	Ger
Mar 27	Ebertbad Oberhausen	Ger
Mar 30	Jazz Haus Freiburg	Ger B
Mar 31	Longhorn Stuttgart	Ger B
Apr 1	Spectrum Augsburg	Ger B
Apr 2	Apeldoorn	Hol
Apr 3	The Roots Meyel	Hol
Apr 4	Spirit Of '66 Verviers	Bel
Apr	Florence	Ita
Apr 30	House Of Blues Chicago	USA B
May 1	The Beaumont Chicago	USA T B
May	St Louis	USA
May	Cleveland	USA
May	Saloon Georgetown	USA
Jun 3	Villa Marina Douglas	Iom
Jun 6	Town Hall Cheltenham	Eng B
Jun 26	University Duisburg	Ger
Jun	Trimedia	Swi
Jun	Peavey Electronics	Eng
Jul 4	Burg Herzburg Festival	Ger
Jul 13	Pont Audemer Festival	Fra
Jul 23	Eichtal Open Air Freilichtbuhne	Ger
Jul 24	Buga Open Air Festival	Ger
Jul 30	Burgergfestival Homberg	Ger
Jul 31	Balou Festival Hamelin	Ger
Aug 7	Nunningen Festival Basle	Swi
Aug 14	Festival Clermont Ferrand	Fra
Oct 1	Centre Culturel Le Havre	Fra B
Oct 2	Salle Oceanis Ploemeurs	Fra
Oct 5	Cabaret Sam Boulogne Sur Mer	Fra
Oct 7	Le Splendide Lille	Fra
Oct 8	La Luciole Alencon	Fra
Oct 9	Run Ar Pens Chateaulin	Fra
Oct 10	Le Bacardi Callac	Fra
Oct 13	L'orange Bleu Vitry Le Francois	Fra
Oct 14	La Forge St Etienne	Fra
Oct 15	L'usine Arles	Fra
Oct 16	Cafe Rex Toulouse	Fra
Oct 17	Valence	Fra
Oct 20	New Morning Paris	Fra R
Oct 21	Eurodisney Paris	Fra
Oct 22	Le Plan Paris	Fra
Oct 23	Festival La Rochelle	Fra
Nov 2	Telford's Warehouse Chester	Eng B
Nov 3	Blues W14 London	Eng
Nov 4	The Stables Milton Keynes	Eng B
Nov 5	Corn Hall Cirencester	Eng
Nov 6	Leisure Centre Mansfield	Eng B V
Nov 7	Robin Hood Dudley	Eng B
Nov 9	The Brook Southampton	Eng B V
Nov 10	Standard Walthamstow	Eng B
Nov 11	Balne Lane WMC Wakefield	Eng
Nov 12	The Dome Whitley Bay	Eng
Nov 13	Rio Rock Club Bradford	Eng B V
Nov 14	King's Head Dursley	Eng
Nov 17	Horn Reborn St Albans	Eng
Nov 18	Festival Hall New Brighton	Eng
Nov 19	Leisure Centre Lochgelly	Sco
Nov 21	Coal Exchange Cardiff	Wal
Dec 3	Schutzenhaus Stuttgart	Ger
Dec 4	Collosaal Aschaffenburg	Ger
Dec 5	Die Weberei Gutersloh	Ger
Dec 6	Jazz Galerie Bonn	Ger
Dec 8	Powerpoint Kehl	Ger
Dec 9	Hirsch Nuremberg	Ger
Dec 10	Juz Schuttdorf	Ger
Dec 11	Hellendorn Lantdtar	Hol
Dec 12	Helmond	Hol B
2000		
Feb 25	Chiddingfold Club Guildford	Eng B
Mar 25	Eurodisney Nr Paris	Fra
Mar 28	Cri Art Auch	Fra
Mar 30	Le Thelonius Bordeaux	Fra B
Mar 31	Le Psyche Cafe Gap	Fra
Apr 1	Le Variete Sommieres	Fra
Apr 4	013 Tilburg	Hol
Apr 5	Blues Cafe Appeldoorn	Hol
Apr 6	Le Terminal Export Nancy	Fra
Apr 7	Reims	Fra
Apr 8	Le Splendide Lille	Fra B
Apr 9	Spirit Of '66 Verviers	Bel
Apr 15	Victoria Inn Pontypridd	Wal
Apr 16	Nighthawks Swindon	Eng B
Apr 17	Guildhall Gloucester	Eng B
Apr 18	The Cavern Liverpool	Eng B
Apr 19	The Dome Whitley Bay	Eng
Apr 22	Shepherd's Bush Empire London	Eng T B
Apr 23	Robin 2 Bilston	Eng
Apr 24	Wedgewood Rooms Portsmouth	Eng
Apr 27	Waterfront Norwich	Eng
Apr 28	Fibbers York	Eng B
Apr 29	Century Theatre Coalville	Eng
Aug 4	Guitar Festival Bath	Eng B
Aug 5	Village Hall East Prawl	Eng B
Aug 7	Riverside Festival Gravesend	Eng V
Aug 12	Eject Garden Party Dreisen	Ger
Aug 19	Festival Kortenarken	Bel

207

Discography

The catalogue numbers given in this discography refer to UK releases unless otherwise stated. The compilers have not attempted to include a complete list of world-wide pressings of Wishbone Ash's standard album releases. We have, however, included overseas albums which were never released in the UK. For a more detailed world-wide discography, please refer to *The Collectors Guide to Wishbone Ash,* published by CGP.

Studio Albums
Wishbone Ash
Recorded at: De Lane Lea, London, England
Producer: Derek Lawrence
Engineer: Martin Birch
Release date: December 4th 1970
Highest UK chart position: No. 34
Tracks: Blind Eye, Lady Whiskey, Errors Of My Way, Queen of Torture, Handy, Phoenix.
LP Catalogue Nos: MCA – MKPS 2014 / MCG 3507 / MCA 2343
CD – MCA MCVM-183 / MCD10661 BEAT GOES ON BGOCD234
Comments: Matthew Fisher of Procol Harum played piano on Blind Eye. This album was released on Decca in the USA.

Pilgrimage
Recorded at: De Lane Lea, London, England (except track 7 recorded live the De Montfort Hall, Leicester, England on June 14th 1971)
Producer: Derek Lawrence
Engineer: Martin Birch
Release date: October 1971
Highest chart position: No. 14 (No. 9 in NME Chart)
Tracks: Vas Dis, The Pilgrim, Jail Bait, Alone, Lullaby, Valediction, Where Were You Tomorrow (live)
LP Catalogue Nos: MCA – MDKS 8004 / MCG 3504 / MCL 1762
CD – MCA DMCL 1762 / MCD 10233 / MCLD 19084 (with bonus track – Jail Bait) (from *Live from Memphis*)
Comments: Alone was originally recorded with words but this version was dropped in favour of the instrumental version. The vocal version appeared on the *Distillation* box set in 1997. This album was released on Decca in the USA.

Argus
Recorded at: De Lane Lea, London, England
Producer: Derek Lawrence
Engineer: Martin Birch
Release date: May 1972
Highest chart position: No 2 (UK) (Gold Disc Status)
Tracks: Time Was, Sometime World, Blowin' Free, The King Will Come, Leaf & Stream, Warrior, Throw Down The Sword
LP Catalogue Nos: MCA MDKS 8006 / MCG 3510 / MCL 1787
CD: MCA DMCL 1787 / MCLD 19085 / MCD 10234 – (with bonus track – No Easy Road) (7 inch single version)
Comments: This was the first Wishbone Ash album to be recorded on 16 track tape. The previous two had been recorded on 8 track tape. John Tout of Renaissance played organ on Throw Down The Sword. This album was released on Decca in the USA.

Wishbone Four
Recorded at: Olympic and Apple Studios, London, England
Release date: May 1973

Producer: Wishbone Ash
Engineer: Keith Harwood
Highest chart position: No.12 (Silver Disc Status)
Tracks: So Many Things To Say, Ballad Of The Beacon, No Easy Road, Everybody Needs A Friend, Doctor, Sorrel, Sing Out The Song, Rock 'n' Roll Widow.
LP Catalogue Nos: MCA MDKS 8011 / MCG 3503
CD: MCA MCLD 19149 / MCD 10350
Comments: This was the first album to feature a photograph of the group on the front cover and also the first to be produced solely by the band. It also featured a colour poster of the band and all the lyrics of the songs. The album sleeve colour varied in different territories.

There's The Rub
Recorded at: Criteria Studios, Miami, Florida, USA
Producer: Bill Szymczyk
Engineers: Alan Blazek/Bill Szymczyk
Release Date: November 1974
Highest chart position: No.16 (Silver Disc Status)
Tracks: Silver Shoes, Don't Come Back, Persephone, Hometown, Lady Jay, F.U.B.B.
LP Catalogue Number: MCA MCF 2585
CD – MCA MCD10448 (US issue) MCLD 19249 (UK 2-on-1 issue with *Locked In*)
Comments: Apart from the usual electric guitars, Andy Powell played Mandolin and Laurie Wisefield played banjo. As Laurie Wisefield was still under contract to CBS records, this and the next six albums would contain the legend, "Laurie Wisefield appears courtesy of CBS Records Ltd". The closing "sound" on the album straight after F.U.B.B. is a growling sound from Martin Turner which he perfected between vocal takes.

Locked In
Recorded at: Atlantic Studios, New York City, USA
Producer: Tom Dowd
Engineers: Geoff Daking/Jay Borden
Release Date: March 1976
Highest chart position: No. 36
Tracks: Rest In Peace. No Water In The Well, Moonshine, She Was My Best Friend, It Started In Heaven, Half Past Lovin', Trust In You, Say Goodbye.
LP Catalogue number: MCA MCF 2750
CD: Repertoire (Germany), also MCA MCLD 19249 (UK 2-on-1 with *There's The Rub*),
Comments: Cissy Houston, the mother of Whitney Houston was one of several backing vocalists on this album, which also featured Peter Wood (ex-Sutherland Brothers) on keyboards. This album was released on Atlantic in the USA.

New England
Recorded at: Laurel Edge, Connecticut, USA Remixed at Criteria Studios, Miami, Florida, USA
Producers: Ron and Howard Albert
Engineers: Ross Alexander, Jack Nuber, Mark Emery
Release Date: November 1976
Highest chart position: No. 22
Tracks: Mother of Pearl, (In all of my Dreams) You Rescue Me, Runaway, Lorelei, Outward Bound, Prelude, When You Know Love, Lonely Island, Candle Light
LP Catalogue numbers: MCA MCG 3523 / MCL 1699
CD: BEAT GOES ON BGOCD405 (UK 2-on 1 CD with *Front Page News*) MCA MCD 02238 (German issue)
Comments: The majority of the album was recorded in the basement of Martin Turner's house and band headquarters, Laurel Edge in Connecticut, NE USA. Ted Turner got a writing credit for the song "Candlelight" which he had helped to write before he left the band in 1974, and which Wishbone Ash subsequently used on this album. This album was released on Atlantic in the USA.

Front Page News
Recorded at: Criteria Studios, Miami, Florida, USA
Producers: Ron and Howard Albert
Engineer: Steve Gursky
Release Date: October 1977
Highest chart position: No.31
Tracks: Front Page News, Midnight Dancer, Goodbye Baby Hello Friend, Surface To Air, 714, Come In From The Rain, Right or Wrong, Heart Beat, The Day I Found Your Love, Diamond Jack.
LP Catalogue Numbers: MCA MCG 3524 / MCL 1655 / MCA 2311
CD: BEAT GOES ON BGOCD405 (UK 2-on 1 issue with *New England*), also MCA MCAD-11027 (US issue)

Comments: This was the first album by Wishbone to feature strings on some of the songs. The back cover showed pictures of Pauline Powell and Maurn Turner and the members of the band leaving a club that supposedly had just caught fire!

No Smoke Without Fire
Recorded at: De Lane Lea, Wembley, London, England
Producer: Derek Lawrence
Engineer: Rafe McKenna
Release Date: October 1978
Highest chart position: No. 43
Tracks: You See Red, Baby The Angels Are Here, Ships In The Sky, Stand And Deliver, Anger In Harmony, Like a Child, The Way of The World (parts 1 and 2).
LP Catalogue no: MCA MCG 3528 / MCA 3060
CD: MCA MCLD 19374 (with bonus tracks: Firesign, Time And Space (remix), Lorelei (live), Come in From The Rain (live), Bad Weather Blues (live).
Comments: The initial pressing of the album contained a free 7 inch single containing the live tracks Lorelei and Come In from The Rain.

Just Testing
Recorded at: Surrey Sound, Leatherhead, England (except 'Helpless' at Kingsway Recorders, London, England)
Producer: Martin Turner, John Sherry and Wishbone Ash
Engineers: Surrey Sound – Martin Moss. Kingsway Recorders – Bob Broglia
Release date: January 1980
Highest chart position: No. 41
Tracks: Living Proof, Haunting Me, Insomnia, Helpless, Pay The Price, New Rising Star, Master of Disguise, Lifeline
LP Catalogue No: MCA MCF 3052
CD: MCA MCLD 19375 (with bonus tracks – Come On, Fast Johnny, Blowin' Free (live), Helpless (live))
Comments: Features Ian Kew on organ and Claire Hamill on backing vocals on some tracks.

Number The Brave
Recorded at: Criteria Studios, Miami, Florida, USA
Producer: Nigel Gray
Engineer: Unknown
Release Date: April 1981
Highest chart position: No. 61
Tracks: Loaded, Where Is The Love, Underground, Kicks On The Street, Open Road, Rainstorm, That's That, Rollercoaster, Number The Brave.
LP Catalogue Number: MCA MCF 3103
CD: Not available in this format
Comments: The only Wishbone Ash album where a member decided to leave the band before material from the album had been played live on tour.

Twin Barrels Burning
Recorded at: Sol Studios, Cookham, England (except for 'My Guitar' at Surrey Sound, Leatherhead, England)
Producers: Ashley Howe, Stuart Epps ('My Guitar' – Nigel Gray, Stuart Epps)
Engineers: Ashley Howe, Stuart Epps ('My Guitar' – Nigel Gray, Stuart Epps)
Release Date: October 1982
Highest chart position: No. 22
Tracks: Engine Overheat, Can't Fight Love, Genevieve, Me And My Guitar, Hold On, Streets Of Shame, No More Lonely Nights, Angels Have Mercy, Wind Up.
LP Catalogue No: AVM Records ASH1
CD: CASTLE COMMUNICATIONS CLACD 389
Comments: The highest charting Wishbone Ash album since 1976's *New England* and their final UK chart placing. Various labels issued the album worldwide. An alternative sleeve design was featured on the US pressing, which was issued on Fantasy. A third sleeve variation was featured on Finland release on Polarvox.

Raw To The Bone
Recorded at: Surrey Sound Studios, Leatherhead, England
Producer: Nigel Gray
Engineer: Jim Ebdon
Release Date: 1985
Tracks: Cell of Fame, People In Motion, Don't Cry, Love Is Blue, Long Live The Night, Rocket In My Pocket, It's Only Love, Don't You Mess, Dreams (Searching For An Answer), Perfect Timing

LP Catalogue number: NEAT 1027
CD: CASTLE COMMUNICATIONS CLACD 390
Comments: The first Wishbone Ash album that failed to reach the album charts. It featured additional musicians Brad Lang, Andrew Brown and Simon Butt. Various labels issued the album worldwide, some using an alternative sleeve design.

Nouveau Calls
Recorded at: Beethoven, Guerrilla, Phoenix Studios, London, England
Producers: William Orbit, Martin Turner
Engineer: Mick Williams
Release date: December 1987
Tracks: Tangible Evidence, Clousseau, Flags Of Convenience, From Soho To Sunset, Arabesque, In The Skin, Something's Happening In Room 602, Johnny Left Home Without It, The Spirit Flies Free, A Rose Is A Rose, Real Guitars Have Wings
LP Catalogue No: IRS Records MIRF 1028
CD: IRS Records SMIRF 1028 / POWERBRIGHT PBV005CD
Comments: The first ever completely instrumental album from Wishbone Ash, released as part of IRS Records' "No Speak" series.

Here To Hear
Recorded at: Beethoven, Terminal and Beat Factory, London, England
Producers: Martin Turner, Adam Fuest
Engineer: Adam Feust
Release date: August 1989
Tracks: Cosmic Jazz, Keeper Of The Light, Mental Radio, Walk On Water, Witness To Wonder, Lost Cause In Paradise, Why Don't We, In The Case, Hole In My Heart (Part One), Hole In My Heart (Part Two)
LP Catalogue No: IRS Records EIRSA 1006
CD: IRS Records IRSD 82006
Comments: The first "vocal" reunion album from the original Mark 1 line up of Wishbone Ash. The US release features an alternative sleeve design.

Strange Affair
Recorded at: Ivy Lane Farm, Buckinghamshire, England
Producer: Martin Turner
Engineer: Martin Turner
Release date: April 1991
Tracks: Strange Affair, Wings Of Desire, Renegade, Dream Train, Some Conversation, Say You Will, Rollin', You, Hard Times, Standing In The Rain
LP Catalogue No: IRS Records EIRSA 1045
CD: IRS Records EIRSACD 1045
Comments: The only Wishbone Ash album to feature two different drummers – Robbie France and Ray Weston – following the departure of original drummer, Steve Upton at the start of the recording sessions.

Illuminations
Recorded at: Studio Unicorn, Redding, Connecticut, USA; Element Studios, Hampton Court, England; Reel Hits, Weston, Connecticut, USA; North Shore Studios, Ridgefield, Connecticut, USA
Producers: Andy Powell, Roger Filgate, Paul Avgerinos
Engineers: Paul Avgerinos, John Etchels, Al Payson
Release date: 28th October 1996
Tracks: Mountainside, On Your Own, Top Of The World, No Joke, Tales Of The Wise, Another Time, A Thousand Years, The Ring, Comfort Zone, Mystery Man, Wait Out The Storm. Bonus instrumental track – The Crack of Dawn
CD Catalogue No: HTD Records HTDCD67
Comments: The picture of the stained glass church window on the front cover was discovered in a library in Salt Lake City, Utah and by pure coincidence, turned out to have come from the church in Soulbury, which could clearly be seen from Andy Powell's old Buckinghamshire village home, Ivy Lane Farm.

Trance Visionary
Recorded at: Far Heath Studios, Guilsborough, Northamptonshire, England
Producer: Mike Bennett
Release date: April 1998
CD catalogue no: INVISIBLE HANDS MUSIC IHCD 12
Tracks: Numerology, Wonderful Stash, Heritage, Interfaze, Powerbright (Black & White Screen), Remnants Of A Paranormal Menagerie, Narcissus Nervosa, Trance Visionary, Flutterby, Banner Headlines, The Loner, Powerbright Volition, Gutterfly, Wronged By Righteousness
(Later reissued on RESURGENCE RES 140 (with bonus tracks: Heritage (remix), Powerbright, Dub-Visionary, Wrong by Right (remix))

Comments: Although credited to Wishbone Ash, Andy Powell was the only member of the band involved at the time of the recording of this album, which mixes classic Wishbone Ash riffs with dance compositions by Andy Powell and producer Mike Bennett. Latter day Wishbone Ash member Bob Skeat guested on Wonderful Stash but was not a band member at the time of recording. Tacye provided vocals on the tracks, Wonderful Stash and Narcissus Nervosa. Samples of interviews with Miles Copeland and Martin Turner were also used.

Psychic Terrorism
Recorded at: Far Heath Studios, Guilsborough, Northamptonshire, England
Producer: Mike Bennett
Release date: November 1998
CD catalogue no: DREAMSCAPE RECORDS (no catalogue number)
Tracks: Transliteration, Narcissus Stash, Sleeps Eternal Slave, Monochrome, Breaking Out, The Son of Righteousness, Psychic Terrorism, How Many Times?, Bloodline, Back Page Muse, Powerbright Conclusion
Comments: A "live" in the studio variation of the "Trance Visionary" theme, this time featuring the entire present day Wishbone Ash band apart from Ray Weston.

Psychic Terrorism – CD ROM
CD catalogue no: RATION – L RALVP 004CD
Details: This was a double CD release with CD 1 being the same as above, whilst CD 2 contained the following tracks: Powerchrome, Dub Visionary, X-Erted, Powerchrome Industrial, Wonderful Nervosa, Power Thrack, Wrong or Write?, Wonderful Stash, Wonderful Stash film

Bare Bones
Recorded at: Spider Hill Studios, Roxbury, Connecticut, USA; Spotlight Studios, Willesden, London, England
Producer: Andy Powell
Engineers: Alec Head, Graham Pilgrim
Release date: October 1999
Tracks: Wings Of Desire, Errors Of My Way, Master Of Disguise, You Won't Take Me Down, Love Abuse, (Won't You Give Him) One More Chance, Baby Don't Mind, Living Proof, Hard Times, Strange Affair, Everybody Needs A Friend.
CD Catalogue No: HTD Records HTDC104
Comments: This reworking of several old Ash numbers in an acoustic setting featured several guest musicians, most notably, Claire Hamill on backing vocals and Andy Powell's' son, Aynsley (AJ) Powell on percussion.

Live Albums
Live From Memphis
Recorded at: Memphis, WMKC studios, 21.8.72
Tracks: The Pilgrim; Jailbait; Phoenix
LP Catalogue Number: Decca 1922 (note: US promo only release)

Live Dates
Recorded at: * Fairfield Hall, Croydon, England (June 17th 1973) ++ Portsmouth Guildhall, England (June 21st 1973) ** Reading University, England (June 23rd 1973) + Newcastle City Hall, England (June 24th 1973) using the Rolling Stones 16 track mobile recorder. Re-mixed at Olympic Studios, London, England
Release Date: December 1973
Producer: Wishbone Ash
Engineer: Keith Harwood
Highest chart position: No: 23 (Silver Disc status)
Tracks: LP 1 – The King Will Come*, Warrior+, Throw Down The Sword+, Rock 'n' Roll Widow**, Ballad Of The Beacon**, Baby What You Want Me To Do++
LP 2 – The Pilgrim*, Blowin' Free+, Jail Bait**, Lady Whiskey**, Phoenix*
LP Catalogue Numbers: MCA ULD1/2 / MCSP 254
CD: MCA MCAD2-10396 (bonus track Phoenix) (*Live From Memphis*) (US 2CD set)
BEAT GOES ON BGOCD293 (single CD)
Comments: The US release contained a free colour booklet showing over 50 photos of the band on the road in America. This was the highest selling Wishbone Ash vinyl album ever, based on the fact that each LP counted as a single unit.

Live In Tokyo
Recorded at Tokyo Sun Plaza, Japan on 10th and 15th November 1976
Producer: Martin Turner
Release date: March 1979
Tracks: FUBB; Way of the World; You See Red; Blowin Free; Jailbait

LP Catalogue number: MCA VIM 6187 (note: Japanese LP)
Live Dates II
Recorded at: *Apollo, Glasgow, Scotland (19th November 1976) +City Hall, Sheffield, England (18th October 1977) -Marquee Club, London, England (19th October 1977), ^Hammersmith Odeon, London, England (25th October 1978), ~Colston Hall, Bristol, England (27th October 1978), ¬Colston Hall, Bristol, England (16th February 1980) \City Hall, Hull, England (1st June 1980), /Civic Hall, Wolverhampton, England (4th June 1980) using the Rolling Stones, Manor and Basing Street mobiles
Producer: Wishbone Ash
Engineers: Rafe McKenna, Neil Black
Release Date: 20th October 1980
Highest Chart Position: No.40
Tracks: LP 1 – Doctor\, Living Proof¬, Runaway/, Helpless/, F.U.B.B.^ , The Way of The World~ LP 2 – Lorelei*, Persephone*, You Rescue Me*, Time Was¬, Goodbye Baby Hello Friend-, No Easy Road+.
LP Catalogue no: MCG 4012
CD: not available in this format
Comments: The first 25,000 copies of this album were a double with an "extra free" album included, the track titles of the second album were on a blue sticker on the front cover. Subsequent copies of the album came in a single sleeve with just the first album. Some early copies of the sleeve were misprinted with the inner gatefold design from the first "Live Dates" album!
Live Dates Vol.II Additional Material
Release date: 1980
Tracks: Lorelei; Persephone; You Rescue Me; Time Was; Goodbye Baby Hello Friend; No Easy Road.
LP Catalogue no: MCA 203.223.270 (note: German LP)
Comments: single album release of the second "bonus" disc from "Live Dates Volume II"
Hot Ash
Recorded at: various UK locations 1976-80
Producer: Wishbone Ash/John Sherry
Release date: 1981
Tracks: Blowin' Free; Living Proof; Goodbye Baby Hello Friend; Bad Weather Blues; Doctor; Way of the World; Helpless; No Easy Road
LP catalogue number: MCA 5283 (note: US release)
Comments: Compilation of live material taken from "Live Dates II" + various single b-sides, etc.
BBC Radio 1 Live In Concert
Recorded at: BBC Paris Theatre, London, England on May 25th 1972
Release date: October 1991
Tracks: Blowing Free, Time Was, Jailbait, The Pilgrim, Warrior, Throw Down The Sword, The King Will Come, Phoenix
CD catalogue number: Windsong International WINCD 004
Comments: The recording featured is in Mono, although stereo bootlegs were already in circulation.
The Ash Live In Chicago
Recorded at: Easy Street, Glenview, Chicago, USA on 24th and 25th January 1992
Producers: Ted Turner, Andy Powell, Fred Breitberg
Engineer: Fred Breitberg
Release date: March 1992
Tracks: The King Will Come, Strange Affair, Standing In The Rain, Lost Cause In Paradise, Keeper Of The Light, Throw Down The Sword, In The Skin, Why Don't We?, Hard Times, Blowing Free (sic), Living Proof.
LP Catalogue No: PERM LP6 (Permanent Records)
CD: Permanent Records PERM CD6 (UK release) GRIFFIN GCD 247 2 (US release)
Comments: Featured Dan Gillogly on Keyboards. This was the last Wishbone Ash album to be released on vinyl.
Note: This release has been re-released under many different titles by several other record companies. This list is not necessarily complete. If you have one of the titles below it is a copy of the original official recordings above.
The Living Proof – Live In Chicago – EMPORIO EMPR CD825
The King Will Come – MCPS CD 447534-2
Keeper Of The Light – TRING JHD075
Live In Chicago – CYCLOPS CYCL 030 (ltd edition boxed with *Collectors Guide To Wishbone Ash* book)
The King Will Come – PILZ 448238-2
Live In The USA – VONO 112008
Living Proof – Live In Chicago – MUSIC DELUXE MDCD012
Wishbone Ash – Live Chicago – STARLING SA CD 021
Wishbone Ash Picture Disc – MASTER TUNE CP6246

Living Proof Live In Chicago – RIGHT RECORDINGS RIGHT 005
Strange Affair – POINT PRODS. 2621342
The Ash Live In Chicago – UNIVERSE CDSP 90893
In Concert – ALL AT ONCE HP93452
Live At The BBC
Recorded at: various BBC studio sessions 1971/72 plus Old Grey Whistle Test 1977
Producers: Mike Harding, Mike Franks, John Walters, Adrian Revill, Jeff Griffin, Michael Appleton
Release date: January 1996
Tracks: Blind Eye, Lullaby, Pilgrim, Jailbait, Blowin' Free, Throw Down The Sword, Vas Dis, Goodbye Baby Hello Friend, Come In From The Rain
CD catalogue number: Band of Joy BOJCD012
Live In Geneva
Recorded at: Arthur's Club, Geneva, Switzerland on 6th April 1995
Release date: 15th March 1996
Tracks: The King Will Come, Strange Affair, Throw Down The Sword, In The Skin, Hard Times, Blowin' Free, Keeper Of The Light, Medley – Blind Eye, Lady Whiskey, Jail Bait, Phoenix, The Pilgrim, Runaway, Sometime World, Vas Dis
CD Catalogue No: HNRCD003 (Hengest Records)
Comments: The first Wishbone Ash album to be recorded digitally. There was a video of this performance but this has never been released. The tracks are not in the same running order as the original concert.
Live -Timeline
Recorded at: The Bottom Line, Nagoya, Japan on 23rd May 1991, plus BBC studio session
Release date: January 1997
Tracks: Lost Cause In Paradise, Standing In The Rain, This Strange Affair (sic), The King Will Come, Throw Down The Sword, In The Skin, Why Don't We, Wings Of Desire, Time Was. The Living Proof (sic), Blowin' Free, Vas Dis, Where Were You Tomorrow
CD catalogue number: Receiver RRCD 216
Comments: Most of the tracks are the same as "The Ash Live In Chicago", though Martin Turner as opposed to Andy Pyle plays on this album.
Archive Series
Recorded at: The Bottom Line, Nagoya, Japan on 23rd May 1991, plus a BBC studio session
Producer: Mike Bennett
Release date: 1998
Tracks: Vas Dis, Phoenix, Where Were You Tomorrow, Blowin' Free, Leaf And Stream, The King Has Come (sic), Lost Cause In Paradise, Standing in The Rain, This Strange Affair (sic), Throw Down The Sword, Time Was, Wings Of Desire, In The Skin
CD catalogue number: Rialto Records RMCD 224
Comments: With the exceptions of Phoenix and Leaf And Stream the tracks are exactly the same as on Live-Timeline.
The King Will Come – Live
Recorded at: Davenport USA in 1976 and Canada in 1973
Release date: October 1999
Tracks: Rest In Peace, The King Will Come, Trust in You, Persephone, Moonshine, Half Past Lovin', Rock 'N' Roll Widow, Time Was, Ballad of the Beacon, The Warrior (sic), Throw Down The Sword, Blowin' Free, Doctor
CD catalogue number: Receiver Records RRCD 276 Z
Comments: The Davenport recordings feature Graham Maitland on keyboards and feature some of the *Locked In* songs in a live setting.
Live in Paris
Recorded at New Morning Club, near Paris, France on 20th October 1999
Release date: Autumn 2000

COMPILATIONS
An Evening Program With Wishbone Ash
Release date: 1972
LP Catalogue No: Decca DL7-1919 (note: US promo only LP)
Tracks: Phoenix, Jailbait, Warrior, Blind Eye, The Pilgrim, Lady Whiskey, Blowin Free
Milestones
Release date: 1975
LP Catalogue no: MCA 503731 4 (note: Dutch LP release)
Tracks: 2LP repackaging of "Argus" and "Pilgrimage"
Masters Of Rock

Release date: 1975
LP Catalogue no: MCA MAPS 7820 (note: Dutch LP release)
Tracks: Queen of Torture, Jailbait, Blowin' Free, Where Were You Tomorrow, Errors of my Way, The King Will Come, Sorrel, Blind Eye
The Best Of Wishbone Ash
Release date: 1975
LP Catalogue no: MCA 62.004 (note: German LP)
Tracks: Queen of Torture, Jailbait, Blowin' Free, Where Were You Tomorrow, Errors of my Way, The King Will Come, Sorrel, Blind Eye
Australian Tour Sampler
Release date: 1975
LP Catalogue no: MCA Astor MA – 12067 (note: Australian promo only LP)
Tracks: Blind Eye, Jail Bait, Warrior, Ballad of the Beacon, The King Will Come, Don't Come Back
Comments: Andy Powell interview interspersed with tracks
Special DJ Copy
Release date: 1975
LP Catalogue no: MCA MLD – 94 (note: Japanese promo only LP)
Tracks: Lady Whiskey, The Pilgrim, The King Will Come, Rock 'N' Roll Widow, Don't Come Back, Persephone, Rest In Peace, Moonshine, Say Goodbye
The Original Wishbone Ash
Release date: 1977
LP Catalogue No: MCA 42.006 (note: German LP)
Tracks: Jailbait, Queen of Torture, Sorrel, Where Were You Tomorrow, The King Will Come, Errors of my Way, Blowin' Free, Blind Eye
That's Wishbone Ash
Release date: 1977
LP Catalogue No: MCA 296.067 245 (note: German LP)
Tracks: Outward Bound, The Pilgrim, Jailbait, Where Were You Tomorrow, Lady Whiskey, Lady Jay, Don't Come Back, Blowin' Free
Classic Ash
Release date: May 1977
LP Catalogue no: MCA MCF 2795
CD: MCD 10578
Tracks: Blind Eye, Phoenix, The Pilgrim, Blowin' Free, The King will Come, Rock And Roll Widow, Persephone, Outward Bound, Throw Down The Sword
Comments: The amusing sleeve notes for this album were written by DJ, John Peel, an early supporter of Wishbone Ash and their music. Japanese release features different sleeve design.
Wishbone Ash
Release date: 1981
LP Catalogue no: MCA VIM 4074 6 (note: Japanese 2LP set)
Tracks: Disc 1: Blind Eye, Errors of my Way, Warrior, Like a Child, Lady Whiskey, Everybody Needs A Friend, Sometime World.
Disc 2: Rest in Peace, Helpless, FUBB, Living Proof, The Way of the World Pt.2, Lifeline
Comments: Eponymous collection – not to be confused with the band's first album
The Best Of Wishbone Ash
Release date: May 1981
LP Catalogue no: MCA MCF 3134
Tracks: Blind Eye, Queen of Torture, Jail Bait, The King Will Come, Blowin' Free, Doctor, Persephone, Silver Shoes, Goodbye Baby Hello Friend, Living Proof
Comments: Steve Upton wrote the sleeve notes for this album
Time Was/The Wishbone Ash Collection
Release date: 1993
Catalogue no: MCA MCD 10765 (note: US 2CD release)
Tracks: CD 1 – Phoenix, Blind Eye, Errors of my Way, Handy, Vas Dis, Lullaby, Where Were You Tomorrow, The Pilgrim (live), Blowin' Free, Time Was
CD 2 – Warrior, Sometime world, The King will Come, So Many Things To Say, Ballad Of The Beacon, Sorrel, Baby What You want Me To Do (live), F.U.B.B, Front Page News, 714, You See Red, Pay The Price, Underground
Comments: The majority of the tracks feature the Mark 1 line-up of the band.
The Very Best Of Wishbone Ash: Blowin' Free
Release date: 1994
Catalogue no: Nectar NTRCD014

Tracks: Blind Eye, Blowin' Free, The Pilgrim, The King Will Come, Time Was, Ballad Of The Beacon, Outward Bound, Throw Down The Sword, Lady Whiskey, Persephone, Jailbait, Phoenix
The Best Of Wishbone Ash
Release date: 1997
CD Catalogue no: MCA MCAD11620
Tracks: Blind Eye, Phoenix, The Pilgrim, Lorelei (live), Sometime World, Warrior, Throw Down The Sword, Persephone, F.U.B.B., Blowin' Free (acoustic), Living Proof
Distillation
Release date: October 1997
CD Catalogue no: REPERTOIRE RECORDS REP 4649 CX
CD 1 – Blind Eye, Lady Whiskey, Phoenix, Jail Bait, The Pilgrim, The King Will Come, Leaf & Stream, Warrior, Throw Down The Sword, No easy Road, Ballad of the Beacon, Sorrel, Persephone
CD 2 – Lady Jay, F.U.B.B., Say Goodbye, (In all of my Dreams) You Rescue Me, Prelude, Candlelight, Front Page News, Goodbye Baby Hello Friend, Surface To Air, You See Red, Ships In The Sky, Living Proof, Lifeline, Underground, Genevieve, Clousseau
CD 3 – Witness to Wonder, Why Don't We, Strange Affair, Dream Train, Standing In The Rain, Alone, Time And Space, Come On, Fast Johnny, She's Still Alive, T-Bone Shuffle, Bolan's Monument, Duffle Shuffle, Mountainside, Crack of Dawn
CD 4 – Outward Bound, Rest In Peace, Lorelei, Come In From The Rain, Bad Weather Blues, Sometime World, Errors of my Way, Blowin' Free, Insomnia, Helpless, The Way of The World, Lookin' For A Reason (all live)
Comments: Quite simply, the most carefully thought-out Wishbone Ash anthology to date – largely thanks to co-operation between band members past and present and the record company's receptiveness to fans suggestions.
Outward Bound
Release Date: October 1998
CD Catalogue no: BMG LC8637 (German release)
Tracks: Blowin' Free, Sometime World, Blind Eye, The Pilgrim, Front Page News, Goodbye Baby Hello Friend, Midnight Dancer, Runaway, Outward Bound, Lonely Island, Jail Bait, Alone, Silver Shoes, Don't Come Back, No Easy Road

Singles
The following is a listing of all Wishbone Ash's UK singles releases. For a detailed listing of overseas singles, please refer to *The Collectors Guide to Wishbone Ash,* published by Collector's Guide Publishing.
7 Inch Vinyl Singles

MCA MK 5061	Blind Eye/Queen Of Torture	Jan 1971
MCA MKS 5097	No Easy Road/Blowin' Free	Aug 1972
MCA MUS 1210	So Many Things To Say/Rock 'N' Roll Widow	Jul 1973
MCA MCA 165	Hometown/Persephone	Nov 1974
MCA MCA 176	Silver Shoes/Persephone	Feb 1975
MCA MCA 261	Outward Bound/Lorelei	Nov 1976
MCA MCA 291	Phoenix/Blowin' Free/Jail Bait	Apr 1977
MCA MCA 326	Front Page News/Diamond Jack	Sept 1977
MCA MCA 327	Goodbye Baby, Hello Friend	Oct 1977
MCA MCA 392	You See Red/Bad Weather Blues (Live)	Sept 1978
MCA MCA 518	Come On/Fast Johnny	Aug 1979
MCA MCA 549	Living Proof/Jail Bait (Live)	Jan 1980
MCA MCA 577	Helpless (Live)/Blowin' Free (Live)	May 1980
MCA MCA 695	Underground/My Mind Is Made Up	Mar 1981
MCA MCA 726	Get Ready/Kicks On The Street	May 1981
MCA MCL 14	Get Ready/Kicks On The Street	May 1981
AVM WISH 1	Engine Overheat/Genevieve	Sept 1982
AVM 1002	No More Lonely Nights/Streets Of Shame	Dec 1982
IRS IRM 164	In The Skin/Tangible Evidence	May 1988
IRS EIRS 104	Cosmic Jazz/T-Bone Shuffle	Jul 1989

7 Inch Flexidisc
MCA Sound For Industry SFI 263 Free Flexidisc With 'New England' Tour Programme Excerpts From:
Outward Bound/Runaway/
Mother Of Pearl/You Rescue Me   Nov 1976
12 Inch Vinyl Singles
MCA 12MCA 392 You See Red/Bad Weather Blues (Live)   Sept 1978
MCA MCAT 577 Helpless(Live)/Blowin' Free(Live)   May 1980

thirty years of Wishbone Ash

IRS EIRS T104 Cosmic Jazz/T-Bone Shuffle/Bolan's Monument   Jul 1989
Invisible Hands Music IHST7 Trance Visionary/Wronged By Righteousness/Heritage/Powerbright   Oct 1998

Fan Club Albums
In the mid to late 1990's "Dr. John" at the US ASH fan club released a series of Archive CD's containing several tracks taken from demo recordings and bootlegs in an attempt "to beat the bootleggers" with all proceeds raised from their sales going to "the band".

From The Archives
Release date: 1994
CD Catalogue no: DJ-61466 (USA)
Reissued and repackaged by Powerbright PBVP001 (UK)
Tracks: Lullaby, Miles' Interview, LA Blues, Steve's Interview, Where Were You Tomorrow, Martin's Interview, Lady Whiskey, Ted's Interview, Phoenix, Martin's Interview, The King Will Come, Andy Martin Andy interviews, Rock 'N' Roll Widow, Andy's Interview, Ballad Of The Beacon, Sometime World, Martin's Interview

Archives Vol. II
Release date: 1995
CD catalogue no: SAT3395 (USA)
Reissued and repackaged by Powerbright PBVP002 (UK)
Tracks: Alone, Steve Upton Interview, Ted Turner Interview, The Pilgrim, Andy Powell Interview, Rest In Peace, Steve Upton Introduction, Silver Shoes, Lifeline, Laurie Wisefield Interview, Persephone, Outward Bound, Lady Jay, Ted Turner Interview, Clousseau, T-Bone Shuffle, Bolan's Monument, Andy & Martin Interview, Alone

Archives Vol. III
Release date: 1996
CD Catalogue no: USASH92956 (USA)
Reissued and repackaged by Powerbright PBVP003 (UK)
Tracks: Open Road, Cell of Fame, Long Live The Night, She's Still Alive, Don't Come Back, Cat & Dog Fight, Danny Don't Go To Ireland, One Time Only, Love Abuse, The Last Time, 70's Rock, Wings Of Desire, Ship Of Dreams, East Coast Boogie, Hard Times, Miles Copeland's Revenge, Ashes From The Table

Transcriptions
The following listing features radio transcription LPs – e.g.. LPs featuring exclusive live in concert or studio tracks and/or interview material by Wishbone Ash, pressed up by radio stations for play as an entire radio show. These items are particularly elusive, largely due to the small number of copies printed of each album. This is usually less than 50 copies per disc.

BBC Show #367
BBC 129474/S (US)
Tracks: (side 2) Jail Bait; Lullaby; Pilgrim
Comments; All studio tracks with other artists including The Move, Mott The Hoople and Mary Hopkin.

BBC Top Of The Pops Show 18
BBC CN 1552/S (UK)
Recorded at: London Paris Theatre 25.5.72
Tracks: Time Was; Blowin Free; Warrior; Throw Down the Sword; The King Will Come; Phoenix

Nightbird & Co
ARMY 74909 (US)
Features: Laurie Wisefield and Andy Powell interview plus studio tracks taken from "Locked In"
Comments: 2LP set also featuring Jethro Tull and Don Harrison Band.

BBC Show #?1977
BBC CN ? (UK)
Recorded at Wembley Empire Pool, London 31.10.77
Tracks: Blind Eye, Lady Whiskey, Warrior, Throw Down The Sword, Front Page News, Goodbye Baby Hello Friend, Come In From The Rain, Phoenix, Blowin' Free

BBC In Concert # 187
BBC TS CN 3214/S (UK)
Recorded at London Hammersmith Odeon 25.10.78
Tracks: The King will Come, You See Red, Front Page News, The Way Of The World, Phoenix, Anger In Harmony, Queen of Torture, Blowin' Free

BBC In Concert 1980
BBC TS CN 3561/S (UK)
Recorded at: London Hammersmith Odeon 2.2.80
Tracks: Doctor; Blind Eye; The Way of the World; Insomnia; Queen of Torture; Lifeline; Blind Eye; Blowin

Free; Helpless; Jailbait
BBC In Concert 1981
BBC TS CN 03849/S (UK)
Recorded at: London Hammersmith Odeon 6.2.81
Tracks: Lady Whiskey; Living Proof; Underground; Warrior; Kicks on the Street; Phoenix; Number the Brave; Helpless
BBC Rock Hour 1982
BBC TS 4136 (US)
Recorded at: London Hammersmith Odeon 6.2.81
Tracks: Lady Whiskey; Underground; Warrior; Kicks on the Street; Phoenix; Number the Brave; Helpless
BBC In Concert 1988
BBC TS Catalogue unknown (UK)
Recorded at: London Hammersmith Odeon 4.3.88
Tracks: Tangible Evidence; Living Proof; Genevieve; No More Lonely Nights; The King Will Come; Throw Down the Sword; Clousseau; In the Skin; Blowin Free

Bootleg Recordings
The following listing details all known Wishbone Ash bootleg vinyl and CD releases. In the case of CDs, this listing is restricted to factory pressed releases and does not include the numerous home made CDR bootlegs which have surfaced since the advent of home CD recording equipment. Neither does it include bootleg cassettes. See the concert listings section for concerts which have been bootlegged.
Disclaimer: This listing is published purely for reference purposes. Neither the authors or publishers wish to condone the illegal act of bootlegging and cannot advise on how the following titles may be obtained.
Sound Quality: We have rated each bootleg for sound quality. Please note ratings are based on the general standards of bootleg releases, not that of official recordings.

LPs
Live 73 Alexandra Palace
OG 732 (Japan)
Recorded at: Alexandra Palace, London 22.12.73
Tracks: So Many Things to Say; Rock n Roll Widow; Everybody Needs a Friend; Ballad of the Beacon; Phoenix.
Sound Quality: Fair – audience recording
Ashes Are Burning
ZAP 7963 (Japan)
Recorded at: Tokyo Sun Plaza 14.10.76
Tracks: The King Will Come; Warrior; Lorelei; Persephone; You Rescue Me; Rest in Peace; Blowin' Free; Bad Weather Blues
Sound Quality: Fair – audience recording
Lorelive Date
Steel Blade 1004 (US)
Recorded at: Metal Hammer Festival, Loreley 14.9.85
Tracks: Don't Come Back; Living Proof; Streets of Shame; Cell of Fame; No Lonely Nights; The King Will Come; Don't Cry; People in Motion; Blowin' Free
Sound Quality: Good – taken from mixing desk
Argus Dates
Montreux (German)
Recorded at: Munich 23.2.72; Heidelberg 22.9.77; Ludwigschafen 4.12.76
Tracks: Time Was; Blowin Free; Jailbait; The King Will Come; Warrior; Throw Down the Sword; Blind Eye; Lady Whiskey; Where Were You Tomorrow; Sometime World; Outward Bound
Sound Quality: Fair – audience recordings
Comments: clear vinyl; cover hand made from South American coffee sack

CDs
Fighters And Warriors
OH BOY 1-9058 (Lux)
Recorded at: BBC Paris Theatre, London 25.5.72
Tracks: Time Was; Blowin' Free; Warrior; Throw Down the Sword; The King Will Come; Phoenix
Sound Quality: Excellent stereo – FM broadcast
In America & Over Japan
OH BOY 1-9077 (Lux)
Recorded at: Tokyo 1978 and Memphis 21.8.72
Tracks: Jailbait; The Pilgrim; Phoenix; FUBB; The Way of the World; You See Red; Jailbait; Blowin' Free.

Sound Quality: Excellent stereo – taken from "Live from Memphis" and "Live in Tokyo" LPs
Super Golden Radio Shows – Live In London
SGRS 038 (Italy)
Recorded at: Hammersmith Odeon, London 2.2.80
Tracks: Doctor; Blind Eye; The Way of the World; Insomnia; Queen of Torture; Lifeline; Living Proof; Blowin' Free; Helpless; Jailbait
Sound Quality: Excellent stereo – FM broadcast
Phoenix From The Ashes
DISCURIOS DIS 116
Recorded at: London Paris Theatre 21.2.74; BBC Session 1971; Hammersmith 1978
Tracks: Ballad of the Beacon; Sometime World; Rock n Roll Widow; Blowin Free; Jailbait; Time Was; Phoenix; Blind Eye; Alone; Errors of My Way
Sound Quality: Good to average.
Volume 1 – Live
IMTRAT 40.95001 (German)
Recorded at: Liverpool 1976 except track one recorded Hammersmith Odeon 1980
Tracks; Helpless; Runaway; Warrior; Lorelei; Persephone; You Rescue Me; Outward Bound; Mother of Pearl; Rest in Peace; Time Was; Bad Weather Blues
Sound Quality: Near excellent – rumoured to be taken from 4-track feed from mixing desk
Wishbone Ash Live
WZ 09115
All details as "Volume 1 – Live", except track list doesn't feature "Bad Weather Blues"
Runaway
K-Point 1621.1027-2 (German)
All details as "Volume 1 – Live"
Live – Mother Of Pearl
MASTERTONE AB 3043
All details as "Volume 1 – Live"
Their Greatest Hits
All details as "Volume 1 – Live"
Playing Free
HM 009 (German)
Recorded at: Hammersmith Odeon, London 2.6.81
Tracks: Where is the Love; Living Proof; Underground; Warrior; Kicks on the Street; Phoenix; Number the Brave; Helpless; Blowin Free; Get Ready; The King Will Come
Sound Quality: Excellent stereo – FM broadcast
Lady Whiskey
GLR 9236
Recorded at: Hammersmith Odeon, London 2.6.81
Tracks: Lady Whiskey; Underground; Warrior; Kicks on the Street; Phoenix; Number the Brave; Helpless
Sound Quality – Excellent Stereo – FM broadcast
No More Lonely Nights
TCC 050
Recorded at: Metal Hammer Festival, Loreley 14.9.85
Tracks: Don't Come Back; Living Proof; Streets of Shame; Cell of Fame; No Lonely Nights; The King Will Come; Don't Cry; People in Motion; Blowin' Free
Sound Quality: Good – taken from mixing desk
Reunion Live 91
WBA 01 (Japan)
Recorded at: Kawasaki, Club Citta 21.5.91
Tracks: Strange Affair; The King Will Come; Lost Cause in Paradise; Standing in the Rain; Blowin' Free; Hard Times; Jail Bait
Sound Quality: Excellent stereo – FM broadcast

Other Projects
The discography below attempts to list the key guest appearances, solo albums and sideline projects featuring the various members of Wishbone Ash which occurred whilst they were members of the band.

Andy Powell
Renaissance – Ashes Are Burning
Release date: 1973
LP catalogue number: Sovereign SVNA 7261
CD: One Way Records CDL 57576

Blowin' Free

Comments: Andy plays lead guitar on the title track
Terry Tonik – Just A Little Mod / Smashed And Blocked
Release date: 1979
Single catalogue number: POSH RECORDS Toff 1
Comments: A novelty single that Andy Powell produced and played on with Ian Harris, who designed some of the Wishbone Ash album covers. The duo also wrote and recorded a tribute single to John Lennon which was distributed via Beatles' fan club magazines, entitled "Dakota".
Blue Law, Featuring Andy Powell – Gonna Getcha
Release date: 1996
CD catalogue no: HENGEST RECORDS HNRCD002
Tracks: Gonna Getcha, Shade Tree Mechanic, Body Talk, For Crying Out Loud, Five O'Clock Whistle, Bicycle Man, Joy Ride, Woke Up This Morning, Hey Miss Bessie, House of Cards, One Too Many Times, One More Mile to Go
Comments: US Blues band featuring Andy Powell as guitarist, co-writer and producer. A fan club only cassette featuring some of the tracks was released in 1994 entitled, The Sure Thing – "First Take".

Martin Turner
Martin Turner – Walking The Reeperbhan
Release date: November 1996
CD cat no: DDDCD001
reissued and repackaged by Blueprint cat no: BP298CD
Tracks: Fire Sign, Walking the Reeperbahn, Hot Surrender, My Brother, Strangers, Psychic Flash to Ginza, You, Passion, Lean on Me, Kelly's Away With the Fairies, Where Will I Go?, The Naked Truth, Heaven Is, Broken Down House
Comments: 1996 solo collection featuring material recorded during 1981-96. Several tracks later adapted as Wishbone Ash material are featured in their original form. "Heaven Is" is an outtake from the "Here to Hear" sessions, featuring Martin, Andy Powell and Steve Upton.
Roy Hollingworth – In The Flesh
Release date: 1996
CD: Bellaphon (German release)
Tracks: Hungry Youth, Love Takes It All, In The Flesh, Good Enough To Bleed For, Mandy Moonshine, Milk Kisses, The Screen Sees All, Don't Wanna Wanna, Hollywood Lines, We The People
Comments: Martin Turner featured both as a producer and as a musician providing bass, keyboards, guitar and drum programming on this solo album by the former *Melody Maker* New York correspondent.

Ted Turner
John Lennon – Imagine
Release date: September 1971
LP catalogue number: Apple
CD: EMI CDP 746 641-2
Comments: Ted Turner plays acoustic guitar on the track "Crippled Inside"

Laurie Wisefield
Claire Hamill – Touchpaper
Release date: 1984
LP catalogue number:
CD : BLUEPRINT RECORDS BP306CD
CODA RECORDS CODA 8
Comments: Laurie featured on guitar on several tracks

Tony Kishman
Tony Kishman – Catch 22
Release date: November 1997
CD catalogue number: PURE RECORDS 003642560-2
Tracks: Heading For a Rough Ride, Catch 22, Let Me Down Easy, How'm I Gonna Get By, Modern Girl, The Lucky One, Classy Kind'a Love, Sky's The Limit, Serenity, Believe In Yourself
Comments: A full scale solo album from the Ash bassist/vocalist in the late 1990's.

Videos
Wishbone Ash In Concert
Trillion Pictures Ltd TPL 0001
Release date: September 1983
Phoenix

Hendring HEN 2244
Release date: April 1990
The King Will Come
Release date: 1989 (Germany)
The above three video cassettes all feature the same concert, recorded at London's Marquee Club on February 23rd 1983, as part of the Marquee's 25th Anniversary celebrations.
Track listing: Can't Fight Love, Living Proof, Open Road, No More Lonely Nights, Underground, The King Will Come, Phoenix, Engine Overheat, Blowin' Free
Group line up: Andy Powell, Laurie Wisefield, Trevor Bolder, Steve Upton
Wishbone Ash Live
PMI MVP 991 210 3
Release date: June 1990
This video was filmed by Central Television, originally for their "Bedrock" series, at Bristol Colston Hall on September 26th 1989.
Track listing: Real Guitars Have Wings, The King Will Come, Cosmic Jazz, Keeper Of The Light, Why Don't We, Blowin' Free, Medley – Blind Eyes, Lady Whiskey, Sometime World, Phoenix, Jailbait.
Group line-up: Andy Powell, Ted Turner, Martin Turner, Steve Upton
Live At Mansfield
Wishbone Ash Fan Club release
Release date: December 1997
This video was filmed at the 4th annual Wishbone Ash convention at the Mansfield Leisure Centre England on 8th November 1997. Features guest appearances by Martin Turner, Chris Auld and Claire Hamill.
Track listing: Acoustic section – Crack of Dawn, East Coast Boogie. Main set – Real Guitars Have Wings, The King Will Come, Top Of The World, Throw Down The Sword, Mountainside, Vas Dis, Sometime World, Strange Affair, On Your Own, The Ring, Leaf & Stream, Another Time, Living Proof, Runaway, Medley – (Blind Eye, Lady Whiskey, Phoenix, The Pilgrim), Blowin' Free, Errors of my Way, Hard Times.
Group line up: Andy Powell, Roger Filgate, Tony Kishman, Mike Sturgis
May Day
Wishbone Ash Fan Club release
Release date: July 1999
This is the official documentary of the first ever US Wishbone Ash convention, which took place on Saturday 1st May 1999 at the Beaumont Club in Chicago. It features behind the scenes footage, interviews with members of the band as well as some live footage.
Track listing: excerpts from: Real Guitars Have Wings, Throw Down The Sword, Ballad of the Beacon, Strange Affair, Mountainside, Blowin' Free, Wings of Desire, FUBB, Master of Disguise
Group line up: Andy Powell, Mark Birch, Bob Skeat, Ray Weston
Shepherd's Bush Empire – 30th Anniversary Concert
To be released autumn 2000

Promotional Material
A promotional film for the "No Easy Road"/ "Blowin' Free" single was shot in the summer of 1972.
A promo video for "In The Skin" was filmed at Hammersmith Odeon, London on 4th March 1988.
A promo video for "Wonderful Stash" from the "Psychic Terrorism" album was made by Christian Guyonnet in 1998. This was featured on the CD Rom version of "Psychic Terrorism"

Family Tree

Mark One (Autumn 1969 To May 1974)
Andy Powell	Ted Turner	Martin Turner	Steve Upton
(Guitar/Vocals)	(Guitar/Vocals)	(Bass/Vocals)	(Drums)

Mark Two (May 1974 – September 1980)
Andy Powell	Laurie Wisefield	Martin Turner	Steve Upton
(Guitar/Vocals)	(Guitar/Vocals)	(Bass/Vocals)	(Drums)

Graham Maitland played keyboards for live shows in the US during 1976

Mark Three (October To December 1980)
Andy Powell	Laurie Wisefield	John Wetton	Steve Upton
(Guitar/Vocals)	(Guitar/Vocals)	(Bass/Vocals)	(Drums)

Mark Four (March 1981 To April 1983)
Andy Powell	Laurie Wisefield	Trevor Bolder	Steve Upton
(Guitar/Vocals)	(Guitar/Vocals)	(Bass/Vocals)	(Drums)

Claire Hamill added backing vocals for live shows in UK/Europe during May/June 1981

Mark Five (April 1983 To December 1985)
Andy Powell	Laurie Wisefield	Mervyn Spence	Steve Upton
(Guitar/Vocals)	(Guitar/Vocals)	(Bass/Vocals)	(Drums)

Mark Six (January 1986)
Andy Powell	Jamie Crompton	Mervyn Spence	Steve Upton
(Guitar/Vocals)	(Guitar)	(Bass/Vocals)	(Drums)

Mark Seven (February 1986 To July 1986)
Andy Powell	Jamie Crompton	Andy Pyle	Steve Upton
(Guitar/Vocals)	(Guitar)	(Bass)	(Drums)

Mark Eight (August 1986 To December 1986)
Andy Powell	Phil Palmer	Andy Pyle	Steve Upton
(Guitar/Vocals)	(Guitar)	(Bass)	(Drums)

Mark Seven (January 1987 To December 1987)
Andy Powell	Jamie Crompton	Andy Pyle	Steve Upton
(Guitar/Vocals)	(Guitar)	(Bass)	(Drums)

Mark One (May 1987 To July 1990)
Andy Powell	Ted Turner	Martin Turner	Steve Upton
(Guitar/Vocals)	(Guitar/Vocals)	(Bass/Vocals)	(Drums)

Jamie Crompton played additional guitar during the February/March 1988 UK Tour

Mark Nine (July 1990 To November 1990)
Andy Powell	Ted Turner	Martin Turner	Robbie France
(Guitar/Vocals)	(Guitar/Vocals)	(Bass/Vocals)	(Drums)

Mark Ten (November 1990 To October 1991)

Andy Powell	Ted Turner	Martin Turner	Ray Weston
(Guitar/Vocals)	(Guitar/Vocals)	(Bass/Vocals)	(Drums)

Mark Eleven (October 1991 To December 1993)

Andy Powell	Ted Turner	Andy Pyle	Ray Weston
(Guitar/Vocals)	(Guitar/Vocals)	(Bass)	(Drums)

Brad Lang deputised on bass for Andy Pyle on several 1992 live dates
Alan Darby played additional guitar/vocals on several 1992 shows

Mark Twelve (March 1995 To September 1995)

Andy Powell	Roger Filgate	Tony Kishman	Mike Sturgis
(Guitar/Vocals)	(Guitar/Vocals)	(Bass/Vocals)	(Drums)

Mark Thirteen (October 1995 To December 1995)

Andy Powell	Roger Filgate	Martin Turner	Mike Sturgis
(Guitar/Vocals)	(Guitar/Vocals)	(Bass/Vocals)	(Drums)

Mark Twelve (January 1996 To September 1996)

Andy Powell	Roger Filgate	Tony Kishman	Mike Sturgis
(Guitar/Vocals)	(Guitar/Vocals)	(Bass/Vocals)	(Drums)

Martin Turner deputised for Tony Kishman on bass/vocals for a one off festival appearance in Hungary in the summer

Mark Thirteen (October 1996 To December 1996)

Andy Powell	Roger Filgate	Martin Turner	Mike Sturgis
(Guitar/Vocals)	(Guitar/Vocals)	(Bass/Vocals)	(Drums)

Tony Kishman deputised for Martin Turner on bass/vocals for several dates of the autumn 1996 UK tour

Mark Twelve (December 1996 To December 1997)

Andy Powell	Roger Filgate	Tony Kishman	Mike Sturgis
(Guitar/Vocals)	(Guitar/Vocals)	(Bass/Vocals)	(Drums)

Chris Auld deputised for Roger Filgate at the Bradford 1997 show

Mark Fourteen (January 1998 To May 1998)

Andy Powell	Mark Birch	Bob Skeat	Mike Sturgis
(Guitar/Vocals)	(Guitar/Vocals)	(Bass/Vocals)	(Drums)

Ray Weston deputised for Mike Sturgis on some of the Jan to March UK/European Tour

Mark Fifteen (May 1998 To The Present)

Andy Powell	Mark Birch	Bob Skeat	Ray Weston
(Guitar/Vocals)	(Guitar/Vocals)	(Bass/Vocals)	(Drums)

Titles available from SAF, Firefly and Helter Skelter Publishing

Firefly, SAF Publishing and Helter Skelter have a wide range of music-related titles which are all available by mail order from the world famous Helter Skelter bookshop.

Either consult the websites below, or phone, fax or write to Helter Skelter to request the latest catalogue.

You can phone or fax Helter Skelter on the following numbers:

Telephone: +44 (0)20 7836 1151 or Fax: +44 (0)20 7240 9880
Office hours: Mon-Fri 10:00am – 7:00pm, Sat: 10:00am – 6:00pm, Sun: closed.

Helter Skelter Bookshop,
4 Denmark Street, London, WC2H 8LL, United Kingdom.
If you are in London come and visit us, and browse the titles in person!!

Email: helter@skelter.demon.co.uk
www.skelter.demon.co.uk

For the latest on SAF and Firefly titles check the SAF website:
www.safpublishing.com